Dollars and Democracy

DOLLARS
and DEMOCRACY

A Blueprint for Campaign Finance Reform

The Association of the Bar
of the City of New York,
Commission on Campaign Finance Reform

RICHARD BRIFFAULT,
Executive Director

Foreword by
JOHN D. FEERICK and ROBERT M. KAUFMAN

FORDHAM UNIVERSITY PRESS
New York • 2000

Library of Congress Cataloging-in-Publication Data

Association of the Bar of the City of New York Special Commission on
  Campaign Finance Reform.
    Dollars and democracy : blueprint for campaign finance reform / the
  Assoication of the Bar of the City of New York, Special Commission on
  Campaign Finance Reform ; introduction by John D. Feerick and
  Robert M. Kaufman ; Richard Briffault, executive director.—1st ed.
      p.   cm.
    ISBN 0-8232-2095-8 (hc.)—ISBN 0-8232-2096-6 (pbk.)
    1. Campaign funds—Law and legislation—United States.   I. Title.
  KF4920.A97   2000
  342.73'078—dc21   00-042676

Printed in the United States of America
00 01 02 03 04 5 4 3 2 1
First edition

CONTENTS

COMMISSION ON CAMPAIGN FINANCE REFORM

CO-CHAIRS

John D. Feerick

Dean, Fordham University School of
Law
Chair, New York State Commission
on Government Integrity
Former President, Citizens Union
Foundation

Robert M. Kaufman

Partner, Proskauer Rose LLP
Former President, American
Judicature Society
Former Legislative Counsel to
Senator Jacob K. Javits

Hon. Cyrus R. Vance

Partner, Simpson Thacher &
Bartlett
Former U.S. Secretary of State
Former Deputy Secretary of
Defense

EXECUTIVE DIRECTOR

Richard Briffault

Vice-Dean and Joseph P.
Chamberlain Professor of
Legislation, and Executive
Director, Legislative Drafting
Research Fund, Columbia
University School of Law

MEMBERS

Hon. Robert Abrams	Partner, Stroock & Stroock & Lavan Former Attorney General of New York State
Mark Alcott	Partner, Paul, Weiss, Rifkind, Wharton & Garrison Former Chair, Downstate New York Committee, American College of Trial Lawyers
Susan Cornick-Allen	Commission Secretary, 1997–1998
Joy Barson	Liaison, Committee on Federal Legislation
Andrea J. Berger	Assistant Corporation Counsel, Division of Legal Counsel, New York City Law Department Former President, New York Women's Bar Association Former Vice Chair, Lawyers Alliance for New York
David M. Brodsky	Managing Director, General Counsel-Americas, Credit Suisse First Boston Former Chair, New York Lawyers for the Public Interest
John W. Campo, Jr.	Transaction and Financial Counsel, General Electric Company Former Council Member, Boston Bar Association
John R. Dunne	Of Counsel, Whiteman Osterman & Hanna Former Assistant Attorney General, Civil Rights Division, U.S. Department of Justice Former New York State Senator

Leonard A. Feiwus	Commission Secretary, 1998–2000
Alexander Forger	Special Counsel, Milbank, Tweed, Hadley & McCloy Former President, Legal Services Corporation
Jerome S. Fortinsky	Partner, Shearman & Sterling Former Assistant to the Governor for Regional Affairs, Office of Governor Mario M. Cuomo Founder and Co-Chair, New York Young Lawyers for Clinton-Gore '96
Marilyn F. Friedman	Former Partner, Patterson, Belknap, Webb & Tyler Former Chair, Association of the Bar of the City of New York Committees on State Legislation and Election Law
Joel M. Gora	Associate Dean, Brooklyn Law School Former General Counsel, New York Civil Liberties Union
Nicole A. Gordon	Executive Director, New York City Campaign Finance Board Former President, Council on Governmental Ethics Laws Former Counsel to the Chairman, New York State Commission on Government Integrity
Hon. Hugh R. Jones	Former Associate Judge, New York Court of Appeals Former President, New York State Bar Association
Lance M. Liebman	Professor and Former Dean, Columbia University School of Law President, American Law Institute

Carlos G. Ortiz	General Counsel, GOYA Foods, Inc. Former National President, Hispanic National Bar Association

Constantine Sidamon-Eristoff	Of Counsel, Lacher & Lovell-Taylor
	  PC
	Vice Chairman, New York League of
	  Conservation Voters
	Former Regional Administrator,
	  USEPA Region II

Peter J. Wallison	Partner, Gibson, Dunn & Crutcher
	Former Counsel to the President of
	  the United States
	Former General Counsel of the
	  Treasury

Paul Windels, III	Partner, Perry & Windels
	Former Member, New York
	  Republican State Committee
	Former Chair and General Counsel,
	  New York County Republican
	  Committee

Michael Weinstock	Official in various political campaigns

Affiliations are listed for informational purposes, and the report does not necessarily reflect the views of the entities listed.

FOREWORD

THE SPECIAL COMMISSION on Campaign Finance Reform was
formed by the Association of the Bar of the City of New York in 1997
on the initiative of its then president Michael Cardozo, and in the
wake of the 1996 presidential and congressional elections. The Commission was directed to examine all aspects of the current system and
recommend appropriate changes.

In selecting members for the Commission, the Association sought
to have different and varied backgrounds and a broad spectrum of
perspectives represented. In pursuing its work, the Commission met
often and had its staff prepare comprehensive papers on the present
system, proposals for change, and applicable constitutional and policy considerations. At its many meetings over the past three years,
the Commission engaged in robust discussions, exchanges, and debates. The results of its deliberations were embodied in a series of
papers that were then reviewed at meetings and changed to reflect
the thinking of the group.

After its exhaustive work, the Commission reached a consensus as
to a blueprint for campaign finance reform in America. This Report
reflects that consensus. The recommendations reflect multiple and
diverse goals and are interrelated. Not every member of the Commission subscribes to every recommendation. There were significant differences, as reflected in the separate statements in this Report. In
the end, however, there was substantial agreement in the Commission that the present system was broken and badly in need of reform.

In this report the Commission submits its recommendations and
dedicates its entire labor to Cyrus Vance, whose health did not permit him to serve during the latter part of our endeavor. His life in
public service has been a model of the legal profession at its very
best.

The work of the Commission could not have been accomplished
without the dedication of those who selflessly devoted many hun-
dreds of hours to its task. We express our gratitude to each member

of the Commission and on behalf of every member to Professor Richard Briffault of Columbia University School of Law, our Executive Director and reporter. He did his work with distinction and an extraordinary commitment. Without Professor Briffault, this Report would not have been possible. We also extend special thanks to Leonard Feiwus for his outstanding efforts as secretary of the Commission, and to Miriam Jimenez and Claire Nee for their superb research and drafting assistance and their painstaking attention to detail.

Our Commission, research assistance, and this publication would not have been possible without the outstanding support we received in the form of grants from the following: the Ford Foundation; Open Society Institute; New York Community Trust (New York Critical Needs Fund, Lucille Gutman Trust, Robert M. Kaufman Fund, and General Charitable Fund); the Bauman Family Foundation; the J. M. Kaplan Fund, Inc.; the Joyce Foundation; Robert M. Kaufman; and the Fordham University School of Law. We thank Fordham University and its Press for publishing this Report.

Finally, the Commission would like to express its gratitude to Association President Michael Cooper for so generously supporting our work and to his predecessor, Michael Cardozo, for seeing a need for such a Commission—one that would build on a long and noble history of the Association in helping Congress deal with subjects of national import. We also thank the staff of the Association for their considerable help so vital to our work. We refer specifically and appreciatively to Barbara Berger Opotowsky and Alan Rothstein.

JOHN D. FEERICK and ROBERT M. KAUFMAN
April, 2000

Dollars and Democracy

Introduction and Summary

A. The Collapse of the Watergate-Era Campaign Finance System

OUR FEDERAL CAMPAIGN finance system is in a state of disarray. In the early 1970s Congress adopted legislation aimed at achieving full disclosure of the sources of campaign money; limits on the size of campaign contributions by wealthy individuals and organized interest groups; public funding, with spending limits, for presidential candidates; and effective enforcement through a new administrative agency, the Federal Election Commission (FEC). The Watergate-Era legislation known as the Federal Election Campaign Act (FECA)[1]—also carried forward longstanding prohibitions on the use of corporation and union treasury funds in federal elections.[2] These provisions of FECA were sustained by the Supreme Court in the leading case of *Buckley v. Valeo*,[3] and in subsequent decisions.

Campaign finance activity in recent federal elections, however, has sharply departed from the framework adopted by Congress. A large and growing percentage of campaign funds is not subject to FECA's disclosure requirements. Wealthy individuals, organized interest groups, corporations, and unions easily, massively, and legally disregard FECA's dollar limitations and source restrictions on campaign funds. Publicly funded presidential candidates actively solicit and control the expenditure of millions of dollars of private contributions.

---

[1] 2 U.S.C. §§ 431–455. The provisions for public funding for presidential candidates are technically separate from the Federal Election Campaign Act and are found in the Presidential Campaign Fund Act, 26 U.S.C. §§ 9001–9012, and the Presidential Primary Matching Payment Account Act, 26 U.S.C. §§ 9031–9042. This Report will use the acronym FECA as a shorthand way of referring to both the Federal Election Campaign Act and the presidential public-funding legislation.

[2] The prohibition on corporate contributions in federal elections dates back to the Tillman Act of 1907. The prohibition on the use of union treasury funds in federal elections dates back to the Smith-Connally Act of 1943.

[3] 424 U.S. 1 (1976).

The FEC has proven incapable of enforcing many of FECA's requirements, restrictions, and prohibitions.

The problems with the current campaign finance system, however, run deeper than evasions of the legal framework, as serious as those evasions are. The parts of the system that work as Congress intended have come to cause problems as well. The dollar limits on the size of contributions to candidates and parties are exactly the same as those enacted in 1974, even as campaign costs have skyrocketed and inflation has eaten away at the value of the statutory limits. (See figures 1-A and 1-B.) The spending limits that are part of the presidential public funding system are adjusted for inflation but were initially set at such a low level that public funds are insufficient in light of the costs of contemporary campaigns. Many of the FEC's problems were built into its structure by Congress.

Most importantly, the current statutory system does nothing to ensure that serious congressional candidates have the resources they need to mount effective campaigns. Nor does it attempt to level the electoral playing field by make it easier for challengers to compete fairly with incumbents. As a result, in many races, one candidate, typically the incumbent, has an enormous financial advantage over his or her opponents.

The current campaign finance system has significant negative ef-

FIGURE 1-A: SPENDING BY CONGRESSIONAL CANDIDATES
1974–1998

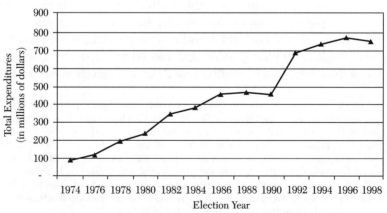

Source: 1974–1980, Citizens' Research Foundation; 1982–1998, FEC.

FIGURE 1-B: SPENDING BY CONGRESSIONAL CANDIDATES
1974–1998
(Adjusted for Inflation in January 2000 Dollars)

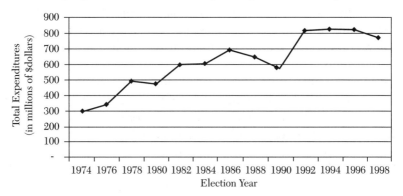

Source: Spending 1974–1980. Citizens' Research Foundation; Spending 1982–1998, FEC. Adjustment for inflation is based on U.S. Department of Labor, Bureau of Labor Statistics, "Consumer Price Index. All Urban Consumers-(CPI-U) U.S. City Average," ftp://ftp.bls.gov/pub/special.requests/cpi/cpiai.txt

fects on our democracy. The system produces many elections in which the incumbent runs without serious competition. A tiny number of very wealthy individuals, organizations, and interest groups have enormous influence over the financing of election campaigns and, ultimately, on the elections themselves. Large campaign donations, and candidates' dependence on these donations for the funds necessary to fuel their campaigns, provide major donors with opportunities for special access to elected officials. The enormous burdens of fundraising on elected officials and candidates discourage many potentially serious candidates from participating in elections, have led many seasoned officeholders to decline to seek reelection, and cause candidates and public officials to devote a disproportionate amount of their time and effort to the campaign money chase. The burden of fundraising also operates as a barrier to participation by women and minority candidates. The widespread and highly publicized evasions of the campaign finance laws insult the integrity of our legal system and contribute to the public's deep and growing cynicism about the campaign finance process, and about the very legitimacy of our democracy itself.

The problems with our current campaign system ought not to come as a surprise. The basic statutory framework was adopted more than a quarter century ago. Tinkered with a few times in the 1970s, it is virtually unchanged over the last two decades. During that time, the political system has evolved, and new and expensive campaign technologies have developed. Candidates, contributors, and other participants in the political process have gained experience with the system, probed its weaknesses, found its loopholes, and exploited its shortcomings.

Campaign finance regulation needs to be a dynamic process that keeps pace with the changing nature of political campaigns. But our federal election laws remain frozen as they were written in the 1970s. Congress has frequently debated campaign finance regulation, and on occasion one house or the other has passed new measures. But the political process has been blocked.[4] Despite growing public alarm and the mounting evidence of the inadequacies of the system under FECA, no significant federal campaign finance legislation has been adopted since 1979.

In addition to political gridlock on Capitol Hill, two significant factors further complicate the task of campaign finance reform. First, the Constitution, as interpreted by the Supreme Court, constrains the regulation of political campaigns. Campaign finance laws affect the communication of campaign messages and are, thus, subject to judicial review under the First Amendment. The Supreme Court has invalidated some campaign finance reforms and indicated that some campaign finance activities may not be regulated.

The limits imposed by the Supreme Court, however, should not be exaggerated. The Court has sustained the authority of Congress to limit contributions, to ban contributions by business corporations, to require the disclosure of campaign contributions and expenditures, to provide for public funding for candidates, and to make a candidate's acceptance of spending limits a condition for public funding. Indeed, the Court has held that many of these reforms—disclosure, limits on contributions, public funding—actually promote

---

[4] No campaign finance bill passed either house in the 1980s. In 1990, 1991, and 1992 the Senate and the House passed different campaign finance reform measures. In 1992 both houses of Congress adopted the Conference Committee's report on the Senate proposal, S. 3, but President Bush vetoed the measure, and the Senate failed by nine votes to override his veto. Since then, the House passed the Shays-Meehan Bill, in 1998 and again in 1999. Action on Shays-Meehan's Senate counterpart, McCain-Feingold, has been blocked by filibuster.

constitutional values. In the Court's most recent campaign finance case, decided in January of this year (see page 30), several of the justices signaled their willingness to revisit campaign finance doctrine in light of the new campaign finance stratagems that have emerged in recent years. The Supreme Court may have foreclosed certain regulatory options, but it has not prevented reform.

Second, campaign finance reform is difficult because of the inherent complexity of the problem. Campaign finance reform involves the consideration and reconciliation of multiple, diverse, and often conflicting goals. A well-functioning campaign finance system must protect freedom of speech, advance competitive elections, curtail special interest influence, and promote the equal political voice of all citizens, while minimizing the burdens of regulation on candidates, contributors, other participants in the process, and the FEC. Campaign finance reform requires respect for the open and dynamic character of the American political process, the evolving nature of campaigns, and the variety of circumstances and campaign styles across the country. Campaign finance reform must avoid burdening particular candidates or groups or providing advantages to their opponents. Reform must also take into account how candidates, contributors, and others will respond to particular efforts to regulate their behavior.

Campaign finance reform must be comprehensive. Limited approaches, targeting just one or another problem in the system, will have only a limited impact and are, in fact, likely simply to produce new forms of evasion and new loopholes. Only an integrated program of reforms can produce a strengthened democratic system. Yet given the range of conflicting values, the role of political interests, and the difficulties of designing reforms that can work in practice, comprehensive reform is by its very nature difficult to achieve.

B. THE ROLE OF THE COMMISSION ON CAMPAIGN FINANCE REFORM

The Association of the Bar of the City of New York believes that it can serve a constructive role in achieving comprehensive campaign finance reform. Formed in 1870 to combat corruption in the selection of judges, the Association has long played a leadership role in providing broad, in-depth, and nonpartisan analysis of major policy issues. The Association has always been particularly interested in questions of government integrity. It has produced landmark studies on conflicts of interest in the executive and legislative branches of the federal government, and on election-law reform in New York City and State.

The Commission on Campaign Finance Reform was created in February 1997, in response to the growing concerns within the membership of the Association about the large unregulated contributions, high levels of fundraising, and high costs of campaigns in the 1996 elections. The Commission is composed of a knowledgeable and diverse group of leaders of the Bar. It consists of men and women, people of different ethnic and racial groups and diverse ideological backgrounds. It includes Republicans, Democrats, and independents. Many members currently hold or previously held elected or appointed office, or ran for elected office, at the federal, state, or local levels. Many have participated in the management and financing of campaigns. Our numbers include three past presidents of the Association (one of whom was also Secretary of State of the United States), a former Counsel to the President of the United States, a former New York State Attorney General, the General Counsel to the New York Civil Liberties Union, the Executive Director of the New York City Campaign Finance Board, academics, and practitioners without direct experience in campaigns who are knowledgeable in the ways of the world, and especially the operations of the legal system.

Over the past three years, the Commission has closely examined the operations of the federal campaign finance system, considered the principles that ought to govern campaign finance regulation, and carefully reviewed many pending reform proposals.[5] The Commission has spoken with people active in the field, and in cooperation with the New York City Campaign Finance Board it sponsored a conference that drew participants from across the country to discuss

---

[5] This report is focused exclusively on the federal campaign finance system, with particular attention to the funding of congressional campaigns. It does not address state or local campaign finance regulation. The Association of the Bar has addressed state and local campaign finance practices in previous reports. See, e.g., Committee on Election Law, "Towards a Level Playing Field—A Pragmatic Approach to Public Campaign Financing." 52 *The Record* 660 (Oct. 1997).

state and local innovations and their implications for reform at the federal level.[6]

The Commission has evaluated a broad range of reform options, including bills currently or recently before Congress; measures adopted or under consideration at the state and local level; and ideas put forward by numerous public policy and academic thinkers. We have extensively deliberated the strengths and weaknesses of a number of different ideas. Our recommendations draw from different, and conflicting, approaches to reform. Nevertheless, we believe that these proposals constitute a comprehensive package that, taken together, will protect free speech, promote competitive elections, curtail special-interest influence, reduce the burdens of fundraising, provide for a more open political process and more representative governance, improve administration, and produce a campaign finance system that is both more consistent with the system adopted by Congress nearly three decades ago and more faithful to our democratic political ideas than the system that is in place today.

C. SUMMARY OF RECOMMENDATIONS

Our recommendations draw from three different approaches to campaign finance reform. First, we would relax some of the restrictions in existing law that, due to the passage of time and the effects of inflation, have become unduly burdensome and unnecessary to advance the goals of campaign finance regulation. Thus, we would raise the current limits on individual contributions to candidates and parties, and we recommend that all contribution limits be, henceforth, indexed for inflation. Second, we would repair weaknesses in the current regulatory framework by addressing two problems that have emerged since FECA's enactment—political party soft money and issue advocacy advertising—and we would strengthen the FEC so that it could be a more effective enforcement agency. Third, we

---

[6] The Conference was held at the Association of the Bar on Nov. 9, 1998. The conference was funded in part by grants from the New York Community Trust and the Joyce Foundation. The proceedings of the conference may be found at "From the Ground Up: Local Lessons for National Reform," 27 *Fordham Urban L. J.* 5–166 (1999).

would go forward to reduce the role of large, unequal private contributions in elections and governance, ameliorate the burdens of fundraising, and enhance candidate competitiveness by providing for a system of partial public funding for congressional elections.

These three approaches are reflected in five specific groups of recommendations:

(1) Public funding for congressional elections;
(2) Adjustment of existing contribution limits;
(3) Controls on soft money;
(4) Redefining electioneering speech to permit regulation of so-called issue advocacy advertising;
(5) Reforming the FEC.

(1) Public Funding

To promote voter equality and competitive elections, to ameliorate the burdens of fundraising, to facilitate political participation by new candidates, women, and minorities, to reduce the potentially corrupting effect of large contributions, and to increase the ability of candidates to get their messages to the voters, the Special Commission recommends that Congress add to the present system of public funding for presidential elections by enacting a system of public funding for elections to the House of Representatives and the Senate.

Candidates would become eligible for public funding by (i) raising a threshold amount of qualifying contributions, (ii) agreeing to limit the use of their personal or family funds in the election, and (iii) agreeing to limit their total campaign expenditures. Public funds would be provided on a matching-funds basis, with two dollars in public funds provided for every dollar in matchable private contributions of up to $250.

Public funding would be accompanied by a spending limit. The purpose of the spending limit is not primarily to limit or reduce the amount of money devoted to campaign activity. Election expenditures provide a valuable function in educating the public and mobilizing the electorate. Challengers, in particular, need to be free to spend enough money to offset the many advantages that incumbents enjoy. The purpose of spending limits is to eliminate the "arms race" mentality that causes candidates to embark on almost endless fundraising in order to be prepared for the possibility that they will be outspent by their opponents. Thus, the spending limit ought to be set high, so as not to interfere with the ability of candidates to mount competitive campaigns. But it needs to be firm to constrain the destructive effects of the current money chase. Consistent with the spending levels of competitive challengers in recent elections, we recommend that the limit in House elections be $1 million, indexed for inflation. The limit in Senate races will vary from state to state, reflecting differences in population and spending patterns. But as with the House, the limits are keyed to spending in competitive races and are not intended to reduce general levels of spending.

Candidates participating in the public-funding program need to be assured that by accepting a spending limit they have not denied themselves the ability to respond to a high-spending opponent who has opted not to participate in the public-funding program. Consequently, we recommend that the spending limit be raised when a publicly funded candidate's opponent raises contributions that would enable him or her to spend over the limit, and that the limit be eliminated altogether when the opponent's receipts are well above the limit.

In addition, we recommend that the public-funding program be financed out of the federal Treasury, not the income-tax checkoff currently used to provide the public funds for presidential campaigns. The checkoff does not provide enough funds to cover the costs of contemporary campaigns. Moreover, no other important public program depends on a checkoff. Public funding is too vital to the health of our democracy to depend on the ups and downs of the checkoff.

(2) Adjustment of Existing Contribution Limits

The Special Commission believes that contribution limits are necessary and appropriate to control the potential for undue influence by large donors and potential donors. But we believe that these limitations ought to be adjusted in light of changes in the cost of campaigns. As campaigns have become more expensive, the size of the maximum contribution an individual can make relative to the total funds the candidate must collect has grown smaller, thereby reducing the corruptive threat of contributions currently at the statutory ceiling. With the costs of campaigns rising but the size of the maximum contribution frozen at 1974 levels, the burdens of fundraising on candidates have grown. With individual contributions capped, candidates have become more dependent on intermediaries—such as PACs and bundlers—to help them raise the funds they need. So, too, the combination of 1974-level limits and 2000 campaign costs has provided both candidates and donors with a powerful incentive to engage in soft money financing. Thus, the current limits on private contributions have not so much limited the role of fat cats as they have enlarged the role of interest groups and contributed to the soft money evasion. Consequently, we recommend that FECA's contribution restrictions be adjusted in light of changes in the costs of campaigns. The amount of money an individual can contribute to a candidate for federal office per election, thus, should be trebled from the 1974 level. This adjustment would be slightly less than the increase in the cost of living over that time. We also recommend that the current law, which provides for separate limits on contributions for primary and general elections, be changed. Realistically, candidates who make it to the general election are participating in one long campaign, not two, and moneys technically contributed for the primary election can be used for the general election. In practice, the current contribution limit is $2000 per election cycle, not the $1000 per election officially written into the statute book. FECA would be more consistent with campaign finance practices, and more honest with the public, if it set one overall limit for the entire election cycle. As a result, we recommend that an individual be permitted to contribute up to $6000 per candidate per election cycle, and that the contribution level be readjusted every two years in light of changes in the cost of living.

With respect to individual contributions to PACs, and contributions by PACs to candidates and party committees, we recommend that the current limits be continued and then indexed for inflation following the enactment of comprehensive campaign finance reform legislation. We see no persuasive basis for the statute's current posture of permitting larger contributions to and by PACs than it permits individuals to give to candidates. By immediately raising the individual limit without raising the PAC limit, we would place individual and PAC donors on a more level playing field.

Consistent with trebling the limit on individual contributions to candidates, we would treble the limit on the aggregate contributions an individual can make for federal election purposes per calendar year, from the 1974 level of $25,000 to $75,000, with the limit again indexed for inflation in the future.

(3) Soft Money and the Political Parties

Soft money is money that, by definition, is not subject to the dollar limitations and source prohibitions of federal law. Soft money is outside of FECA's regulation because it is technically used for purposes other than the support of federal candidates. But in practice, soft money has come to play an important role in federal elections. Soft money undermines the central goal of reducing the impact of special-interest influence on officeholders and the electoral process. Indeed, the very existence of soft money mocks campaign finance law.

We recommend that Congress ban the use of soft money in federal elections. We would prohibit federal officeholders and candidates for federal office from soliciting, receiving, directing, transferring, or spending any money that does not comply with the source and dollar limits applicable to federal campaign contributions. We also recommend that Congress prohibit the national committees, including the congressional campaign committees of the political parties, their officials, and their agents, from soliciting, receiving, directing, transferring, or spending any money that does not comply with the source and dollar limitations applicable to federal campaign contributions.

These proposals are not intended to reduce the role of the political parties in federal election campaigns. We recognize that parties are important participants in the financing of federal election campaigns. Party spending can have many benefits. Party money reflects a broader range of interests and concerns than money provided by PACs; party committees typically devote a greater share of their resources to competitive challengers and marginal incumbents than do other contributors; and parties give considerable attention to registering and mobilizing voters. But soft money permits unlimited participation by large donors, special interest groups, corporations, and unions. In so doing, soft money flouts the law and gives an excessive role to monetary influences within the parties. Soft money must be prohibited to restore the integrity of federal election law.

The prohibition of soft money, however, ought to be accompanied by a loosening of the rules governing hard money contributions to and by the parties. The Commission recommends that Congress raise the limit on individual hard money donations to political parties. An individual donor could give to party committees in total any amount up to the proposed aggregate ceiling on individual contributions of $75,000 per calendar year. We would also raise the limits on donations by parties to candidates, and on party spending that is coordinated with candidates. We would allow candidates who participate in the proposed congressional public-funding system to receive party financial support up to the public-funding spending limit.

The Commission would also restore the integrity of the limitations on party spending in support of candidates by clarifying when a party expenditure ought to be considered independent and when it ought to be considered coordinated with a candidate. Once a party committee has made a direct contribution to, or a coordinated contribution with, a candidate, then all subsequent expenditures by that committee and by all committees of that party with respect to that candidate are to be treated as coordinated with the candidate and as subject to the limits on party support for candidates. In addition, once a party has nominated a candidate, all party expenditures supporting that candidate are to be treated as coordinated.

(4) Express Advocacy

FECA's rules and requirements apply only to campaign messages that constitute express advocacy of the election or defeat of federal candidates. The courts have generally defined express advocacy narrowly, by holding that only messages that contain literal words of electoral advocacy—such as "vote for," "vote against," "elect," "defeat"—may be treated as express advocacy. Ads that praise or condemn clearly identified federal candidates but that carefully avoid using the magic words of express advocacy are labeled issue advocacy and are considered to be beyond the scope of regulation. Many so-called issue advocacy ads contain no discussion of issues at all. Most television viewers or radio listeners find these so-called issue ads indistinguishable from ads that contain the magic words of literal advocacy.

Electioneering ads that are deemed issue ads avoid federal reporting and disclosure requirements and may be funded by donations from corporate and union treasuries. Parties may pay for issue ads with corporate and union donations, and with individual donations that exceed FECA's limits. Party spending on issue ads is not subject to FECA's limits on coordinated expenditures, even when the ads benefit a candidate who has accepted public funding and spending limits.

The Commission recommends that FECA be amended to provide that:

(1) any advertisement that is coordinated with a candidate shall be treated as a contribution to that candidate even if the content of the advertisement avoids words of express advocacy;

(2) any communication by a committee of a major political party that mentions by name or includes the likeness of a clearly identified federal candidate shall be treated as express advocacy subject to the expenditure limitations and reporting and disclosure requirements applicable to such advocacy; and

(3) any communication that clearly identifies by name or likeness a candidate for federal office shall be presumed to be express advocacy if broadcast or published within the 30 days prior to a primary or general election; this presumption, however, may be rebutted by a showing that, based on the content and context of the speech, viewers, listeners, or readers are unlikely to treat the communication as election-related.

We recognize that these recommendations present important constitutional questions and that they depart from the current judicial definition of express advocacy. Nevertheless, for the reasons we lay out in the body of this Report, we believe that these proposals are constitutional and will withstand judicial scrutiny.

(5) Federal Election Commission

Effective enforcement is essential to any system of campaign finance law, but the current Federal Election Commission has failed to provide effective enforcement. Many of the problems with the FEC are built into its basic structure, including the even number of commissioners, the lack of a long-term chair, and the partisan appointments process, as well as congressionally imposed restrictions on the FEC's investigatory and enforcement powers. As a result, the FEC is frequently incapable of taking effective action against the major parties or their candidates.

We recommend that the FEC be restructured, with an odd number of commissioners, a chair who is appointed to serve for at least two years, and at least one member who is not affiliated with any major political party. We also recommend simplifying the FEC's cumbersome multistep enforcement process, increasing its ability to detect violations by empowering it to conduct random audits, and providing for enforcement during the real time of a contested election by allowing the FEC to go to court and seek expedited relief in appropriate cases.

Finally, we urge Congress and the President to take seriously their responsibility for effective enforcement of the campaign finance laws by depoliticizing the appointments process and by providing the FEC with the additional resources necessary for it to discharge its many tasks.

We emphasize that all the elements of this comprehensive program are closely intertwined and interdependent. Raising contribution limits is desirable only if the other steps are taken to eliminate soft money, strengthen FECA, and provide public funding, thereby balancing the effects of larger private donations with more effective enforcement of the new limits and with public money that can dilute the impact of special-interest influence. Banning soft money and regulating issue advocacy assume both an increase in the hard dollar contributions and the provision of public funding as well as effective enforcement of the new rules to ensure that these restrictions do not make it more difficult for candidates to fund their campaigns and do not create incentives for the future development of campaign finance techniques that would evade these desirable regulations. Public funding assumes effective and enforceable controls on soft money and issue advocacy, lest the public-funding system be overwhelmed by large and unregulated donations from outside the system. Higher, but effective, restrictions on private contributions may be desirable to ensure that the proposed public-funding system is, as the Supreme Court has said the Constitution requires, truly a voluntary option for participating candidates.

We believe that our package of proposals, taken together, can produce a campaign finance system that is more open and competitive, provides voters with greater information, reduces the burdens of fundraising, reduces the undue influence of large donors on governance, better respects the norm of voter equality, and is more effectively enforced than the current system. (See table 1.)

TABLE 1: SUMMARY OF RECOMMENDATIONS

Public Funding

Authorize voluntary, partial public funding in Congressional elections
- for primary and general elections
- for qualifying candidates
- $2:$1 match for each private donation up to $250 per individual donor

Qualifying by raising
- House—$25,000 (with only $250 per individual in-state donor counting)
- Senate—between $25,000 and $75,000, depending on state population (with only $250 per individual in-state donor counting)

Limit on candidate's use of personal/family funds

Spending limit
- House—$1 million per election cycle, subject to cost of living adjustment
- Senate—in states with voting-age population (VAP) less than one million, limit of $1 million + $2.00 per voting-age person. In states with VAP greater than one million, limit of $1 million + $1.50 per voting-age person

Spending limit raised if participating candidate has high-spending non-participating opponent

Contribution Limits

Limit on individual donation to candidate raised from $2000 per election cycle to $6000 per election cycle.
- and adjusted for future inflation

Limit on individual donations to party committees removed, subject only to limit on total donations by an individual

Limit on total donations by an individual to candidates, PACs, and parties raised from $25,000 per calendar year to $75,000 per calendar year
- and adjusted for future inflation

Limits on donations to and by PACs unchanged, but in the future to be adjusted for inflation

Soft Money and the Political Parties

Federal officeholders and candidates forbidden from dealing with soft money

National party committees forbidden from dealing with soft money

State party committees forbidden from dealing with soft money for federal election activity

State party committees may use soft money for mixed federal-nonfederal activities subject to allocation,

- with approximately 60% of funds in hard money

Limits on party contribution/coordinated expenditures in support of candidates to be doubled

Party spending in support of a nominated candidate defined as a coordinated expenditure

All party spending in support of a candidate who has received a party contribution or benefited from a party coordinated expenditure is defined as coordinated

Issue Advocacy/Express Advocacy

All communications coordinated with a candidate are express advocacy

All communications by a political party that mention by name, or include the likeness of, a clearly identified federal candidate are express advocacy

Rebuttable presumption that all communications by any individual or organization that mention by name, or include the likeness of, a clearly identified federal candidate within 30 days of a federal election are express advocacy

Federal Election Commission

Seventh commissioner to be appointed; must not be affiliated with a political party

Strong chair to be appointed for a two-year term

Civil enforcement process to be simplified

Random audit authority to be restored

Power to seek expedited relief authorized

Additional resources to keep pace with level of federal campaign activity

2

The Federal Campaign Finance System

A. THE STATUTORY FRAMEWORK

FEDERAL CAMPAIGN finance law has four principal elements:

(1) Contribution and expenditure restrictions in connection with elections for federal office
(2) Reporting and disclosure requirements for federal candidates and for organizations that raise and spend money in connection with federal election campaigns
(3) Enforcement by the Federal Election Commission
(4) Voluntary public funding for presidential candidates

(1) Contribution and Expenditure Restrictions

FECA imposes dollar limits on contributions to candidates, political committees, and political parties. It limits certain expenditures by political parties, as well as by candidates who choose to accept public funding. FECA also completely prohibits campaign contributions and expenditures by certain organizations and individuals, specifically corporations, labor unions, government contractors, and foreign nationals.

LIMITS ON CONTRIBUTIONS BY INDIVIDUALS   A person[7] may contribute up to $1000 to a federal candidate per election. As the Act treats primaries and general elections as separate elections,[8] the effective limit on contributions per election cycle is $2000.

A person may also give $5000 per calendar year to a "political

---

[7] "Person" includes an individual, partnership, committee, association, corporation, labor union, or any other organization or group of persons. 2 U.S.C. § 431 (10).

[8] 2 U.S.C. § 431 (1)(A). A runoff election is also considered to be a separate election with its own set of limits.

committee," that is, an organization that either receives more than $1000 in contributions to be used in federal election campaigns or spends more than $1000 in connection with federal election campaigns.

The Act treats party committees as political committees, but it permits individuals to make a total of $20,000 in contributions to the national committees of a political party per calendar year. This $20,000 limit covers a party's Senate campaign committee and its House of Representatives campaign committee as well as the party National Committee itself.

The Act imposes an aggregate cap of $25,000 on the total contributions an individual can make to all candidates, political committees, and party committees for federal election purposes within a calendar year.

LIMITS ON CONTRIBUTIONS BY POLITICAL ACTION COMMITTEES (PACs)   Contributions by a political committee to a candidate, another committee, or a political party are subject to the same limitations that apply to contributions by individuals,[9] but a "multicandidate political committee"—that is, a political committee that receives contributions from 50 or more persons and makes contributions to five or more candidates for federal office—enjoys the benefit of a higher contribution limit. Such a PAC can contribute up to $5000 per candidate per election (or $10,000 per election cycle); $5000 in contributions per calendar year to any other political committee; and $15,000 per calendar year to a national political party committee. There is no aggregate limit on the amount of contributions a PAC can make to all candidates, committees, or parties in an election cycle. All PACs established, financed, maintained, or controlled by the same corporation, union, or other person are subject to one contribution limit, so that parent organizations cannot proliferate PACs to avoid the statutory ceiling.

LIMITS ON POLITICAL PARTY CONTRIBUTIONS AND EXPENDITURES   Party committees—including the national committees, the Senate and House campaign committees, and state and local party

---

[9] There is, however, no aggregate limit on the total amount of contributions a political committee can make in a calendar year.

committees that make sufficient contributions or expenditures in connection with federal elections to fall within the Act—can contribute up to $5000 per election per candidate. In addition, each party's national committee, or its Senate campaign committee, may contribute up to $17,500 to a candidate for election to the Senate.[10]

FECA offers the parties two additional opportunities, unavailable to individuals or PACs, for providing candidates with financial support:

1. *Coordinated Expenditures:* The parties may engage in "coordinated expenditures" in support of their candidates. Money that is not given to a candidate but is spent by an individual or organization in coordination with a candidate is treated as though it were a contribution to that candidate and is subject to the statutory contribution ceiling.[11] However, the Act authorizes party committees, and only party committees, to engage in coordinated expenditures with candidates that do not count against the contribution caps. Coordinated expenditures are subject to dollar limits, but these limits are much higher than the limits on contributions. Moreover, unlike the limits on contributions, the coordinated expenditure caps are adjusted for inflation.

A party national committee may spend two cents per voting age population, inflation-adjusted from a 1974 base, in support of the party's presidential ticket.[12] Under this formula, each of the two major national parties will be able to spend $13.3 million in coordinated spending in support of its presidential ticket in 2000.[13] The national and state parties may also each spend the greater of $20,000 in 1974 dollars, or two cents in 1974 prices times the voting-age population of the state, in coordinated expenditures in connection with the general election campaigns of party Senate candidates, or for the House of Representatives candidates in a state that has only one House seat.[14] The coordinated spending limit for party spending in support of other House candidates is $10,000, inflation-adjusted

---

[10] There is no similar rule governing contributions to candidates for the House of Representatives.

[11] 2 U.S.C. § 441a(a)(7)(B)(i).

[12] 2 U.S.C. § 441a(d)(2).

[13] FEC Release, "If the Presidential Election Were Held in 1999," July 7, 1999, http://www.fec.gov/press/spend99.htm

[14] 2 U.S.C. § 441a(d)(3)(A).

from a 1974 base.[15] In 1998 the coordinated spending limit for House races in states with one House district was $65,100, and $32,550 in states with two or more House districts. FECA permits both national and state party committees to undertake coordinated expenditures in congressional elections. The state committee typically designates a national party committee—such as the Senate campaign committee for Senate elections or the House campaign committee for elections to the House of Representatives—to act as its "agent" for coordinated expenditures.[16] Such an "agency agreement" effectively doubles the national committee's coordinated expenditure limit and enhances the overall impact of party spending. As a result, in 1998, limits on party coordinated spending for Senate races ranged from $130,200 in Alaska to $3,035,874 in California.[17]

2. *Grassroots Expenditures:* State and local party committees may undertake certain "grassroots" expenditures in support of federal candidates. These include payments for (i) campaign materials "such as pins, bumper stickers, handbills, brochures, posters, party tabloids, and yard signs" used in connection with volunteer activities on behalf of party nominees; (ii) voter-registration activities; and (iii) get-out-the-vote drives.[18] These expenditures can be made only with contributions that comply with FECA's dollar caps and source limits, but the amount state and local parties can spend on these activities is unlimited.

CORPORATIONS AND LABOR UNIONS   It is unlawful for any national bank or any corporation organized under federal law to engage in any campaign finance activities, and for any other corporation or any labor organization to make any contributions or expenditures in connection with an election for federal office. The ban on corporate contributions is our oldest federal campaign finance law. The ban was first enacted in 1907 in response to disclosures about the role of large

---

[15] 2 U.S.C. § 441a(d)(3)(B).

[16] See, for example, Frank J. Sorauf, *Inside Campaign Finance: Myths and Realities,* 227 (1992). The Supreme Court upheld the transfer of such spending authority in *FEC v. Democratic Senatorial Campaign Comm.,* 454 U.S. 27 (1981).

[17] FEC Release, "FEC Announces 1998 Party Spending Limits: Amounts Range from $130,200 to $3 Million," Mar. 6, 1998, http://www.fec.gov/press/441ad.htm

[18] 2 U.S.C. § 431(8)(B)(xi),(xii),(9)(B)(viii),(ix).

corporate contributions in the 1904 presidential election campaign.[19] The ban on union campaign finance activities dates back to 1943.[20]

FECA, however, makes three exceptions from the ban on corporate and union contributions and expenditures. The first two— exemptions for "internal communications" and for nonpartisan registration and get-out-the-vote drives—track the Act's general exemptions from the definitions of contribution and expenditure. Communications by a corporation to its stockholders and executive or administrative personnel and their families, and by a union to its members and their families, are not subject to restriction. Similarly, nonpartisan registration and get-out-the-vote campaigns by a corporation aimed at its stockholders and executive or administrative personnel and their families, or by a union aimed at its members and their families, are not subject to restriction.

Corporate and Union PACs: The third exemption authorizes corporations, unions, membership organizations, trade associations, and cooperatives to use their funds to establish, administer, and solicit contributions to "a separate segregated fund to be utilized for political purposes."[21] Although corporations and unions cannot use funds from their corporate or union treasuries to contribute directly to federal candidates or to spend in support of or opposition to federal candidates, the corporations and unions can use their funds to set up PACs and to enable their PACs to solicit funds from persons affiliated with the corporation (such as shareholders and executive and administrative personnel and their families) or the union (union members and their families). The PACs, in turn, can make contributions to candidates and spend money in support of or opposition to federal candidates.[22]

---

[19] See Robert E. Mutch, *Campaigns, Congress, and Courts: The Making of Federal Campaign Finance Law*, 1–8 (1988).

[20] Id. at 153–57.

[21] 2 U.S.C. § 441b(b)(3).

[22] In general, a corporate PAC may solicit only its stockholders and senior personnel (and families), and a union PAC may solicit only its members and their families. But corporate PACs may make two written solicitations a year of other employees, and unions may make two written solicitations per year of stockholders and executives. Membership organizations, cooperatives, and corporations without capital stock may solicit only their members. Trade association PACs may solicit contributions from the stockholders and executive or administrative personnel of a member corporation of the trade association, so long as the member corporation has ap-

Contributions to a PAC sponsored by a corporation or union must be voluntary. It is unlawful to obtain contributions by force, job discrimination, financial reprisal, or threats. Any person soliciting an employee for a contribution to a fund is required to inform the employee, at the time of solicitation, of the right to refuse to contribute.

Although a corporate or union PAC is required to keep its funds separate from the parent organization, that requirement is intended to ensure only that the funds actually given to candidates, or spent in support of or opposition to candidates, are actually the result of voluntary contributions. The parent corporation or union can determine how its PAC spends its money, which candidates it supports, and how large a contribution the candidate receives. The parent organization can also pay the administrative costs of the PAC, including its fundraising expenses.

FOREIGN NATIONALS AND FEDERAL CONTRACTORS   FECA prohibits federal contractors and foreign nationals from making contributions in connection with any election to any political office. Foreign citizens who have been lawfully admitted to permanent residency in the United States are not subject to the ban on contributions by foreign nationals.[23] Federal contractors, however, can establish, administer, and solicit contributions to PACs, which are governed by the general rules applicable to PACs.[24] The law does not permit foreign nationals to create PACs.

LIMITS ON SPENDING BY CANDIDATES AND INDEPENDENT COMMITTEES   The 1974 amendments to FECA originally provided for limits on campaign spending by candidates and on spending by individuals or organizations operating independently of candidates' committees in support of or opposition to candidates. These restrictions were held unconstitutional by the Supreme Court in *Buckley v. Valeo* two years later. The Court, however, upheld the spending limits that presidential candidates were required to accept as a condition for public funding.

---

proved, and so long as the member corporation does not approve any solicitation by more than one such trade association in a calendar year.
[23] 2 U.S.C. § 441e(b)(2).
[24] 2 U.S.C. § 441c.

(2) Reporting and Disclosure Requirements

FECA imposes detailed reporting requirements on candidates and on political committees that raise and spend money in connection with federal elections. Disclosure requirements have been a central feature of federal campaign finance law since 1911, but earlier laws were riddled with exceptions and poorly enforced. Under FECA, a candidate for federal office is required to designate a principal campaign committee within 15 days of becoming a candidate. All candidate campaign committees—indeed, all political committees—are required to keep detailed records of contributions and expenditures, including the name and address of any person who makes any contribution in excess of $50 or a total of $200 in contributions in a calendar year, and the name and address of every person to whom a disbursement greater than $200 is made.

CANDIDATE COMMITTEES   Campaign committees of candidates for Congress have to file pre-election, post-election, and quarterly reports during an election year, and semiannual reports in non-election years. Campaign committees of candidates for President must file monthly, pre-election, and post-election reports in an election year, and monthly or quarterly reports in a non-election year. Other political committees must file periodic reports.

These reports must disclose total contributions from persons, from the candidate, from political party committees, and from other political committees, and they must identify: (i) any person who contributes more than $200 in the reporting period; (ii) any political committee that makes a contribution in the period; and (iii) any transfer of funds among affiliated committees. Candidate committee reports must also disclose all expenditures to meet candidate or committee operating expenses and must include the name and address of each person who received $200 in expenditures in a calendar year.

POLITICAL COMMITTEES   Political committees other than candidate committees must report contributions to other political committees and identify any person who receives a disbursement of $200 in connection with an independent expenditure by the reporting committee.

PARTY COMMITTEES   Party committees that make expenditures in connection with elections of candidates for federal office must report the name and address of each person who receives such an expenditure.

OTHER PARTICIPANTS IN FEDERAL ELECTION CAMPAIGNS   Every person or organization other than a political committee that spends more than $250 in a calendar year in connection with a federal election campaign must also file a statement identifying any person who makes a contribution greater than $200, indicating whether an expenditure is in support of or opposition to a candidate, and a certification under penalty of perjury whether the independent expenditure was made in cooperation, consultation, or concert with a candidate. Any expenditure aggregating $1000 or more made after the 20th day, but more than 24 hours, before an election must be reported to the FEC within 24 hours after it was made. The FEC is required to develop a filing, coding, and cross-indexing system for these reports. Within 48 hours of the FEC's receipt of reports and statements filed with it, the FEC must make them available for public inspection and copying.

(3) Enforcement

Although federal campaign finance laws have included disclosure requirements since 1911, prior to the enactment of FECA these laws were poorly enforced. Disclosure "meant nothing more than submitting reports of general election contributions and expenditures to the House clerk and Senate secretary; there were no regulations standardizing reporting forms or defining violations, and little provision for enforcement. . . . [T]he act made no provision for publicizing reported financial data. As candidates and committees ignored it, and attorneys general failed to enforce it, the law became a dead letter."[25] A central feature of FECA is the creation of an independent agency to enforce the Act's contribution restrictions and reporting requirements, and to disclose campaign finance information to the public.

FEDERAL ELECTION COMMISSION   The FEC consists of six members appointed by the President, with the advice and consent of the

---

[25] Mutch, supra, at 84.

Senate, for six-year terms. As a result of an amendment enacted in 1997, newly appointed or reappointed members are henceforth limited to a single term. No more than three of the members appointed by the President may be affiliated with the same political party. In practice, three members of the FEC are Democrats and three are Republicans, and despite the President's formal power to nominate, the Democratic and Republican congressional leaders have "enormous influence" in selecting the appointees who "represent" their respective parties.[26]

The FEC has exclusive jurisdiction with respect to the civil enforcement of FECA. The FEC has the power to initiate, defend, and appeal civil actions; render advisory opinions; make, amend, and repeal rules; subpoena the attendance and testimony of witnesses and compel the production of documents; and conduct audits and field investigations.

CIVIL PENALTIES   Penalties for violation of FECA's requirements are a maximum of $5500 or the amount of the contribution or expenditure involved in the violation, whichever is greater. For knowing and willful violations, the penalty doubles to $11,000, or twice the amount of the contribution or expenditure involved in the violation, whichever is greater.

CRIMINAL PENALTIES   Any person who knowingly and willfully commits a violation of the Act that involves the making, receiving, or reporting of any contribution or expenditure aggregating $2000 or more in a calendar year may be fined, imprisoned for not more than one year, or both. The fine shall not exceed the greater of $25,000 or 300 percent of the contribution or expenditure involved in the violation. In the case of a knowing and willful violation of the rules governing solicitations by the PACs of corporations, unions, and membership organizations—particularly the rules designed to ensure that contributions to such funds are voluntary—these penalties may apply to violations involving $250 or more in a calendar year.

Criminal enforcement falls within the exclusive jurisdiction of the Department of Justice. FECA's criminal penalties are rarely invoked,

---

[26] Brooks Jackson, *Broken Promise: Why the Federal Election Commission Failed,* 29 (1990).

however, because of the difficulty of proving a knowing and willful violation, as well as the statute's short three-year statute of limitations.[27]

(4) The Presidential Public Funding System

The presidential election campaign public funding system has three components: funding for the general election campaign, funding for pre-nomination campaigns, and funding for the nominating conventions of the national parties. All three components are funded by the voluntary income-tax checkoff established by 26 U.S.C. § 6096. The checkoff—originally $1 for an individual return and $2 for a joint return—was raised to $3 and $6 in 1993.

GENERAL ELECTION PUBLIC FUNDING   The Act provides for a system of voluntary but, at least theoretically, full general election public funding for participating candidates. The candidates of major parties may receive public funds for their campaigns if they agree not to make campaign expenditures greater than the public funds they receive, furnish the FEC with a complete record of campaign expenses, and agree to audit and examination by the FEC.

Major party candidates—that is, candidates of those parties that received 25 percent or more of the vote in the prior presidential election—are entitled to receive $20 million, adjusted for inflation from a 1974 base. The public grant was $61.8 million in 1996 and is expected to be at least $66.12 million for the 2000 election.[28] Since the adoption of the public funding system, the only parties that have qualified as major parties are the Republican and Democratic parties.

---

[27] See generally Kenneth A. Gross, "The Enforcement of Campaign Finance Rules: A System in Search of Reform," 9 *Yale Law & Pol. Rev.* 279 (1991); Michael W. Carroll, "When Congress Just Says No: Deterrence Theory and the Inadequate Enforcement of the Federal Election Campaign Act," 84 *Geo. L. J.* 551 (1996). Criminal cases growing out of campaign finance abuses are more likely to be brought under the Federal False Statements Act (for failure to disclose an excessive contribution, or using a conduit to hide it), as conspiracy to defraud the United States (for misrepresenting the true source of a contribution), or embezzlement (when funds that cannot be used for a political contribution are diverted to that purpose) than under FECA's criminal provisions. See Carroll, supra, at 557.

[28] FEC, "If the Presidential Election Were Held in 1999," http://www.fec.gov/press/spend99.htm (July 7, 1999). Final determination of the 2000 federal grant will not occur until final figures for cost-of-living adjustments are available in early 2000.

A *minor party candidate*—that is, the candidate of party whose candidate for president received more than 5 percent but less than 25 percent of the popular vote in the preceding presidential election—is also eligible to receive public funds. Minor party candidates receive a fraction of the funds paid to the major party candidates. That fraction is based on the ratio of the number of popular votes the minor party's candidate received in the last presidential election to the average number of popular votes received by the major party candidates in the preceding presidential election. Thus, Ross Perot, who received 19 percent of the total vote in 1992 as the candidate of the Reform Party (in an election in which the Republican and Democratic candidates received an average of about 40 percent of the vote each), received $29.1 million. In order to receive public funds, minor party candidates also have to agree to accept the spending cap and other conditions applicable to major party candidates. As the Reform Party received 8.4 percent of the popular presidential vote in the 1996 election, it will be eligible to receive approximately $11 million for the 2000 general election.

The candidate of a *new party*—that is, a party that failed to receive 5 percent of the vote in the preceding presidential election—may also receive public funds. The payment to new party candidates will be made only after the election and only if the candidate receives more than 5 percent of the popular vote. The payment to a new party candidate is based on the ratio of the candidate's votes to the average vote for the candidates of the major parties. Under this provision, John Anderson received public funds after the 1980 election. In order to be eligible for public funds, a new party candidate must abide by the spending cap and agree to the other conditions applicable to the major party candidates during the election.

Spending Limits The public grant comes with a spending limit. The presidential ticket may not spend more than the public grant. There are two exceptions to this rule.

First, the public funding law provides that candidates can raise and spend without limitation funds for general election legal and accounting compliance (GELAC). These funds must comply with FECA's contribution restrictions and reporting requirements, but they are not subject to spending limits. In 1996 the two major and one minor party candidates eligible for public funds supplemented their combined $152.7 million in public grants with $13.6 million in GELAC funds.[29]

Second, the law authorizes the parties to engage in coordinated expenditures in support of their presidential tickets. The coordinated spending limit is two cents per voting-age population adjusted from a 1974 base. In 1996 the coordinated spending limit was $12.1 million for each of the major parties. Interestingly, neither party actually spent at the limit level. The Republican Party, at $11.6 million, came close, but the Democratic Party, at $6.7 million, spent only a little more than half its permitted coordinated expenditures.[30]

The decision of a presidential candidate to accept public funding and a spending limit cannot operate to limit the spending by independent organizations in support of that candidate or in opposition to that candidate's opponent. Provided the organization is truly operating independently of the publicly funded presidential candidate, its spending cannot be limited.[31]

Nominating Conventions   The parties can receive public funds to defray the costs of their nominating conventions. Provided they agree not to make expenditures greater than the payments from public funds, major parties may receive the inflation-adjusted equivalent of $4 million in 1974 dollars.[32] In 1996 each of the major parties received $12.4 million for its convention costs. They will each receive $13.2 million in 2000.[33] A minor party may receive a fraction, based on the same ratio used for calculating payments to the minor party presidential candidate, provided the minor party also agrees to a convention spending cap. The Reform Party is scheduled to receive $2.5 million for its 2000 convention.[34]

---

[29] Anthony Corrado, "Financing the 1996 Presidential General Election," in *Financing the 1996 Election,* John C. Green, ed., 74–79 (1999).

[30] Id. at 79–81.

[31] *FEC v. National Conservative Political Action Comm.,* 470 U.S. 480 (1985).

[32] 26 U.S.C. § 9008. Originally, the limit was $2 million, subject to cost of living adjustment. That figure was increased to $3 million plus COLA for 1980, and then to $4 million plus COLA for the 1984 conventions and thereafter.

[33] FEC, "Both Major Parties to Receive Public Funding for 2000 Conventions," http://www.fec.gov/press/conv00.htm (June 28, 1999).

[34] FEC, "Reform Party to Receive Public Funding for 2000 Convention," http://www.fec.gov/press/refconv.htm (Nov. 22, 1999). The grants to the major parties are supposed to fully fund their convention costs, but the parties may create host-city committees that can raise private donations to cover certain convention-related costs. Host-city committee expenditures now rival the public grant.

PRESIDENTIAL PRIMARY CAMPAIGNS For the presidential general election, the public grant is largely intended to replace private funding for major party candidates. For the primaries, public funding is intended to cover only part of a candidate's costs. A candidate is eligible for presidential primary public funds if he or she raises at least $5000 in contributions from residents of each of at least 20 states, although no more than $250 from any one donor can be counted toward the qualification threshold. A candidate ceases to be eligible for payments 30 days after the second consecutive primary election in which he or she receives less than 10 percent of the votes cast for all the candidates of the candidate's party in that primary. The candidate may become reeligible if he or she receives 20 percent or more of the total vote for candidates of his or her party in a subsequent primary.

Public funds are provided as a dollar-for-dollar match for each private contribution the candidate receives, up to $250 from each donor. Total matching payments to a candidate are capped at 50 percent of the limitation on total prenomination spending imposed as a condition for participation in the primary matching program. The prenomination spending ceiling, originally set at $10 million subject to inflation adjustment, is one-half the ceiling on general election spending for major parties. Thus, in 1996 the prenomination spending cap was $30.9 million, and the most public funds a candidate could receive was $15.45 million. In 2000, the prenomination spending cap is likely to be a little above $33 million. In addition, primary candidates may raise an amount equivalent to 20 percent of the spending cap to cover fundraising costs in the preconvention period. That effectively raises the 2000 spending limit to about $39.7 million. Moreover, like general election candidates, primary candidates may spend unlimited amounts for legal and accounting costs they incur to comply with the law.

The primary matching program also limits the amount a candidate can spend in each state. A presidential candidate can spend no more than the greater of 16 cents multiplied by the voting-age population of the state, or $200,000, adjusted for inflation from a 1974 base.

For both primary and general election public funding, a candidate who accepts public funding may not spend more than a total of $50,000 in funds that come from the candidate's personal resources or from the resources of members of the candidate's immediate family.

B. THE CONSTITUTIONAL LAW OF CAMPAIGN FINANCE

Federal campaign finance law and the possibilities of reform are shaped and constrained by constitutional law. The constitutional law of campaign finance first emerged with the Supreme Court's landmark 1976 decision of *Buckley v. Valeo*.[35] The *Buckley* case involved a wide-ranging challenge to the key provisions of the Federal Election Campaign Act of 1971 and the 1974 amendments. *Buckley* and its progeny have dominated judicial review of campaign finance regulation for a quarter century. The Supreme Court's recent decision in *Nixon v. Shrink Missouri Government PAC*[36] underscores *Buckley*'s continuing significance to campaign regulation.

The basic elements of the *Buckley* doctrine are[37]:

- Campaign finance regulations implicate the First Amendment's protections of political speech and association.
- Campaign finance may be regulated to prevent corruption or the appearance of corruption but not to equalize the spending of competing candidates or the influence of different voters or groups, or to limit the resources devoted to campaigns.
- Contributions and expenditures are to be treated differently; expenditures enjoy the highest level of constitutional protection, while contributions are less protected and, because they more clearly raise the danger of corruption, are more easily limited.
- Reporting and disclosure requirements are generally constitutional because they perform the valuable role of informing voters about the sources of the funds financing campaign activity.
- Contribution and expenditure limits and reporting and disclosure

---

[35] 424 U.S. 1 (1976).

[36] 120 S. Ct. 897 (2000).

[37] *Buckley* also invalidated the structure of the FEC. As originally created in 1974, the FEC would have consisted of six commissioners, two (one Republican and one Democrat) appointed by the President, one each by the Majority and Minority Leaders of the Senate, and one each by the Speaker and the Minority Leader of the House. The Supreme Court held that vesting law-enforcement authority in a body that included appointees of the legislative leaders violated the separation of powers. Congress responded in 1976 by providing for an FEC composed of six members appointed by the President, subject to the advice and consent of the Senate.

requirements can be applied only to those activities that expressly advocate the election or defeat of federal candidates, and not to general political speech.

- Public funding of candidates is constitutional; indeed, public funding furthers First Amendment values by facilitating public discussion and electoral communication and reducing the influence of large private contributions; and candidates can be required to accept spending limits, which would otherwise be unconstitutional, as a condition for receiving public funds.

One significant component of FECA not considered in *Buckley* is the ban on the use of corporation and union treasury funds for contributions and expenditures in federal elections. That ban was upheld in later cases.

Applicability of the First Amendment to Campaign Finance Regulation

Buckley determined that campaign finance regulations impinge on the values of political expression and freedom of association protected by the First Amendment. *Buckley* did not conclude that "money is speech," but it did find that in our large, complex, and heterogeneous society money is often essential for the dissemination of political speech:

> The distribution of the humblest handbill or leaflet entails printing, paper, and circulation costs. Speeches and rallies generally necessitate hiring a hall and publicizing the event. The electorate's increasing dependence on television, radio, and other mass media for news and information has made these expensive modes of communication indispensable instruments of effective political speech.[38]

Justice Breyer recently restated the point in his concurring opinion in *Nixon v. Shrink Missouri Government PAC*, when he observed that campaign finance restrictions are a "matter of First Amendment concern not because money *is* speech (it is not), but because it *enables* speech."[39]

Having situated campaign finance regulation within the domain of the First Amendment, however, *Buckley* did not consider all cam-

---

[38] *Buckley,* supra, 424 U.S. at 19.

[39] *Shrink Missouri Government PAC,* supra, Breyer, J., concurring, 120 S. Ct. at 911 (emphasis supplied). Justice Ginsburg joined Justice Breyer's opinion.

paign finance activities exempt from regulation, nor did it apply a uniform standard of review to campaign restrictions and requirements.

Justifications for Regulating Campaign Finance Activities

Buckley rejected three proposed justifications for restrictions on campaign finance activities. First, the Court determined that campaign contributions or expenditures could not be limited in order to promote equality of political influence among individuals or groups supporting or opposing different candidates. Second, the Court found that campaign contributions or expenditures could not be restricted in order to equalize the financial resources of candidates competing for federal office. The Court did not challenge the importance of these concerns but held that they could not be advanced by the imposition of limits on the use of campaign money. Third, the Court rejected the argument that restricting the cost of campaigns could justify limits on spending. Indeed, the Court denied there was any constitutional interest in limiting campaign spending: "[T]he mere growth in the cost of federal election campaigns in and of itself provides no basis for governmental restrictions on the quantity of campaign spending and the resulting limitation on the scope of federal campaigns. The First Amendment denies government the power to determine that spending to promote one's political views is wasteful, excessive, or unwise."[40]

The Court, however, found that campaign finance activities could be limited to prevent "corruption and the appearance of corruption spawned by the real or imagined coercive influence of large financial contributions on candidate's positions and on their actions if elected to office."[41] As the Court acknowledged, "[t]o the extent that large contributions are given to secure political quid pro quos from current and potential officeholders, the integrity of our system of representative government is undermined." Moreover, "[o]f almost equal concern as the danger of actual quid pro quo arrangements is the impact of the appearance of corruption stemming from public awareness of the opportunities for abuse inherent in a regime of large individual

---

[40] *Buckley,* supra, 424 U.S. at 57.
[41] Id. at 25.

financial contributions." Congress could act to stem the erosion in public "confidence in the system of representative government" by imposing some restrictions on campaign finances.

The Contribution/Expenditure Distinction

Closely related to its rejection of political equality and its endorsement of preventing corruption as justifications for campaign finance limits, the *Buckley* Court distinguished between two different forms of regulatory techniques: restrictions on *expenditures*—that is, spending by candidates, organizations, and individuals on communications to the voters—and restrictions on *contributions*—that is, payments by an individual or organization to a candidate, which the candidate then uses to fund political communications with the voters.

Expenditures were given the greatest degree of constitutional protection. Expenditures were held to be the highest form of campaign finance activity because they involve direct communication to the voters. The Court rejected the egalitarian arguments for limiting campaign spending and determined that limits on candidates' expenditures could not be justified as necessary to limit the danger of corruption. As a result, *Buckley* invalidated dollar limitations on expenditures by candidates.

Contributions were given less constitutional protection. First, the Court viewed contributions as a lesser form of political speech. Unlike an expenditure, a contribution does not entail an expression of political views; "it serves as a general expression of support for the candidate and his views but does not communicate the underlying basis for the support." In a sense, a contribution is "speech by proxy": "While contributions may result in political expression if spent by a candidate or an association to present views to the voters, the transformation of contributions into political debate involves speech by someone other than the contributor."[42]

Second, contributions, unlike expenditures, raise the specter of corruption. The transmission of money from a donor to a candidate raises both the danger and the appearance of a quid pro quo. Contributions can undermine the integrity of the public process in a way that expenditures, which are simply the communication of political ideas, do not.

---

[42] Id. at 21.

Consequently, *Buckley* upheld FECA's limits on individual contributions to candidates, on contributions by PACs to candidates, and on aggregate campaign contributions by an individual.

Buckley's contribution/expenditure distinction is central to the jurisprudence of campaign finance. The distinction has been controversial. Three members of the *Buckley* Court rejected the distinction: Chief Justice Burger and Justice Blackmun would have invalidated contribution limits as well as expenditure limits. Justice White, who found that promoting equality and limiting campaign costs could justify restrictions on campaign spending, would have upheld both sets of limits. Justice Marshall, who supported the distinction in *Buckley*, subsequently rejected it and indicated he would uphold limits on campaign expenditures as well as contributions.[43]

In 1996, in *Colorado Republican Federal Campaign Committee v. FEC*,[44] three justices broke with the distinction: Justices Stevens and Ginsburg determined that the important interest in leveling the electoral playing field could justify expenditure limitations, while Justice Thomas indicated he would invalidate restrictions on contributions as well as on expenditures. In *Shrink Missouri Government PAC*, Justice Scalia joined Justice Thomas in condemning contribution restrictions, while Justice Kennedy, articulating deep dissatisfaction with the basic *Buckley* framework, indicated both sympathy with Justice Thomas's criticism of contribution restrictions and a willingness to support some limits on expenditures as well as contributions. Justice Breyer, joined by Justice Ginsburg, suggested that *Buckley* might be reinterpreted in light of the post-*Buckley* experience to make less absolute the contribution/expenditure line and permit some limitations on expenditures. Justice Stevens went further, implicitly questioning the First Amendment basis for *Buckley*'s invalidation of spending limits.

Nevertheless, in these two recent cases, majorities reaffirmed the basic elements of the contribution/expenditure distinction that expenditures enjoy the highest level of constitutional protection and may not be limited in order to equalize candidate spending or to equalize the influence of the different groups supporting different candidates, but that contributions are less protected and may be subject to dollar limits in order to ameliorate the dangers of corruption.

---

[43] *FEC v. National Conservative Political Action Committee*, 470 U.S. 480, 518 (1984).

[44] 518 U.S. 604 (1996).

Shrink Missouri Government PAC, in particular, reiterated *Buckley*'s conclusion that contribution restrictions are much less of a burden on First Amendment interests than expenditure restrictions, and reemphasized the importance of contribution limitations in avoiding both corruption and the perception of corruption. As Justice Souter wrote, "there is little reason to doubt that sometimes large contributions will work actual corruption of our political system, and no reason to question the existence of a corresponding suspicion among voters."[45] The Court treated voter concerns about corruption as a powerful justification for contribution limitations: "Leave the perception of impropriety unanswered, and the cynical assumption that large donors call the tune could jeopardize the willingness of voters to take part in democratic governance."[46]

Applying the Contribution/Expenditure Distinction

The contribution/expenditure distinction is not always easy to apply. Some forms of campaign money have elements of both contributions and expenditures.

Candidates' Personal Funds: A candidate's use of his or her personal funds or family funds in his or her own campaign is in form a contribution, but since these fund the candidate's own speech they also resemble an expenditure. *Buckley* treated a candidate's contribution of personal funds to his or her own campaign as an expenditure and invalidated FECA's limits on a candidate's use of personal or family funds.[47] Justice Marshall, who joined all other aspects of *Buckley*, dissented from this point.[48] Justice Breyer, in *Shrink Missouri Government PAC*, hinted that candidates' expenditures from personal funds "might be considered contributions to their own campaigns."

Independent Expenditures: Expenditures by individuals or organizations not affiliated with a candidate that expressly support or oppose a candidate for federal office are formally expenditures, but since they benefit a candidate they raise the possibility that the candidate who is benefited thereby will feel an obligation to the spender comparable to that created by a contribution. *Buckley* concluded that

---

[45] *Shrink Missouri Government PAC*, 120 S. Ct. at 908.
[46] Id. at 906.
[47] 424 U.S. at 51–54.
[48] Id. at 286–87.

independent expenditures ought to be treated like candidate expenditures, rather than as contributions to a candidate. The Court discounted the likelihood that such expenditures pose the dangers of corruption, finding that "the absence of prearrangement and coordination of the expenditure with the candidate or his agent not only undermines the value of the expenditure to the candidate, but also alleviates the danger that expenditures will be given as a quid pro quo for improper commitments from the candidate."[49] Consequently, *Buckley* invalidated a FECA provision that would have limited spending by an independent committee in support of or opposition to a federal candidate. Subsequently, in 1984, in *FEC v. National Conservative Political Action Committee*,[50] the Court invalidated the provision of the presidential public funding law that would have imposed a $1000 limit on spending by an independent committee supporting a publicly funded presidential candidate. In 1996, in *Colorado Republican*, a plurality of the Court held that a political party may engage in spending that is independent of that party's candidate, and when it does so, such spending cannot be subject to limitation.

Contributions to Political Committees: Many of FECA's contribution restrictions apply not simply to contributions to a candidate but to organizations that in turn make contributions to a candidate. Such donations are not expenditures as they do not entail direct communications with the voters, but they are not direct contributions to candidates either. *Buckley* did not address this question, but the Court subsequently upheld restrictions on donations to PACs on the theory that such restrictions prevent the donor from using the PAC as a conduit for donations to a candidate and thus prevent circumvention of FECA's limits on donations to candidates.[51]

Defining and Proving Corruption: The prevention of corruption and the appearance of corruption is a central concern of campaign finance doctrine, but the Court has never precisely defined corruption. *Buckley* focused on the "quid pro quo" quality of corruption, but it declined to limit the notion of corruption to outright vote-buying. As the Court recently explained in *Shrink Missouri Govern-*

---

[49] Id. at 47.

[50] 470 U.S. 480 (1984).

[51] See, for example, *California Medical Assn. v. FEC*, 453 U.S. 182 (1981); *FEC v. National Right to Work Committee*, 459 U.S.197 (1982).

ment PAC, "We recognized a concern not confined to bribery of public officials, but extending to the broader threat of politicians too compliant with the wishes of large contributors."[52] *Buckley* held that Congress could use contribution restrictions to curtail the power of money "to influence governmental action" in ways less "blatant and specific" than bribery.[53] The Court emphasized the significance of public concern about the effects of large donations on government in its assessment of the dangers posed by large contributions. Acknowledging that most large contributors "do not seek improper influence over a candidate's position or an officeholder's action," the Court held that limits on large contributions are still constitutionally valid: "Not only is it difficult to isolate suspect contributions, but more importantly, Congress was justified in concluding that the interest in safeguarding against the appearance of impropriety requires that the opportunity for abuse inherent in the process of raising large monetary contributions be eliminated."[54] *Buckley* was relatively deferential to Congress's judgment concerning the size of the contributions that raise the danger of corruption. Quoting the opinion of the court of appeals, *Buckley* concluded, " '[i]f it is satisfied that some limit on contributions is necessary, a court has no scalpel to probe, whether, say, a $2000 ceiling might not serve as well as $1000.' . . . Such distinctions in degree become significant only when they can be said to be differences in kind."[55]

Shrink Missouri Government PAC reiterated this relatively deferential approach in the context of limits imposed by a state legislature on state candidates: "The quantum of empirical evidence needed to satisfy heightened judicial scrutiny of legislative judgments will vary up or down with the novelty and plausibility of the justification raised. *Buckley* demonstrates that the dangers of large, corrupt contributions and the suspicion that large contributions are corrupt are neither novel nor implausible."

Reporting and Disclosure Requirements

Buckley sustained all of FECA's reporting and disclosure requirements. It found that disclosure serves three substantial interests: (i)

---

[52] *Shrink Missouri Government PAC,* 120 S. Ct. at 905.
[53] *Buckley,* supra, 424 U.S. at 28.
[54] Id. at 30.
[55] Id.

providing the electorate with information concerning the sources of a candidate's financial support and, thus, helping the electorate to evaluate the candidate; (ii) deterring corruption and the appearance of corruption "by exposing large contributions and expenditures to the light of publicity"; and (iii) gathering the data necessary to detect violations of the contribution limits.[56]

Buckley also upheld the requirement that independent committees disclose contributions and expenditures in excess of $100. Although independent expenditures may not be limited, disclosure serves an "informational interest" and "increases the fund of information concerning those who support candidates." Even for independent spending, this "informational interest can be as strong as it is in coordinated spending, for disclosure helps voters to define more of the candidates' constituencies."[57]

Finally, the Court upheld FECA's very low reporting thresholds. At the time of the *Buckley* decision, FECA required political committees to keep the names and addresses of those who made contributions in excess of just $10 and to obtain and report the occupations and principal places of business of those who contributed more than $100. The Court acknowledged these thresholds "are indeed low. Contributors of relatively small amounts are likely to be especially sensitive to recording or disclosure of their political preferences. These strict requirements may well discourage participation . . . in the political process." Nevertheless, as in its consideration of contribution limits, the Court deferred to Congress on the question of the precise reporting thresholds. "We cannot require Congress to establish that it has chosen the highest reasonable threshold. The line is necessarily a judgmental decision, best left in the context of this complex legislation to congressional discretion." That particular line Con-

---

[56] Id. at 67–68. *Buckley* acknowledged that minor parties with more precarious financial bases may be vulnerable to the chilling effect of the disclosure of the identity of donors and vendors, and that "the government interest in disclosure is diminished when the contribution in question is made to a minor party with little chance of winning an election." The Court declined to create a blanket exemption for minor parties but indicated it would exempt a minor party from disclosure on a showing that disclosure might subject the party's donors or vendors to harassment. In *Brown v. Socialist Workers '74 Campaign Committee*, 459 U.S. 87 (1982), the Court found that the Socialist Workers Party, which had been harassed by the government in the past, was constitutionally entitled to an exemption from a state campaign finance law disclosure requirement.

[57] *Buckley*, supra, 424 U.S. at 81.

gress drew was not "wholly without rationality"[58] and, hence, constitutional.

The Definition of Election-Related Activity

The importance of the prevention of corruption and the appearance of corruption, and the significance of the information that the disclosure of the sources of campaign funds provides to the voters, led the Court to uphold regulations in the election context that it most likely would have invalidated if applied to political speech generally. As a result, *Buckley* created a need to distinguish between election-related activity and other forms of political activity.

Congress sought to have FECA apply to expenditures "relative to a clearly identified candidate." The Court concluded that "relative to" is "so indefinite" that it "fails to clearly mark the boundary between permissible and impermissible speech."[59] Looking to other language in the statute and to the legislative history, the Court determined that to save "relative to" from the charge of unconstitutional vagueness, the provision could apply "only to expenditures that in express terms advocate the election or defeat of a clearly identified candidate for federal office." In a footnote, the Court stated that under this construction the statute would apply to "communications containing express words of advocacy of election or defeat, such as 'vote for,' 'elect,' 'support,' 'cast your ballot for,' 'Smith for Congress,' 'vote against,' 'defeat,' 'reject.' "[60]

The Court's narrowing construction of "relating to" failed to save FECA's dollar limit on independent expenditures but played a critical role in saving the reporting and disclosure requirements for independent expenditures. As drafted by Congress, FECA required the disclosure of expenditures "for the purpose of . . . influencing" nomination or election of candidates to federal office. This definition posed the danger of "encompassing both issue discussion and advocacy of a political result." Although the requirement could be safely imposed on candidates and on organizations whose "major purpose . . . is the nomination or election of a candidate," when applied to

---

[58] Id. at 83.
[59] Id. at 41.
[60] Id. at 44 n.52

other individuals or organizations, it raised the possibility of requiring disclosure concerning the sources or expenditure of funds used in connection with issue discussions "remote" from the purposes of the Act. To avoid that possibility, the Court read the expenditure disclosure provision to reach "only funds used for communications that expressly advocate the election or defeat of a clearly identified candidate." That would ensure that the spending subject to disclosure "is unambiguously related to the campaign of a particular federal candidate."[61] On that reading, the Court upheld the disclosure requirement.

The Court subsequently broadened slightly its definition of "express advocacy." In *FEC v. Massachusetts Citizens for Life, Inc. (MCFL)*,[62] the Court considered a "Special Edition" of a right-to-life organization's newsletter that listed all the candidates for state and federal office in Massachusetts and identified each one as either supporting or opposing the organization's position on three issues. The publication generally exhorted voters to vote for "pro-life" candidates and provided photographs of only those candidates whose records consistently favored MCFL's positions. The Court found that this constituted "express advocacy": "The Edition cannot be regarded as a mere discussion of public issues that by their nature raise the names of certain politicians. Rather, it provides in effect an explicit directive: vote for these (named) candidates. The fact that this message is marginally less direct that 'Vote for Smith' does not change its essential nature. The Edition goes beyond issue discussion to express electoral advocacy."[63]

Presidential Public Funding System

Buckley sustained presidential public funding without reservation. Public funding was held to fall within the scope of Congress's power to promote the general welfare and did not constitute an "establishment" of any political views. In the Court's view, "to use public money to facilitate and enlarge public discussion and participation in the electoral process, goals vital to a self-governing people, . . . fur-

---

[61] Id. at 80.
[62] 479 U.S. 238 (1986).
[63] Id. at 249.

thers . . . pertinent First Amendment values." Indeed, "public financing as a means of eliminating the improper influence of large private contributions furthers a significant governmental interest." The Act's provision of greater funding to major parties than to minor or new parties was not invidious discrimination as "the Constitution does not require Congress to treat all declared candidates the same for public financing purposes." Congress could choose to tie funding to electoral strength and to rely on the vote in past elections in order to determine eligibility.[64]

The Court also held that Congress could condition the provision of public funds on a candidate's agreement to abide by expenditure limits, so long as the candidate's agreement is voluntary: "Just as a candidate may voluntarily limit the size of the contributions he chooses to accept, he may decide to forgo private fund-raising and accept public funding."[65] In a later case, the Republican National Committee challenged the ancillary restriction on political party coordinated expenditures in support of its presidential ticket, contending that, as a practical matter, candidates had no choice but to accept public funding and that conditioning public funding on the waiver of the First Amendment right to engage in unlimited expenditures constituted an unconstitutional condition. The district court rejected these arguments, and the Supreme Court summarily affirmed.[66]

On the other hand, as previously noted, the Court invalidated limits on independent spending in support of a candidate who chose to accept public funding. A candidate cannot waive the rights of others to engage in independent expenditures on behalf of the candidate.

Special Restrictions on Corporations and Unions

Buckley did not consider the provisions of FECA that prohibit corporations and unions from making contributions and expenditures in connection with federal elections, but provide that corporations and unions may participate in federal elections only by creating "separate, segregated funds" that may solicit voluntary contributions that may be used for federal election contributions and expenditures.

---

[64] *Buckley,* supra, 424 U.S. at 92–98.

[65] Id. at 57 n.65.

[66] *Republican National Committee v. FEC,* 487 F. Supp. (S.D.N.Y.), aff'd mem 445 U.S. 995 (1980).

In *FEC v. National Right to Work Committee (NRWC)*,[67] the Court upheld the provision of FECA that provides that a corporation without capital stock may solicit contributions to its separate, segregated fund only from "members" of the corporation. In so doing, *NRWC* more broadly validated FECA's restrictions on corporate campaign activities.

NRWC found that the restrictions on corporate and union activities have two purposes: (i) "to ensure that substantial aggregations of wealth amassed by the special advantages which go with the corporate form of organization should not be converted into political 'war chests' which could be used to incur political debts," and (ii) to protect the individuals who have paid money into a corporation or union for purposes other than the support of candidates from having that money used to support candidates to whom they may be opposed. These purposes were deemed "sufficient to justify the regulation at issue." Acknowledging that the National Right to Work Committee, although corporate in form, did not exactly fit the stereotype of the wealthy corporation, the Court emphasized that FECA's restriction "reflects a legislative judgment that the special characteristics of the corporate structure require particularly careful regulation." Although FECA "restricts the solicitation of corporations and labor unions without great financial resources, as well as those more fortunately situated, we accept Congress' judgment that it is the potential for such influence that demands regulation."[68]

Subsequently, *MCFL* reiterated that "concern over the corrosive influence of concentrated corporate wealth reflects the conviction that it is important to protect the integrity of the marketplace of political ideas."[69] Corporate spending is problematic because it "raises the prospect that resources amassed in the economic marketplace may be used to provide an unfair advantage in the political marketplace." "Political 'free trade' " does not require that competing candidates or interests possess equal resources as "relative availability of funds is . . . a rough barometer of public support." But a business corporation's resources "are not an indication of popular support for

---

[67] 459 U.S. 197 (1982).
[68] Id. at 207–10.
[69] 479 U.S. at 257.

the corporation's political ideas. They reflect instead the economically motivated decisions of investors and customers. The availability of these resources may make a corporation a formidable political presence, even though the power of the corporation may be no reflection of the power of its ideas."

MCFL created a limited exception from the ban on the use of corporate treasury funds for the expenditures of organizations that, although corporate in form, do not present the dangers of political activity of corporations organized for economic gain. When an organization is formed for the express purpose of promoting political ideas, cannot engage in business activities, has no shareholders or other persons with claims on corporate earnings, and does not accept contributions from corporations or unions, then its resources reflect political support for the organization's political positions, not success in the economic marketplace. Consequently, FECA's prohibition on corporate spending could not be constitutionally applied to ideological corporations.[70]

In 1990, in *Austin v. Michigan Chamber of Commerce*,[71] the Court upheld a state law, comparable to FECA, that banned the use of corporate treasury funds to pay for independent expenditures in support of or opposition to a candidate. Tracking *NRWC* and *MCFL*, the Court determined that the "unique state-conferred" advantages that corporations enjoy, and the fact that corporate resources "have little or no correlation to the public's support for the corporation's political ideas," created a danger of corruption sufficient to justify a prohibition on the expenditure of corporate treasury funds in support of or opposition to candidates.[72] *Austin* refused to extend *MCFL's* exemption for non-business corporations to the Michigan Chamber of Commerce, which described itself as a "non-profit ideological corporation." Unlike the MCFL, the Chamber engaged in business promotion as well as political activities, and the Chamber was largely funded by contributions from for-profit business corporations, raising the danger that it could "serve as a conduit for corporate political spending."[73]

---

[70] Id. at 263–64.
[71] 494 U.S. 652 (1990).
[72] Id. at 659–61.
[73] Id. at 661–65.

C. FEDERAL CAMPAIGN FINANCE ACTIVITIES OUTSIDE OF FECA

In recent years two major new forms of campaign finance activity have emerged that are largely beyond the scope of federal regulation. These are known as *soft money* and *issue advocacy*. Soft money and issue advocacy are often intertwined, and soft money pays for much of the issue advocacy undertaken by political parties. The explosive growth of soft money and issue advocacy has eroded the Act's reporting and disclosure requirements, the dollar limitations on contribution levels, the prohibitions on corporate and union donations, and the spending limits applicable to publicly funded presidential candidates.

Soft Money

The term "soft money" emerged in contrast to "hard money," that is, money that complies with the dollar amount and source limitations of FECA. Contributions and expenditures that are subject to FECA's restrictions, such as those that involve express support for or opposition to federal candidates, must be made with "hard money." But money that is arguably for some other purpose—even though it predictably and intentionally affects federal elections—is soft money exempt from the Act's requirements.

Soft money emerged out of the complications of political federalism. FECA regulates only federal elections, but federal and state elections typically occur concurrently, with candidates for federal and state elections appearing on one state ballot. Political party committees may undertake campaign efforts that assist their federal and state candidates simultaneously. Spending with respect to federal candidates must satisfy FECA, but assistance to state candidates is subject only to state law. Many state campaign finance laws are less restrictive than FECA: some permit corporations or unions to support candidates; some do not limit individual or PAC contributions.[74]

---

[74] In 1998, 14 states had no limits on the amount of contributions by individuals, eight states had no limits on the amount of contributions by corporations, nine states had no limits on the amount of contributions by unions, and 14 states had no limits on the amount of contributions by PACs. Other states had only nominal restrictions or contribution limits much higher than those in FECA. See Edward D. Feigenbaum and James A. Palmer, *Campaign Finance Law 98: A Summary of State Campaign Finance Laws With Quick Reference Charts*, Chart 1A (1998).

Following the enactment of FECA, some state party committees began to press the FEC to allow them to use funds that do not comply with FECA to finance part of the cost of campaign efforts that help the party ticket as a whole, including both federal and state candidates. In 1976 the FEC considered a request for an advisory opinion from the Illinois Republican State Central Committee concerning the allocation of party expenditures for overhead (rent, utilities, office supplies, salaries) and for general campaign activities like voter-registration drives and precinct training courses intended to benefit the entire state Republican ticket. The FEC determined that expenditures for general expenses should be allocated one-third to candidates for federal office, two-thirds to candidates for state office. This allocation reflected the 25/188 (or 15 percent/85 percent) split in the number of federal/nonfederal candidates, modified by the FEC's view that the federal offices "should be given proportionately more weight." The FEC required the state committee to set up separate federal and nonfederal accounts to accept separately contributions for the federal and nonfederal components of the shared programs. The FEC, however, also determined that the party could not permit corporate and union treasury contributions (lawful under Illinois law) to defray the nonfederal portion of voter-registration drives. Only contributions lawful under FECA could be used for the nonfederal portion of party-supported voter-registration activity.[75]

Two years later, the FEC abandoned the effort to prevent the use of corporate funds for party activities that support both federal and nonfederal candidates. In response to a request from the Republican State Committee of Kansas concerning party expenditures for voter registration and get-out-the-vote drives aimed at helping both federal and nonfederal candidates, the FEC advised the state party that it could use corporate and union funds (lawful for political activity under Kansas law) for the nonfederal share of the voter drives, provided the party allocated its costs into separate federal and nonfederal accounts and limited the corporate and union funds to the nonfederal share of the program.[76]

Subsequently, in 1979 the FEC determined that national party

---

[75] FEC Advisory Opinion 1976–72.

[76] FEC Advisory Opinion 1978–10. Commissioner Thomas Harris took the unusual—for the FEC—step of filing a written dissent.

committees could establish nonfederal accounts to be used "for the deposit and disbursement of funds designated specifically and exclusively to finance national party activity limited to influencing the nomination or election of candidates for public office other than elective 'federal office.'" National party committees could accept corporate contributions—and other contributions ordinarily barred by FECA—"for the exclusive and limited purpose of influencing the nomination or election of candidates for nonfederal office."[77] National party committees could finance expenses that benefit both federal and state candidates—such as administrative overhead, voter registration, voter targeting and get-out-the-vote drives, production and distribution of sample ballots, fundraising expenses—by setting up separate federal and nonfederal accounts, allocating expenses between the accounts, and accepting funds prohibited by FECA in the nonfederal accounts, provided those funds were lawful in the states in which, or for the purposes for which, they were used. Soft money was born.

Soft money took on a quiet but growing importance during the 1980s. It is estimated that soft money spending rose from $19 million in 1980 to $45 million in 1988,[78] but because the FEC treated soft money as outside the scope of FECA, there is little hard data concerning the amount of soft money raised and spent by the parties in that decade. In 1990 the FEC responded to years of prodding by Common Cause and the courts and issued rules, which became effective in 1991, requiring party committees to report their soft money receipts, expenditures, and transfers and regulating the allocation of expenses for shared activities between federal and nonfederal accounts.[79] The rules limited the ability of party committees to shelter funds for shared expenses in nonfederal accounts, but "[t]he general effect of the guidelines was . . . to give party organizations a clearer sense of how to spend soft money legally, and, at least in some instances, to permit them . . . to pay a greater share of their costs with soft money than they had been before."[80]

---

[77] FEC Advisory Opinion 1979–17.

[78] See Herbert E. Alexander and Monica Bauer, *Financing the 1988 Election*, 37 (1991).

[79] 11 C.F.R. § 106.5.

[80] Anthony Corrado, "Party Soft Money," 175, in *Campaign Finance Reform: A Sourcebook*, by Anthony Corrado et al. (1997). Even the FEC has acknowledged "there are . . . indications that the allocation rules themselves may have increased

A central issue with soft money has been the allocation of expenses for shared activities between federal and nonfederal accounts. The 1991 rules replaced the FEC's prior practice of permitting party committees to use "any reasonable basis" for allocating expenses. Now the national party committees are required to allocate at least 60 percent of their administrative expenses and costs for generic voter drives to their federal accounts in most years, and 65 percent to their federal accounts in presidential election years.[81]

Senate and House campaign committees are required to allocate their administrative and generic voter drive expenditures on a "funds expended" basis—that is, administrative and generic expenses are allocated to federal and nonfederal accounts in the same ratio as a committee's expenditures for specific federal and nonfederal candidates—except that at least 65 percent of shared expenditures must be allocated to federal candidates.[82]

State and local party committees must also allocate administrative and generic voter-drive costs, but they may use the "ballot composition" method, that is, the percentage allocated to the federal account must reflect the proportion of federal offices to the total offices on the general election ballot. Direct candidate support activities are allocated according to the time or space devoted to federal and non-federal candidates in the communication.[83]

Soft money exploded in the 1990s. In 1991–92 the two national parties raised $86 million in soft money, or double the amount for 1987–88. Soft money accounted for approximately 17 percent of total national party receipts in the 1992 election cycle.[84] By 1995–96, national party soft money receipts had trebled to $263.5 million and accounted for 30 percent of total national party income. In 1996 the national party committees' "nonfederal accounts received nearly 1000 individual contributions in excess of $20,000, and also

the amount of soft money raised by the national party committees." FEC, Proposed Rules, "Prohibited and Excessive Contribution; 'Soft Money,'" 63 Fed. Reg. 37722, 37724, July 13, 1998.

[81] 11 C.F.R. §106.5(b).

[82] 11 C.F.R. §106.5(c).

[83] 11 C.F.R. §106.5(c),(e). All committees are required to allocate fundraising costs based on the relative amounts of federal and nonfederal money raised as a result of a particular solicitation or event. 11 C.F.R. 106.5(f).

[84] FEC, "Political Party Fundraising Continues to Climb," Jan. 26, 1999, http://www.fec.gov/press/pty3098.htm

received approximately 27,000 contributions from FECA-prohibited sources"[85]—presumably corporations, unions, and federal contractors.

In 1997–98 the soft money share of national party income rose to 33 percent, although actual party soft money receipts declined to $224.4 million with the cyclical drop in fundraising from a presidential to a nonpresidential election.[86] National party soft money receipts in 1997–98, however, were nearly five times the $45 million in soft money receipts in 1993–94, the prior nonpresidential election, and more than treble the 10 percent soft money share of party receipts in 1993–94.[87] (See figure 2.) The 1997–98 election marked the first time in which soft money played a critical role in congressional elections; in previous years, the primary use of soft money was to enable presidential candidates participating in the public funding system to evade the spending limits that are a condition for the provision of public funds. Preliminary figures for the 1999–2000 election cycle indicate the dollar volume of soft money is continuing to grow.[88]

The growth in soft money and its expansion into congressional races reflect three developments. First, there is now a substantial number of donors of very large soft money contributions. In 1997–98 there were 390 individuals or organizations—including business corporations, labor unions, American Indian tribes, and ideological groups—that gave $100,000 or more to the soft money accounts of the national political parties. This reflected a 113 percent increase in the number of $100,000+ donors from 1993–94, the prior nonpresidential election cycle. Twenty-six donors gave $500,000 or more; the top four donors gave more than $1 million each. Corporate contribu-

---

[85] FEC Proposed Rules, supra, Fed. Reg. at 37727.

[86] FEC, "FEC Reports on Political Party Activity for 1997–98," Apr. 9, 1999, http://www.fec.gov/press/ptyye98.htm (visited 10/25/99).

[87] The data on party hard money receipts in 1993–94 comes from "FEC Reports on Political Party Activity for 1997–98," supra. The data on soft money for that year is from FEC Info/Public Disclosure, Inc., "Soft Money Summary" (issued 12/28/98), http://www.tray.com/fecinfo/smrpt.htm (visited 11/17/99).

[88] FEC, "FEC Releases Fundraising Figures of Major Political Parties—Large Gain in 'Soft Money' Contributions," Sept. 22, 1999 (Republicans raised 42 percent more in soft money during the first six months of 1999, compared to the first six months of 1997, and Democrats raised 93 percent more in the first half of 1999, compared to the first half of 1997. By contrast, party hard money receipts were up only 16 percent compared to 1997).

FIGURE 2: NATIONAL PARTY NON-FEDERAL ACTIVITY
(SOFT MONEY)
1992–98

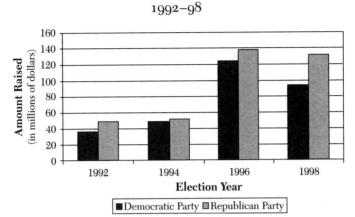

Source: FEC, "National Party Non-federal Activity Through the Complete Two Year Election Cycle," http://www.fec.gov/press/sftlong.htm

tions—prohibited by FECA—dominated the soft money growth, with 218 corporations giving more than $100,000 in 1997–98 and 16 corporations giving more than $500,000 in that period. In the prior nonpresidential election cycle, only 96 corporations broke the $100,000 mark, and only four gave more than $250,000. Thirty-five trade associations also broke the $100,000 mark in 1997–98. Wealthy individuals or couples provided most of the other large soft money donations, with 114 individuals or husband-and-wife pairs giving $100,000 or more, 26 individuals or couples giving $250,000 or more, and four giving $500,000 or more.[89]

Second, public officials have become far more aggressive in pursuing soft money contributions for their parties. "Federal officeholders, in particular, appear to be directly involved in soliciting contributions for the party committees' soft money accounts."[90] President Clinton and Vice President Gore were prominently involved in raising money for the Democratic Party's soft money operations, and Bob Dole raised soft money in connection with his 1996 presidential bid. Dem-

[89] FEC Info/Public Disclosure, Inc., "Soft Money Summary" (issued 12/28/98), http://www.tray.com/fecinfo/smrpt.htm (visited 11/17/99).
[90] FEC Proposed Soft Money Rules, supra, at 37728.

ocrats offered their $50,000 + donors intimate dinners with the president and small-group coffees in the White House Map Room.[91] Republicans provided members of their Team 100—those who gave $100,000—with a three-day opportunity to golf with Senate Majority Leader Lott, Speaker Gingrich, and then-House Appropriations Committee Chair (and briefly Speaker-designate) Livingston at The Breakers at Palm Beach.[92] As the *Wall Street Journal* recently reported, "Cash-for-access confabs on pending bills are business as usual in Washington."[93]

Third, the parties have developed new and more ambitious ways of using soft money in their campaigns. "Generally speaking, it is easier to raise soft money than hard money,"[94] since restrictions on corporations and unions and FECA's dollar limitations do not apply. As a result, the parties seek to use soft money whenever possible, to free up the hard money that must be used for direct support of federal candidates. In addition to using soft money to cover a portion of overhead, voter identification, or turnout expenses, the national parties can stretch their soft dollars by transferring funds to state and local committees and instructing them to use the funds for a particular shared activity. The FEC's allocation rules usually permit a state or local party committee to pay a higher percentage of its mixed activity costs with soft dollars than a national party is able to when conducting the same activity.[95] Roughly half the soft money raised by the Democrats and nearly one-third of the soft money raised by Republicans in 1995–96 was transferred to state and local parties. Even after the money is transferred to a state or local organization, the national party is often able to control its use.

The Democratic National Committee (DNC) was particularly effective at raising substantial sums of soft money, transferring that money to state and local parties and then directing how state party officials could use the money. Thus, it has been reported that in the 1996 campaign, the DNC directed state parties to use soft money

[91] Alison Mitchell, "The Making of a Money Machine: How Clinton Built His War Chest," *The New York Times* (Dec. 27, 1996).

[92] Katharine Q. Seelye, "GOP's Reward for Top Donors: 3 Days With Party Leaders," *The New York Times* (Feb. 20, 1997).

[93] Phil Kuntz, "Cash-for-Access Policy Forums on Bills Are Common, Controversial in Senate," *Wall Street Journal* (Jan. 25, 2000):A20.

[94] FEC Proposed Soft Money Rules, supra, at 37727.

[95] Id.

funds transferred by the DNC to make payments to media consultants hired by the national party or the Clinton-Gore staff to produce generic party advertising.[96] Because of the FEC's ballot-allocation rules, the state parties could use soft money to pay for a higher percentage of these costs than could the national party.[97]

Of the new uses for soft money the most significant is so-called issue advocacy advertising—that is, advertising that evades the judicial definition of electioneering speech.

The Definition of Electioneering Speech

Buckley sought to limit FECA to electioneering speech and to prevent FECA from unconstitutionally curtailing the discussion of political ideas and issues. The Court construed FECA to apply only to "expenditures for communications that in express terms advocate the election or defeat of a clearly identified candidate."[98] Such expenditures became known in campaign finance jargon as "express advocacy"; all other political communications are now called "issue advocacy," including many advertisements that do not discuss issues at all.[99]

Buckley's express advocacy test reflects two concerns. First, despite—or perhaps because of—the close connection between elections and politics, the Supreme Court sought a standard that clearly distinguished election-related spending from other political spending. To avoid vagueness and the chilling effect on political speech that can result from vague regulation, *Buckley* requires the definition of election-related speech to be sharply drawn. Second, the Court seemed worried about unwelcome administrative or judicial probing

---

[96] See Jill Abramson and Leslie Wayne, "Democrats Used the State Parties to Bypass Limits," *The New York Times* (Oct. 2, 1997).

[97] There have been allegations that both national and state party committees transferred soft dollars to nonprofit organizations for the latter to use for voter registration drives and get-out-the-vote campaigns that benefit federal candidates. As nonprofit organizations are not subject to the FEC's allocation rules, the effect of such transfers is to finance certain activities entirely out of soft dollars. FEC Proposed Rules, supra, Fed. Reg. at 37727. See also Albert Eisele, "Your Money, Their Views: Playing Partisan Politics With Nonprofits," *The New York Times* (Dec. 9, 1997):G4.

[98] 424 U.S. at 44, 79–80.

[99] See Richard Briffault, "Issue Advocacy: Redrawing the Elections/Politics Line," 77 *Tex. L. Rev.* 1751 (1999) (discussing issue advertisement that focused on candidates' personal character not issues).

of the intentions of speakers. Extensive intrusion into the internal communications of an organization or the inner workings of a speaker's mind to determine whether the speaker intended to influence an election would raise serious First Amendment problems.

The Supreme Court has considered the distinction between election-related speech only twice—in *Buckley* and in *MCFL*. Most of the lower federal courts that have considered whether a particular communication is engaged in express or issue advocacy have applied the so-called "magic words" test, limiting the definition of express advocacy —and the scope of FECA regulation—to communications that literally ask voters to "vote for," "elect," "cast your ballot for," "vote against," or "defeat" a candidate. As a result, ads that effectively advocate or oppose the cause of a candidate but stop short of the use of the magic words avoid FECA's restrictions and requirements.

This tendency is clearly illustrated by the decisions in *Federal Election Commission v. Christian Action Network*.[100] That case considered a 1992 television advertisement that (as described by the district court) referred to Bill Clinton's support for " 'radical' homosexual causes," presented a "series of pictures depicting advocates of homosexual rights, apparently gay men and lesbians, demonstrating at a political march," and combined "the visual degrading of candidate Clinton's picture into a black and white negative," "ominous music," and "unfavorable coloring" in a manner that "raised strong emotions" among viewers. Both the district court and the court of appeals concluded that the message did *not* constitute express advocacy. Although the advertising named Clinton and used his picture, was broadcast in the weeks immediately preceding the November general election, and was "openly hostile" to the gay-rights positions it attributed to Clinton, the ad was "devoid of any language that directly exhorted the public to vote."[101] Indeed, the court of appeals subsequently determined that the message fell so far short of express advocacy that it slapped the FEC with fees and costs under the Equal Access to Justice Act for bringing the case at all.[102]

Only the Ninth Circuit has taken a somewhat more expansive approach to the determination of whether a communication is express

---

[100] 894 F. Supp. 946 (W.D. Va. 1995), aff'd mem. 92 F.3d 1178 (4th Cir. 1996).
[101] Id. at 948, 953–56.
[102] *FEC v. Christian Action Network,* 110 F.2d 1049 (4th Cir. 1997).

advocacy. In *FEC v. Furgatch*,[103] the court found that a newspaper advertisement, published on the eve of the 1980 presidential election, that combined heated criticism of President Carter's record with the caption and exhortation "Don't Let Him Do It" constituted express advocacy. The ad made no reference to voting against Carter, but the court found that " 'Don't let him' is a command. The words 'expressly advocate' action of some kind." Voting against Carter in the upcoming election "was the only action open to those who would not 'let him do it.' " *Furgatch* emphasized the need to look at the communication "as a whole . . . with limited reference to external events," such as the timing of the ad, in determining whether the message constituted an exhortation to vote for or against a candidate. But *Furgatch* constituted only a modest expansion of the definition of express advocacy. A message could constitute express advocacy only so long as it is "susceptible of no other reasonable interpretation but as an exhortation to vote." It must be "unmistakable and unambiguous, suggestive of only one plausible meaning." If "reasonable minds could differ as to whether it encourages a vote for or against a candidate or encourages the reader to take some other kind of action," it is not express advocacy.[104]

Other federal courts that have considered the issue have rejected *Furgatch*'s slight broadening of express advocacy and, especially, its call to assess whether the message as a whole, with some reference to its timing, constitutes an exhortation to vote. They have, instead, rigidly insisted on the presence of words that explicitly call for the election or defeat of a candidate.[105] The Fourth Circuit, in *Christian Action Network*, sharply chastised the FEC for attempting to find express advocacy in "the combined message of words and dramatic moving images, sounds and other non-verbal cues such as film editing, photographic techniques, and music, involving highly charged rhetoric and provocative images . . . taken as a whole" rather than in explicit words of advocacy.[106] These courts have recognized that the magic words approach will exempt much election-related spending

---

[103] 807 F.2d 857 (9th Cir. 1987).

[104] Id. at 863–65.

[105] See, for example, *Christian Action Network*, supra; *Faucher v. FEC*, 928 F.2d 468 (1st Cir. 1991); *Maine Right to Life Committee, Inc. v. FEC*, 98 F.3d 1 (1st Cir. 1996). See also *Clifton v. FEC*, 114 F.3d 1309 (1st Cir. 1997).

[106] 110 F.3d at 1049.

from regulation. Even as it punished the FEC with fees and costs for its effort to look to the message as a whole rather than for explicit words of advocacy, the Fourth Circuit in *Christian Action Network* acknowledged, quoting from the FEC's brief, that "metaphorical and figurative speech can be more pointed and compelling, and can thus more successfully express advocacy, than a plain, literal recommendation to 'vote' for a particular person."[107] The federal district court in Maine agreed that "language . . . is an elusive thing" and that communication depends "heavily on context"; yet in the same breath, it held that the FEC's effort to define express advocacy with some reference to context was unconstitutional. The court found the result "not very satisfying from a realistic communications point of view and does not give much recognition to the policy of the election statute to keep corporate money from influencing elections" but concluded that such an unrealistic "express advocacy" standard was constitutionally required.[108]

The current definition of "express advocacy" is a standing invitation to evasion of FECA's reporting and disclosure requirements and its prohibitions on the use of corporate and union treasury funds in connection with federal elections. It has proven to be child's play for political advertisers and campaign professionals to develop ads that effectively advocate or oppose the cause of a candidate but stop short of the formal express advocacy that the courts have made a prerequisite for regulation. The most common tactic for political advertisers is to include some language calling for the reader, viewer, or listener to respond to the ad by doing something other than voting. In *Christian Action Network*, for example, the ad called on viewers to telephone the sponsor "for more information on traditional family values." Other ads have urged voters to telephone the candidate and ask him why he or she opposes tax cuts or term limits.[109] The Annenberg Public Policy Center's survey of 107 issue advocacy advertisements that aired on television or radio during the 1996 election cycle found that 70.1 percent urged the viewer or listener to either contact a public official or the advocacy organization sponsoring the ad about

---

[107] Id. at 1064.

[108] *Maine Right to Life Comm.*, supra, 914 F.Supp. at 12–13.

[109] See, for example, *Wisc. Mfrs & Commerce v. Wisc. Elec. Bd.*, 978 F. Supp. 1200 (W. D.Wisc. 1997).

their views concerning a particular policy position.[110] By combining sharp criticism of a candidate with an exhortation to call the sponsor or the candidate criticized, these ads can inoculate themselves from the charge that they constitute express advocacy. (See table 2.)

The combination of a crabbed legal definition of express advocacy and the skill of political advertisers in developing electioneering messages that effectively advocate the cause of a candidate while carefully refraining from explicit exhortations to vote has led to an explosion of issue advocacy. In the 1996 elections, between $135 million and $150 million was spent on issue advocacy.[111] The numbers are necessarily imprecise, and the identities of the sources of funds unknown, because issue ads are not subject to reporting and disclosure requirements. The Annenberg Center estimates that between $275 million and $340 million was spent on issue advertising in connection with the 1998 congressional elections—roughly a doubling from 1996 and a remarkable increase in spending from a presidential to a nonpresidential election year.

Issue ads were initially the province of independent organizations, with distinctive ideological or economic agendas. By the 1996 elec-

TABLE 2: EXPRESS ADVOCACY AND ISSUE ADVOCACY COMPARED

Express Advocacy	John Smith voted to raise your taxes. Don't let him do it again! Vote for Jane Doe on November 3.
Issue Advocacy	John Smith voted to raise your taxes! Call 1-800-123-4567 to find out more about Smith's "tax and spend" policy.

Express Advocacy	*Issue Advocacy*
√ No corporate or union treasury money.	√ Corporate and union treasury money may be used.
√ Hard money rules apply.	√ Soft money may be used
√ Subject to disclosure.	√ Not subject to disclosure.

---

[110] See Deborah Beck et al., *Issue Advocacy Advertising During the 1996 Campaign*, 7–8 (1997).

[111] Id. at 3.

tion cycle, however, the major political parties had become actively involved in issue advocacy in support of their candidates or in opposition to the candidates of the other party. The Democratic National Committee undertook an extensive advertising program to trumpet the accomplishments of the Clinton administration and criticize the Republican Congress without explicitly calling for the election or defeat of particular candidates. In addition, in response to a request from the Republican National Committee (RNC), the FEC determined that the RNC could use soft money to defray a portion of the costs of advertising that combined discussion of issues with criticism of President Clinton by name.[112] One early study of the 1996 election cycle estimated that the parties spent an estimated $68 million on issue ads, thereby accounting for nearly half of all issue ad spending in that election.[113] Another, more recent, study estimated major party issue ad spending in 1995–96 at nearly $110 million, or more than two-thirds of the issue ad spending in that cycle.[114] In 1996 party issue ad spending was comparable to—and if the higher estimates of party issue ad spending are accurate, actually greater than—the total of party spending in direct contributions to candidates, coordinated expenditures, and independent expenditures.[115] In 1998 party issue ad spending far exceeded party contributions to candidates, coordinated expenditures with candidates, and independent expenditures expressly supporting or opposing candidates.[116]

---

[112] FEC Adv. Opn 1995–25.

[113] See Beck, supra, at 3.

[114] See Paul S. Herrnson, "Financing the 1996 Congressional Elections," in Green, *Financing the 1996 Election,* supra, at 122. According to Herrnson, the Democratic National Committee and the Democratic congressional campaign committees together spent $60 million on issue ads in 1995–96, while the Republican National Committee and Republican congressional campaign committees together spent $49 million.

[115] Party coordinated and independent expenditures in the 1996 presidential election came to $19.2 million. See Anthony Corrado, "Financing the 1996 Presidential General Election," in Green, supra, at 75. Party contributions to candidates, coordinated expenditures, and independent expenditures in the 1996 congressional elections came to $70.9 million. See Robert Biersack and Melanie Haskell, "Spitting on the Umpire: Political Parties, the Federal Election Campaign Act, and the 1996 Campaigns," in id. at 163.

[116] Total party contributions to, coordinated expenditures with, and independent expenditures concerning federal candidates in 1997–98 came to $40.8 million. See FEC, "Political Party Fundraising Continues to Climb," Jan. 26, 1999, http://www/fec/gov/press/pty3098.htm (visited 9/17/99).

Issue advocacy advertising has, thus, become an important means of enabling corporations and unions to use treasury funds to participate in federal elections. It has also enhanced the appeal of soft money for the parties, since, according to an FEC advisory opinion, issue ads can be paid partially from soft money. A pending lawsuit would make it even easier for the parties to engage in issue advocacy. The FEC's 1995 advisory opinion on the use of soft money to fund issue advocacy provided that party issue advocacy costs are subject to the FEC's rules for allocating mixed federal–nonfederal activity between hard and soft money. As a result, national party issue advocacy spending must be funded 60 percent by hard money and 40 percent by soft money in nonpresidential election years, and 65 percent by hard money and 35 percent by soft money in presidential election years.[117] The FEC's rules are more generous to state and local parties. For those parties, the hard/soft allocation is based on the number of federal offices as a share of the total number of offices on the ballot in the state in the next election. As there are, typically, far more state than federal offices on the ballot, the state parties may fund most issue advocacy with soft money.[118] This explains the large numbers of multimillion dollar transfers of soft money by the national party committees to state committees that so struck election observers in 1996, as the national parties tried to direct soft money to those states where it could defray the greatest share of issue advocacy and other joint federal–nonfederal expenses.[119] In 1998, however, the Ohio Democratic Party and the RNC sued the FEC, asserting that any limit on the use of soft money to fund issue advocacy is unconstitutional. In their view, party issue advocacy—including advocacy that mentions candidates for federal office—is beyond the scope of FECA so that the FEC cannot force them to use any hard money to

---

[117] 11 C.F.R. §106.5(b)(2).

[118] In New York, for example, in the Year 2000 elections, there will be 33 federal offices—President, Senator, and 31 Representatives—and 211 state offices (61 state senate seats and 150 assembly seats) on the ballot. The federal share of the federal-state total is just 13 percent.

[119] See, for example, Jill Abramson and Leslie Wayne, "Democrats Used the State Parties to Bypass Limits," *The New York Times* (Oct. 2, 1997):A1; Robert Biersack and Melanie Haskell, "Spitting on the Umpire: Political Parties, the Federal Election Campaign Act, and the 1996 Campaigns," in Green, supra, at 179–81. National party committees will also transfer soft money to state and local parties in exchange for hard money, which the national committees can use to make contributions to federal candidates.

fund issue ads. The parties failed to obtain injunctive relief in time for the 1998 elections,[120] but the suit is still pending. If the parties prevail, party issue advocacy is likely to surge.

D. CAMPAIGNING UNDER FECA

FECA and its principal amendments have now been in place for more than a quarter of a century. The campaign finance regime created together by Congress, in FECA, and the Supreme Court in *Buckley* and its progeny has six salient characteristics:

- Sharply rising congressional candidate campaign costs
- An increasingly burdensome fundraising process
- A dominant role for PACs and individual donors who make large donations
- In many elections, an extreme imbalance in the campaign funds available to competing candidates, especially in races involving incumbents and challengers
- An increasing role for political parties in financing campaigns, with a growing share of that attributable to soft money
- A growing portion of campaign costs, particularly the costs of challengers, financed by the candidates' personal resources

Rising Costs

The average cost of congressional races has risen dramatically over the last quarter century. According to the Committee for Economic Development (CED), the average cost of a House race rose from $73,000 in 1976 to over $500,000 in 1998, and the average cost of a Senate race rose from $596,000 to $3.8 million in the same period. In 1976 no House campaign cost more than $500,000, but in 1998 there were 309 campaigns in which expenditures broke the half million mark. Indeed, there were 104 House campaigns in 1998 that

---

[120] *Republican National Committee v. FEC*, 1998 U.S. App. LEXIS 28505, D.C. Cir., Nov. 6, 1998 (affirming district court order denying preliminary injunction against application of FEC soft money allocation regulation to party issue advocacy expenditures).

cost more than $1 million.[121] These averages, moreover, included the spending of losers as well as winners. As we explain below, average spending by candidates who manage to win elections is much higher than the overall average.

Total congressional campaign spending has risen steadily over the last two decades. House and Senate candidates in the aggregate spent $342 million in the 1982 elections, $451 million in the 1986 elections, $680 million in the 1992 elections, and $765 million in the 1996 elections. Total spending dropped slightly in 1998—to $740 million—but that appears to reflect a drop in the total number of candidates[122] rather than any reduction in the costs incurred by active candidates.

This sharp growth in spending is not simply a reflection of inflation. The publicly funded portion of the presidential general election campaign, which is tied to the consumer price index, rose by 176 percent from 1976 to 1996, but the spending of all congressional general election candidates rose 667 percent in the same period.[123]

Nor do these figures take into account soft money and nonparty issue advocacy spending in connection with congressional elections. Before the 1990s, soft money and issue advocacy were negligible factors in congressional elections, but in 1997–98 the national committees of the two major parties collected $224 million in soft money, which is equal to about 30 percent of the total spending by candidates, not counting soft money. The amount of issue advocacy spending targeted on federal races is simply not knowable since issue advocacy is not subject to FECA's reporting and disclosure requirements, but it has been estimated at more than $200 million.

Burdens of Fundraising

The explosion of congressional campaign costs has occurred during an era when limits on contributions to candidates were largely frozen

---

[121] Committee for Economic Development, "Investing in the People's Business: A Business Proposal for Campaign Finance Reform, A Statement by the Research and Policy Committee of the Committee for Economic Development," 13 (1999) (hereinafter CED Report).

[122] The number of candidates dropped from 2605 in 1995–96 to 2100 in 1997–98. "FEC Reports on Congressional Fundraising for 1997–98," http://www.fec/gov/press/canye98.htm, Apr. 28, 1999.

[123] Frank J. Sorauf, "What *Buckley* Wrought," in E. Joshua Rosenkranz, ed., *If Buckley Fell: A First Amendment Blueprint for Regulating Money in Politics*, 52 (1999).

at the levels set by Congress in 1974—$1000 from an individual per election ($2000 per election cycle); $5000 from a PAC or party political committee per election ($10,000 per election cycle); and $17,500 from a national political party to a U.S. Senate candidate per election cycle. Only the limits on party coordinated expenditures have risen with inflation.

The collision between the irresistible force of rising costs and the immovable object of frozen contribution limits has made fundraising an enormous burden for many candidates. As political scientist Thomas E. Mann has pointed out, "The cost of mounting a major campaign is a huge disincentive to candidacy for people of ordinary means who lack the stomach for nonstop fund-raising."[124]The burdens of fundraising affect not only potential challengers but incumbents exhausted by the process. As the CED notes, "In recent years, a growing number of retiring senators and representatives have cited the demands of fund-raising as one of the factors in their decisions to leave office. They have noted that fund-raising has become too arduous and demeaning, has taken too much time and energy away from the work they were elected to do, and has diminished the quality of their representation."[125]

The ever-present need to raise huge sums of money in donations that qualify under FECA "structures how elected officials spend their time, where they travel, with whom they speak, and how they focus their legislative energies."[126] The campaign money chase drives party agendas, scheduling, committee assignments, and the allocation of personal time and staff resources. The burdens are especially acute in the House of Representatives, since members have just two years to collect the $500,000 to $1 million or more they may need for their next election campaign. "Some legislators have reported spending hours *every day* seeking contributions."[127] But senators are also heavily burdened. Although senators have six years, rather than two, to raise their funds, the average Senate race costs seven to ten times the cost of the average House race—and individual and PAC contribu-

---

[124] Thomas E. Mann, "The U.S. Campaign Finance System Under Strain," http://www.brookings.edu/views/Articles/Mann/SNP.htm

[125] CED Report, supra, at 13–14.

[126] Mann, supra.

[127] CED Report, supra, at 13.

tions to Senate candidates are subject to the same limits as apply to House candidates.

Dominant Role of Large Individual Donors and PACs

The single largest source of funds for the war chests of congressional candidates is donations from individuals. In 1996 contributions from individuals constituted 53 percent of the funds received by all candidates for the House of Representatives, 65 percent received by Senate incumbents, 60 percent received by Senate challengers, and 52 percent received by Senate candidates for open seats.[128] In 1998 individual contributions accounted for an estimated 54 percent of total congressional election spending and 64 percent of hard money spending.[129]

Within the category of individual donations, large contributions tend to play a bigger role than smaller ones. In 1996 House candidates raised two-thirds of their individual donations in large donations, defined as those between $200 and $1000, and one-third in donations of less than $200.[130] In 1996 Senate races, incumbents received 60 percent of their individual donations in large contributions; challengers received 65 percent of their individual donations in large contributions; and open-seat candidates received 75 percent of their individual donations in large contributions.[131] In 1998 total large indi-

---

[128] Herrnson, "Financing the 1996 Congressional Elections," supra, at 119–20.

[129] Center for Responsive Politics, "The Big Picture: Who Paid for This Election?" http://www.opensecrets.org/pubs/bigpicture2000/overview/whopaid.ihtml

[130] Herrnson, supra, at 119. Herrnson considers the sources of candidate resources based on the status of the candidate, that is, whether a candidate is an incumbent, challenger, or seeking an open seat. Individuals provided 53 percent of House incumbent resources, with 35 percent of total contributions coming from large individual donations and 18 percent from small donations, for a ratio of 2:1. Similarly, in open-seat races, individuals again provided 53 percent of total campaign resources, with 36 percent coming in large donations and 17 percent in small donations, for a ratio of approximately 2:1. Individuals provided 54 percent of the funds for House challengers, but a larger share of that money came from smaller donors. Large individual donors provided 32 percent of challenger resources, and small individual donors 22 percent, for a ratio of 3:2. Given the relatively small share of campaign resources that went to challengers (challengers spent on average $279,000, compared to $750,000 by incumbents and $690,000 by open-seat candidates), it is reasonable to conclude that large individual donations accounted for two-thirds of all individual donations.

[131] Id. at 120.

vidual donations to candidates and parties came to $464 million, compared with $351 million in small individual donations to candidates and parties.[132] Overall, large individual donations account for roughly two-fifths of the funding for Senate candidates, one-third of the funding for House candidates, and one-third of the total amount provided to all candidates and party committees.

After large individual donors, the principal participants in federal congressional election finance are PACs. (See figures 3 and 4.) Over the last two decades, PACs have consistently provided between one-quarter and one-third of the total contributions received by congressional candidates.[133] In 1996 PACs provided 19 percent of the funding for House challengers, 24 percent of the funding of candidates for open House seats, and 39 percent of the funding for House incumbents. PACs were the largest single source of funds for House incumbents and the second largest source (after large individual donors) for open-seat candidates that year. PACs loomed a little less large in Senate races in 1996, providing just 9 percent of the funds for challengers, 18 percent of the funds for open-seat candidates, and 22 percent of the funds for incumbents. As in the House, PACs were the second largest source, after large individual donors, of funds for

FIGURE 3: HOUSE: CONTRIBUTIONS BY SOURCE (1998)

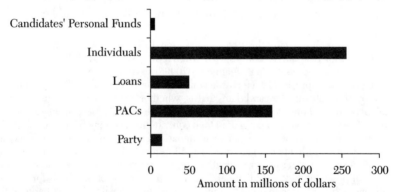

Source: FEC, "Financial Activity of All Senate and House Campaigns", http://www.fec.gov/press/allsu,98.htm
*Coordinated expenditures are included under "Party".

---

[132] Center for Responsive Politics, supra.

[133] Anthony Corrado, Thomas E. Mann, Daniel R. Ortiz, Trevor Potter, Frank J. Sorauf, eds., *Campaign Finance Reform: A Sourcebook,* 141 (1997).

FIGURE 4: SENATE: CONTRIBUTIONS BY SOURCE (1998)

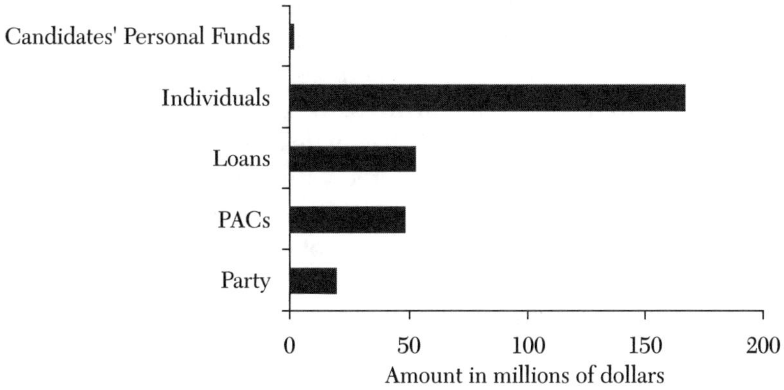

Amount in millions of dollars

Source: FEC, "Financial Activity of All Senate and House Campaigns", http://www.fec.gov/press/allsu,98.htm
*Coordinated expenditures are included under "Party".

open-seat Senate candidates. In 1998 PACs spent $269 million in connection with congressional elections, including over $200 million in contributions to candidates. PACs provided 41 percent of the average winning House candidate's total receipts and 23 percent of the average winner's funds in Senate races.[134]

The rise of PACs is a direct consequence of FECA. Although the PAC device predated the Act, the number of PACs was relatively limited, and the legal status of corporate and labor PACs relative to their parent organizations uncertain. FECA clarified that parent corporations could cover the administrative and fundraising expenses of their PACs and could control PAC contribution decisions. FECA allows a PAC to make five times the contribution that an individual can make, and FECA imposes no limit on the total contributions a PAC can make to all candidates and parties in the aggregate.

Most importantly, while FECA limited the size of individual contributions, the Supreme Court held that Congress could not limit the total of candidates' expenditures. With contributions limited but expenditures unlimited, FECA created a new and significant need for intermediary organizations that could help carry the burden of raising campaign funds. PACs, along with political party committees, have filled this niche.

---

[134] Center for Responsive Politics, supra.

From just 608 PACs in 1974, when PACs were first required to register with the FEC, the number of PACs rapidly grew to 1653 in 1978, 2551 in 1980, 3371 in 1982, and 4009 in 1984.[135] Total PAC contributions to congressional candidates rose rapidly in the same period, too, from $22.6 million in 1976 to $111.5 million in 1984. Since 1984 the number of PACs has plateaued; as of December 31, 1999, there were 3835 PACs registered with the FEC.[136] (See table 3.) Again since about 1984, the level of PAC contributions has stabilized, growing at roughly the same rate as total congressional campaign costs.

PACs are not homogeneous. There are corporate PACs, labor PACs, trade association PACs, membership organization PACs, and PACs not connected to any parent organization. In 1996, 64 percent of all PACs were sponsored by business interests, 8 percent by labor unions, and 28 percent were not connected to any parent organizations. The unconnected PACs are generally ideological organizations. Business PACs also account for most PAC contributions, about 68 percent. Labor PACs provide a larger fraction of PAC contributions than the number of labor PACs would suggest—about 22 percent. Conversely, ideological PACs account for 11 percent of total PAC dollars.[137]

A relative handful of PACs appear to dominate PAC giving. Of the PACs registered in the 1997–98 election cycle, 35 percent made no

TABLE 3: NUMBER OF PACs

Year	Number
1974	608
1978	1653
1980	2551
1982	3371
1984	4009
1999	3835

Source: Center for Responsive Politics. *The Big Picture: Who Paid for this Election?* http://www.opensecrets.org/pubs/bigpicture2000/overview/who_paid.html

---

[135] Id. at 140.

[136] "FEC Issues Semi-Annual PAC Count," http://www.fec.gov/press/paccn-t12000.htm, Jan. 14, 2000.

[137] Herrnson, supra, at 104.

contributions at all, 20 percent made total contributions of less than $5000, and 27 percent made contributions of between $5000 and $50,000.[138] In other words, 82 percent of PACs gave collectively just $25 million, which is a very small fraction of total PAC giving. At the other end of the spectrum, there were 34 PACs that each made contributions of $1 million or more. These 34 PACs (less than 1 percent of all registered PACs) contributed a total of $52.6 million, or just shy of one-quarter of spending by all registered PACs. An additional 51 PACs made contributions ranging from $500,000 to $1 million, for a total of $35.7 million. The next 94 PACs made contributions in the range of $250,000 to $500,000, for a total of $33.2 million. In other words, the top 179 PACs (3.8 percent of all PACs) made $118.5 million in contributions, or 56.1 percent of all PAC contributions.[139] To make $1 million in legal contributions, a PAC has to contribute to at least 200 candidates (or taking into account separate $5000 contributions for a primary and for a general election, at least 100 candidates).

Unequal Resources for Competing Candidates

The rise of PACs has contributed to a central feature of the current campaign finance system: the existence of dramatically unequal campaign resources for competitors. In many campaigns, one candidate, usually the incumbent, significantly outspends his or her opponent. In 1998 the average House incumbent spent $657,000 and the average House challenger spent $265,000, so that, on average, incumbents outspent challengers by 2.4 to 1.[140] Similarly, in 1996 the average incumbent spent $750,000 and the average House challenger spent just $279,000, for an imbalance of 2.7 to 1.[141] (See figures 5, 6, and 7.)

More importantly, in 1998 half of all House challengers raised less than $100,000 and only one-third raised as much as $200,000. Altogether 60 percent of House incumbents either had no significant opposition or outspent their opponents by a margin of ten to one or more. As the Research and Policy Committee of the Committee for

---

[138] CED Report, supra, at 16.
[139] Id.
[140] CED Report, supra, at 17.
[141] Herrnson, supra, at 119.

FIGURE 5: EXPENDITURE GAP WINNERS-LOSERS, 1982–1998
(ALL CONGRESSIONAL RACES)

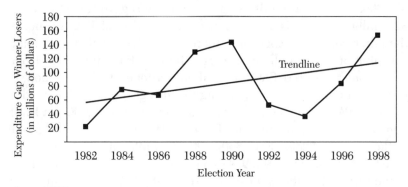

Source: FEC.

FIGURE 6: HOUSE: WINNERS' AND LOSERS' AVERAGE SPENDING
1996–98 (MAJOR PARTIES)

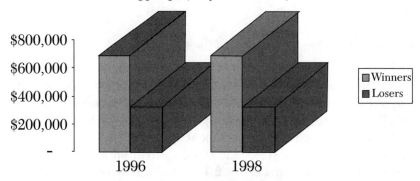

Source: FEC. Data includes spending for the entire election cycle (primary and general election) for all candidates who appeared on the general election ballot. It does not include data for those candidates who lost in the primary and did not appear on the general election ballot

*Major parties are those whose candidates obtained more than 5% of the general election vote.

Economic Development recently observed, "The majority of House challengers now raise and spend so little that they cannot wage a viable campaign. . . . As a result, most House elections were financially uncompetitive."[142]

Absolute funding parity is not essential for competitive elections.

---

[142] CED Report, supra, at 17.

FIGURE 7: SENATE: WINNERS' AND LOSERS' AVERAGE SPENDING
1990–98
(MAJOR PARTIES)

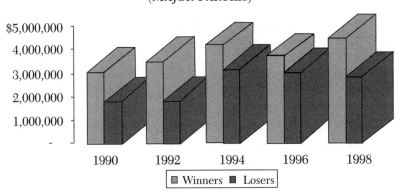

Source: FEC. Data includes spending for the entire election cycle (primary and general election) for all candidates who appeared on the general election ballot. It does not include data for those candidates who lost in the primary and did not appear on the general election ballot.

*Major parties are those whose candidates obtained more than 5% of the general election vote.

A challenger may do well if she or he can muster a critical mass of funds.[143] Nor are campaign finances the sole determinant of election results. Partisan gerrymandering, the issues of the day, the personalities and records of the candidates are all critical variables. But it appears to be the case that if an election is financially noncompetitive, it is likely to be politically noncompetitive, too. The House challengers who spent less than $200,000 generally received less than 40 percent of the two-party vote.[144]

Overall, in the last three congressional election cycles the average winner (including successful open-seat candidates and the rare successful challenger, as well as winning incumbents) outspent the average loser by between 2.5 to 1 and 3 to 1; in 1998 the average winner spent $650,000 while the average loser spent just $211,000.[145] In 95 percent of House races, the biggest spender won.

Conversely, politically competitive elections are marked by financially competitive challengers. In 1998 the relatively small number

---

[143] See Gary C. Jacobson, *Money in Congressional Elections* (1980).

[144] CED Report, supra, at 18.

[145] Center for Responsive Politics, supra.

of House challengers who managed to obtain as much as 40 percent of the major party vote spent an average of $639,000, or approximately the median level of spending by all House incumbents. These unusually well-funded challengers, however, faced incumbents who spent an average of almost $1 million.[146] Still, challengers in that range had a more realistic opportunity to win. In 22 of the 25 races where the biggest spender lost, neither candidate had more than a 2-to-1 edge over the other.[147]

In the Senate, incumbents also tend to benefit from a financial advantage, albeit one less lopsided than that enjoyed by their House counterparts. In 1996 and 1998 Senate incumbents outspent challengers by a ratio of approximately 1.5 to 1.[148] Overall, in 1996 Senate winners outspent their major party opponents by 1.7 to 1, and in 1998 Senate winners outspent their major party opponents 1.8 to 1.[149]

The dominant role of PACs and large donations by individuals contribute to the fiscal edge of incumbency. (See figures 8 and 9 and table 4.) Most PACs make contributions in order to obtain or secure access to elected officials

who are in a position to influence regulations, appropriations, or treaties that affect the environment in which the PAC's industry or work-

FIGURE 8: PAC CONTRIBUTIONS TO CANDIDATES, 1998 ELECTION.

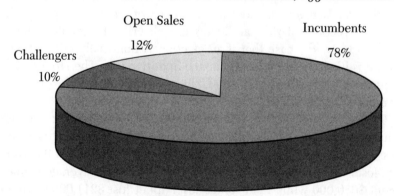

Open Sales
12%

Incumbents
78%

Challengers
10%

Source: FEC, "FEC Releases Information on PAC Activity for 1997–1998, June 8, 1999.

[146] CED Report, supra, at 17.

[147] Center for Responsive Politics, "Money and Incumbency Win Big on Election Day," http://www.crp.org/pressreleases/nov0498.htm, Nov. 4, 1998.

[148] Herrnson, supra, at 120; CED Report, supra, at 18.

[149] Center for Responsive Politics, "Election Statistics at a Glance," http://www.o-pensecrets.org/pubc/bigpicture2000/overview/stats.ihtml

force operates. These groups consider campaign contributions an important tool for reaffirming or strengthening their relationships with influential lawmakers. They recognize that contributions can create good will with representatives and senators, thereby making it easier for the group's lobbyists to influence the legislative process.[150]

PACs that follow access strategies overwhelmingly favor incumbents with their contributions. In 1996, for example, 88 percent of contributions by corporate PACs in House elections went to incumbents, with 52 percent of total corporate PAC contributions going to incumbents considered shoo-ins. Another 9 percent went to candidates in open-seat contests; just 7 percent went to challengers. Similarly, 81 percent of trade and membership association PAC contributions went to incumbents (with 45 percent of total contributions going to incumbents considered shoo-ins), 12 percent went to candidates in open-seat races, and just 8 percent went to challengers.

FIGURE 9: PERCENTAGE OF PAC CONTRIBUTIONS ACCORDING TO CANDIDATE STATUS, 1985–86 TO 1997–98

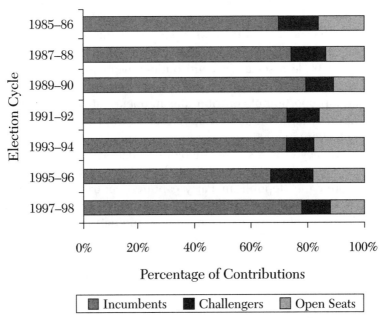

Source: FEC, "FEC Releases Information on PAC Activity for 1997–98," June 8, 1999.

---

[150] Herrnson, supra, at 105.

TABLE 4: AMOUNT AND PERCENTAGE OF PAC CONTRIBUTIONS
ACCORDING TO CANDIDATE STATUS (HOUSE AND SENATE)

Election Cycle	Incumbents		Challengers		Open Seats	
	Amount	%	Amount	%	amount	%
1997–98	170.9	78%	22.1	10%	27.0	12%
1995–96	146.4	67%	31.6	15%	39.8	18%
1993–94	137.2	72%	19.0	10%	33.4	18%
1991–92	135.3	72%	22.9	12%	30.7	16%
1989–90	125.8	79%	16.2	10%	17.1	11%
1987–88	118.2	74%	18.9	12%	22.2	14%
1985–86	96.2	69%	19.9	14%	23.8	17%

Source: FEC, "FEC Releases Information on PAC Activity for 1997–98," June 8, 1999.

The pro-incumbent bias of corporate and trade association PAC giving in 1996 Senate elections was less dramatic but still substantial, particularly when compared with contributions to challengers: 53 percent of corporate contributions went to incumbents, 38 percent to open-seat candidates, and just 10 percent to challengers; and 48 percent of trade association contributions went to incumbents, 41 percent to open-seat candidates, and just 10 percent to challengers.[151] The large proportion of contributions in open-seat races may reflect the unusually large number of open seats (14 out of 34 Senate seats up for election) in 1996.

The primacy of access over ideology in patterns of business PAC giving is also reflected in the shift in the partisan distribution of PAC money after the Republican Party captured control of Congress in 1994. Going into the 1994 elections, with the Democrats in control of both houses of Congress, Democratic candidates received 57 percent of corporate PAC contributions and 59 percent of trade association PAC contributions in House races, and Democratic candidates received 42 percent of corporate PAC and 43 percent of trade association PAC contributions in Senate races. In 1996, with Republicans in power in Congress, Democratic candidates received just 30 percent of corporate PAC contributions and 37 percent of trade association

---

[151] Id. at 109–11.

contributions in House races, and only 20 percent of corporate PAC contributions and 28 percent of trade association PAC contributions in Senate races.

Many large individual contributors also appear to be motivated by business-related access concerns, albeit to a lesser degree than PACs. In 1996 donors who gave between $750 and $1000 to House candidates distributed their money 62 percent to incumbents, 20 percent to challengers, and 18 percent to open-seat candidates. The allocations by large donors in Senate races were closer but still reflected a pro-incumbent tilt relative to challengers: 34 percent to incumbents, 25 percent to challengers, and 41 percent in open-seat races.

Looking back over the last quarter century, according to campaign finance scholar Frank Sorauf, "the years of FECA have been years of incumbent riches. For more than a majority of election cycles they enjoyed more than three to one ratios." This is not due to the restrictions or requirements of FECA itself. Incumbents benefited "from the aggressive use of office and access in raising money, but their chief asset was the overwhelming odds of reelection, more than nine to one in House races."[152] The preferences of PACs and large individual donors for incumbents over challengers and for likely winners in general reflect the built-in advantages of incumbency. By the same token, however, these donors' actions reinforce the incumbents' edge.

FECA did not produce this system. But it does nothing to offset it. As Sorauf has put it, "the campaign finance system offers challengers no weapons with which to overcome the advantages of incumbency."[153]

The Growing Role of Party Committees

The national political parties have done well under FECA. The Act's limits on donations to candidates, coupled with the rising costs of political campaigns, place a premium on organizations that can help candidates obtain funds and defray some of their campaign costs. Aided by the coordinated expenditure provision, in the 1980s party committees emerged as key financial intermediaries in the federal

---

[152] Sorauf, supra, at 55.
[153] Frank J. Sorauf, *Inside Campaign Finance,* 178 (1992).

elections, providing candidates with funds and valuable campaign services and working with them to obtain funds from other donors. For the first time, the national party committees built up a mass financial base, accumulating large aggregates of money through relatively small donations from a large number of donors.[154] The congressional campaign committees, in particular, have become significant players in congressional races. These committees are now involved in recruiting candidates, managing campaigns, producing and placing candidate ads, mobilizing voters, and both providing funds to candidates and assisting candidates in raising funds from PACs and other donors.

In the 1997–98 election cycle, the national committees of the two major parties raised nearly $630 million, or not much less than the $780 million raised in the aggregate by all the candidates for Congress. Although the parties spent most of that money for their own activities or transferred it to state and local party committees, the parties reported providing individual federal candidates with approximately $40 million in hard dollar support, mostly in coordinated expenditures. Although this is less than a fifth of the more than $200 million in PAC contributions to Senate and House candidates, the benefits from party support are probably greater than the value of the reported contributions. Most coordinated expenditures consist of in-kind services: polling data, mailing lists, assistance with fundraising, campaign management, opposition research, and preparation and placement of advertising. These services are often obtained from consultants who provide them to the parties, as repeat participants in the political process, at a discount, so their value to the candidate is likely to exceed the cost to the party.[155]

Most importantly, the $40 million figure does not count soft money spending, which is ostensibly for purposes other than the direct sup-

---

[154] See, for example, Herrnson, "National Party Organizations," in L. Sandy Maisel, ed., *The Parties Respond: Changes in American Parties and Campaigns*, 59 (3d ed. 1998) (the national party organizations raise most of their hard money in the form of direct mail contributions under $100); Leon Epstein, *Political Parties in the American Mold*, 276–78 (1986) (contrasting historic dependence of the parties on a small number of very large donors with the post-FECA development of a mass financial base).

[155] See Anthony Gierzynski, *Legislative Party Campaign Committees in the American States*, 53–54 (1992); Herrnson, supra, at 73 (party in-kind campaign services are worth many times more than their reported value).

port of federal candidates but in fact provides substantial benefits to party candidates. In 1997–98 the national committees of the major parties collected $224 million in soft money, or about one-third of the combined total of hard and soft money. Much of that money aids federal candidates although it is not so reported. Party assistance to candidates is, thus, much greater than the sum of direct contributions to candidates and coordinated expenditures with candidates.

To be sure, the parties are still secondary players in the campaign finance system. The financing of election campaigns remains candidate-centered, with candidates responsible for raising and spending their own funds. The candidates, in turn, raise far more of their money from individuals, from PACs, and from their own personal resources than they do from parties.[156] Nevertheless, the national party committees are much better funded and better organized than before FECA's enactment and are no longer dependent on state parties for financing. Instead, they now provide state parties with financial assistance. Party funds typically account for 7 percent of House candidate funds and 10 percent of Senate candidate funds.[157] But due to the higher limits on party coordinated expenditures than on PAC or individual donations, party committee donations "currently compose the largest single source of campaign money for most candidates."[158] Moreover, more than PACs and individual donors, parties are willing to dedicate a significant portion of their financial support to challengers—at least to challengers who appear to have a decent shot at ousting the incumbent.[159] So party money is likely to loom especially large in the funding of competitive challengers.

Self-Funded Candidates

The combination of FECA's limits on contributions to candidates and *Buckley's* invalidation of limitations on candidate spending and on a

---

[156] In the 1997–98 election, individuals provided 54 percent of all the contributions collected by candidates; PACs accounted for 26 percent of total candidate funds; and 14 percent of candidate funds came from the candidates' own wealth. FEC, "FEC Reports on Congressional Fundraising for 1997–98," http://www.fec.gov/press/canye98.htm, Apr. 28, 1999.

[157] Herrnson in Green, at 119–20.

[158] Paul S. Herrnson, "National Party Organizations at the Century's End," in Maisel, supra at 73.

[159] See Michael J. Malbin and Thomas L. Gais, *The Day After Reform: Sobering Campaign Finance Lessons from the American States*, 145–52 (1998).

candidate's contributions to his or her own campaign has led to an increase in the portion of campaign costs covered by a candidate's personal resources and to a rise in the number of very wealthy individuals who run for office by funding their own campaigns. This is particularly true in Senate races, where self-financing has risen from 5 percent in 1988 to 11 percent in 1998. In 1998, 18 Senate candidates and 69 House candidates put $100,000 or more of their own money into their campaigns.[160]

Self-funding is particularly characteristic of challengers and open-seat candidates. In 1996 House challengers paid one-sixth of their campaign costs (or an average of more than $40,000) out of their own money, and House open-seat candidates spent, on average, more than $90,000 of their own money on their campaigns. In the Senate, the average challenger had to pay nearly one-quarter of the costs of his or her campaign, or approximately $645,000, out of his or her own pocket, and the average Senate open-seat candidate contributed $470,000 to his or her own campaign.[161]

Given the reluctance of large individual donors and PACs to contribute to challengers, the opportunity for self-funding can be crucial for challengers. Nevertheless, the growing dependence of challengers on their own money underscores the limits the current system places on political participation by individuals of ordinary means. Political newcomers unable to self-fund a substantial portion of their campaigns are effectively excluded from the process. In addition, the political parties and other organizations active in elections may treat personal wealth as a factor determining which candidates they will support. As the Research and Policy Committee for the Committee for Economic Development observed:

> The increasing reliance on self-financing also makes personal wealth a more important qualification for seeking public office. National party leaders naturally seek out wealthy candidates to run against better-known, better-financed incumbents. This trend further discourages less-affluent individuals from becoming candidates, since they would now face two major financial hurdles—a primary opponent with a substantial financial advantage and a well-financed incumbent. Indeed, the prospect of challengers with large financial resources may also discourage some incumbents from seeking reelection.[162]

---

[160] CED Report, supra, at 18.
[161] Herrnson in Green, supra, at 119–20.
[162] CED Report at 20.

E. The Problem of Enforcement

Even the best campaign finance laws will have little impact unless they are effectively enforced. The FEC has long been subject to criticism from journalists, academics, public-interest groups, and election-law practitioners as weak and ineffective. It has been called a "toothless tiger"[163] and a "wobbly watchdog"[164] that has "neither the will nor the means to deter wanton violators."[165] According to these critics, the FEC catches few election law violations; fails to penalize most of those it catches; and imposes penalties that are so small, and come so long after the election, that they do not have a meaningful deterrent effect.

Some commentators have praised the FEC for its work in processing disclosure reports, disseminating campaign finance information, and administering the presidential public funding system.[166] A recent external audit, required by Congress in 1997, performed by PricewaterhouseCoopers LLP, concluded that the "FEC is basically a competently managed organization with a skilled and motivated staff," which "accomplishes its disclosure responsibilities" and "operates in a fair, impartial manner, maintaining strict confidentiality and a low tolerance for error." "Productivity has increased in the processing, review, and dissemination of campaign finance transactions in the face of increasing workloads," and deadlines for public release of campaign finance reports are "routinely met."[167] But even the PricewaterhouseCoopers study noted that the FEC was unable to ensure compliance with FECA's contribution restrictions and disclosure requirements.

The FEC's problems appear to result from a combination of structural, political, and legal factors. Enforcement is hobbled by the pro-

---

[163] Note, "The Toothless Tiger—Structural, Political and Legal Barriers to Effective FEC Enforcement: An Overview and Recommendations," 10 *Admin. L. J.* 351 (1996).

[164] James A. Barnes, "Wobbly Watchdog," *The National Journal* (Apr. 2, 1994).

[165] Jackson, *Broken Promise*, supra, at 1.

[166] Id. at 62. See also Report of the American Bar Association Standing Committee on Election Law (Report No. 100, 1994, approved at the ABA Midyear Meeting, 1995).

[167] PricewaterhouseCoopers LLP, "Technology and Performance Audit and Management Review of the Federal Election Commission," vol. 1 Final Report, Jan. 29, 1999, at ES-2–ES-3.

visions of FECA, limited staff and political resources, the increasing complexity of campaign finance practices, and the inherently difficult mission of regulating the very politicians who appoint the FEC's members, determine its powers, and control its budget.[168]

FEC's Structure

The FEC consists of six commissioners, appointed by the President, with the advice and consent of the Senate, for six-year terms. As a result of an amendment adopted in 1997, FEC commissioners will henceforth be limited to a single term. Previously, there had been no limit on the number of terms a commissioner might serve. Indeed, at the end of 1997, one of the original members of the Commission first appointed in 1975 was still a member, and three others had been initially appointed by or before 1981.[169]

No more than three members of the FEC may be affiliated with the same political party. In fact, the Commission is always composed of three Democrats and three Republicans. Commissioners' terms are staggered, with two terms expiring every other year. This has led to the practice of the President's nominating commissioners in Democrat-and-Republican pairs, and with the Senate considering the nominees in pairs rather than as individuals. It also appears to be the practice that the President defers to the political parties and congressional leaders in selecting FEC nominees.

The FEC's even-numbered membership is unusual among federal agencies. Only the International Trade Commission (ITC) also has an even number of members, but the ITC is empowered to act on the affirmative vote of three out of six commissioners. The FEC, by contrast, is required to act by majority vote, with an affirmative vote of four members required for most enforcement actions.[170] This membership structure is also unusual for election-law-enforcement agencies. According to the Center for Responsive Politics, 26 out of 34

---

[168] Internal management issues also have a role to play. Those issues are thoroughly analyzed in the PricewaterhouseCoopers audit and are beyond the scope of this Report. For a further review of campaign finance law enforcement issues, see "From the Ground Up," supra, 27 Fordham Urb. L. J. at 126–56.

[169] See FEC, Annual Report 1997, at 81–82. The incumbent commissioners will be eligible for reappointment to one additional six-year term.

[170] 2 U.S.C. § 437c (c).

federal, state, and local election regulatory structures consist of an odd-numbered commission.[171]

Also departing from the usual practice of federal agencies, the FEC does not have a presidentially appointed chair who serves as such for a full term. Instead, the Commission elects its own chair and vice-chair, who each serve in those capacities for one year. In effect, the positions of chair and vice-chair rotate around the membership of the FEC. The lack of a strong chair may hamper the ability of the Commission to focus its resources; set investigative, enforcement, or policy priorities; and establish an effective and visible public presence that would encourage compliance with legal requirements.

Resources and Workload

The FEC appoints a staff Director, a General Counsel, and a staff. In 1998 the Commission had a full-time-equivalent staff of 313. Of those, one-third were assigned to work on FECA disclosure; another third worked on FECA compliance; about 10 percent administered the presidential public funding program; and the remainder were involved in election administration, data processing and electronic filing projects, and FEC policy-making.[172]

The FEC was hard hit by budget cuts in 1995–96, and the 1998 staff was actually slightly smaller than the staff in 1994 despite the sharp growth in FEC filings and federal election spending generally. The agency has been adding staff in the last two years and is projected to grow modestly in the near future. Although there has been growth in the agency's staff and budget since the 1970s, that growth has been much less than the increase in federal campaign spending subject to regulation.

The agency's budget has also lagged behind the increase in campaign spending, although the budget has grown more than staffing levels. The appropriation for the FEC was $6 million in 1976 and $26.5 million in 1996. As a result, the ratio of campaign finance dollars subject to regulation relative to the agency's budget went from

---

[171] Center for Responsive Politics, "Enforcing the Campaign Finance Laws: An Agency Model" (Carol Mallory and Elizabeth Hedlund, 1993), http://www.opensecrets.org/pubs/lawenforce/enforceindex.html

[172] PricewaterhouseCoopers Audit at ES-5, 2–13.

about $48:$1 in 1976 to $86:$1 in 1996.[173] In recent years, some of the cutbacks have been restored, and the FEC's budget was grown relative to the rate of inflation.

The increase in federal campaign spending and the growing complexity of campaign finance practices has had a direct impact on the FEC's workload. During Fiscal Year (FY) 1997 through FY 1998, the FEC coded and entered roughly 1.9 million transactions, compared with 800,000 transactions entered during the FY 1990–91 period. More than 8000 committees filed approximately 82,000 reports. To clarify reported transactions, approximately 17,000 requests for additional information were sent to committees during this period.[174] The activities of 200 committees were referred for "for cause" audits, compared with roughly 100 referrals each made after the 1994 and 1992 cycles, and the activities of 70 committees were referred for enforcement action.[175]

In addition, there were 18 publicly funded primary and general election presidential candidates subject to audit. In 1995–96 the FEC received more than 300 external complaints alleging violations of FECA by individuals, organizations, and political committees. With these complaints added to pending cases at the beginning of the election cycle, and the 70 referrals from the audit analysis division, the enforcement docket grew to 566 cases.

Due to a lack of enforcement staff and resources, however, only 260 cases were "activated," that is, assigned to enforcement attorneys. Three hundred and six cases were held as " inactive"; of these, 206 were dismissed with no action taken. Similarly, of the 200 referrals for consideration for "for cause" audits, only 15 such audits were actually conducted, and of the 18 presidential candidates subject to audit, only 15 were actually audited.[176] As the PricewaterhouseCoopers audit found, "with its current level of resources and escalating workloads, the FEC accomplishes its disclosure responsibilities, but struggles to meet its compliance mission."[177]

---

[173] The 1996 figures were actually a small improvement over the previous presidential elections in which the activity/agency appropriation ratios were $99:$1 (1984); $96:$1 (1988); and $95:$1 (1992).

[174] Pricewaterhouse Coopers Audit at 4–1.

[175] Id. at 4–3.

[176] Id.

[177] Id. at ES-3.

The Enforcement Process

Campaign finance law enforcement is hampered by the FEC's cumbersome multistep enforcement process, the requirement that a majority of the commissioners approve advancing a case from one step to the next, the requirement that the Commission offer respondents the opportunity to engage in a time-consuming conciliation process in all cases, and the FEC's lack of authority to impose sanctions.

The enforcement process begins either by the receipt of a complaint from an external source or a referral to the enforcement staff from another arm of the agency, such as the audit division. Such a complaint or referral triggers the opening of a "matter under review" (MUR). Once an MUR is activated, the enforcement staff prepares an initial legal and factual analysis. Based on that initial analysis, the Office of General Counsel may decide either to close the case or to find that there is a "reason to believe" (RTB) a violation has occurred. If, based on this preliminary analysis, the staff concludes there is an RTB, the complaint, the staff analysis, and the recommendation are submitted to the commissioners, who must decide, with four affirmative votes,[178] that an RTB exists. If the FEC finds an RTB, an investigation of the MUR is formally initiated. If not, the matter is closed.

If the FEC finds an RTB, the respondent is notified and provided with the basis for the finding. The Commission's regulations provide that at this point the respondent and the staff may enter into what is known as "pre-probable cause conciliation." If that occurs, the result is an agreement that includes an admission of violation by the respondent, remedial steps the respondent must take, and provisions for the payment of a civil penalty. If the FEC approves the agreement, the MUR is resolved.

If the case is not resolved by pre-probable cause conciliation, the FEC may undertake a full investigation. The Commission has subpoena power and can order production of documents, depositions, and interrogatories. The exercise of each of these formal discovery powers requires a vote of the FEC. Ultimately, the Commission's General Counsel submits a brief to the FEC contending there is "probable cause to believe" (PCTB) that a violation was committed, and the respondent submits a response brief. The Commission must

---

[178] 2 U.S.C. § 437g(a)(2).

decide, with the affirmative vote of at least four commissioners required, whether there is PCTB that a violation occurred.

If the FEC finds PCTB, it must once again attempt to conciliate the violation. The statute requires that the conciliation effort last at least 30, but not more than 90, days,[179] but in practice the conciliation period may run well beyond 90 days. Many respondents are skilled at protracting the negotiation process. As with pre-probable cause conciliation, any conciliation agreement must include an admission of violation, a civil penalty, and, where appropriate, corrective measures. Any agreement must be approved by the affirmative votes of at least four commissioners.

If the FEC fails to secure a conciliation agreement, it may authorize the filing of a civil action for relief in federal district court. Again, the decision to go to court requires the affirmative votes of at least four Commission members. A judicial proceeding is a de novo action. The burden is on the FEC, through its General Counsel, to prove its case. The Commission's finding of PCTB receives no deference.

Caseload

The FEC considered nearly 1200 enforcement cases in 1994–98. Of these, 59 percent were dismissed before reaching the Reason to Believe stage; 3 percent resulted in a finding of No Reason to Believe; 12 percent (140 cases) produced a finding of RTB, but no further action was taken; 1 percent produced a finding of Probable Cause to Believe, but no further action was taken; 22 percent were resolved by conciliation; and 2 percent (or 29 cases) resulted in the authorization of a civil suit.[180]

It is difficult to assess the significance of the large number of cases dismissed before the RTB. Many may have been trivial or frivolous, brought by opponents or political enemies of a candidate or committee with the intention to embarrass but without adequate legal or factual foundation. On the other hand, many may have been dismissed simply due to the FEC's lack of resources. In the late 1980s and early 1990s the Commission developed an enormous backlog. To address that backlog, in 1993 the FEC implemented a new "Enforce-

---

[179] 2 U.S.C. § 437g(a)(4).
[180] PricewaterhouseCoopers Audit at 4–67.

ment Priority System," which rated cases according to a variety of factors, including "impact on the process," "intrinsic seriousness of the violation," "development of the law," and the amount of time that had passed since the initial complaint/referral.[181] Although this has allowed the FEC to target its scarce resources on more significant cases, it has also led to the dismissal of many cases simply because they were stale or involved smaller sums of money, not because of the lack of merit. Indeed, due to resource constraints, many cases are never actively pursued. In three of the last four calendar years fewer than half of the FEC's enforcement cases were considered "active"—in 1997 only one-third were "active."[182]

Private Suits

There is no private right of action under FECA. That is, an individual aggrieved by a candidate's or committee's violation of federal election finance law may only complain to the FEC and may not sue directly under the Act. To be sure, the agency's failure to take action on an externally generated case may be challenged, as may its dismissal of a complaint. If the Commission does not take final action on a complaint within 120 days after it was filed, the complainant may seek judicial review in the federal district court of the District of Columbia.[183] Similarly, a complainant may petition for judicial review of the dismissal of a complaint. The complainant, however, will have to show that the FEC's failure to act, or its dismissal of a complaint, was contrary to law and arbitrary and capricious. Few complainants have succeeded in challenging the agency's failure to act or dismissal of a case, although in some cases the reviewing court may require the Commission to submit periodic reports concerning its progress in handling an MUR.

Penalties

Penalties for violations of FECA are a maximum of $5500 or the amount of the contribution or expenditure involved in the violation, whichever is greater. For knowing and willful violations, the penalty

---

[181] Id. at 4–71.
[182] Id. at 4–68.
[183] 2 U.S.C. § 437g(a)(8).

doubles to $11,000, or twice the amount of the contribution or expenditure involved in the violation, whichever is greater. Median civil penalties resulting from negotiated conciliation agreements have risen sharply in recent years, from around $1000 in the 1990–92 period, to more than $7000 in 1995 and 1996, to $9000 in 1997. However, the total penalties from conciliation agreements in 1997 was $863,000, or about half the sum collected in 1994.[184] This may suggest that the agency is concentrating on fewer but more important cases.

Detecting Violations

Due to legislation adopted in 1979, the FEC is banned from undertaking random audits. The FEC initially had random-audit authority, and following the 1976 election it undertook random audits of 10 percent of House and Senate candidates. Those audits "turned up minor but embarrassing inaccuracies in the reports of many incumbents."[185] As a result, Congress stripped the FEC of the authority to conduct audits other than (i) "for cause" or (ii) of candidates who accept presidential public funding.

With respect to audits "for cause"—that is, because of gaps, mistakes, or violations apparent on the face of a report—the FEC lacks the resources to audit more than a fraction of the reports considered for audit. Of the 194 committee reports filed in the 1995–96 election cycle that were considered for a for-cause audit, the Commission referred just 15 (and only one filed by an incumbent candidate) for such an audit.[186] According to PricewaterhouseCoopers, the FEC "does not appear to have enough resources to conduct a sufficient number of audits for cause to have a deterrent effect throughout the filing community."[187] Typically, only about 8 to 10 percent of the reports considered for audit are actually subject to audit. From 1990 through 1997 only 71 for-cause audits were completed, or only about 9 per year.[188]

---

[184] FEC, Annual Report (1997) at 12.
[185] Jackson, supra, at 12.
[186] PricewaterhouseCoopers Audit at 4–44 to 4–45.
[187] Id. at 4–52.
[188] 1997 FEC Annual Report at 93.

3

Basic Principles of Campaign Finance Regulation

THE STRENGTHS and weaknesses of the current campaign finance system cannot be analyzed, nor can potential reforms be evaluated, without a clear understanding of the values that ought to go into the design of a campaign finance structure. We cannot know how well the system is working or whether or how it can be improved until we have a definition of what good working order would mean. Thus, early in its deliberations the Commission on Campaign Finance Reform articulated a set of fundamental principles intended to focus its examination of the present system and guide its consideration of new reforms. These principles grow out of past and present legislation, judicial opinions, and our own sense of the relationship between campaign finance and democratic government.

Some of these principles may, at times, be in tension with other principles. It may not be possible to satisfy completely all of the values implicated by the financing of elections in a democratic political system. Nevertheless, these values must be given a central place in the assessment of the system and in the consideration of its reform. We believe that we as a society can make progress in advancing those campaign finance principles that currently receive inadequate attention without jeopardizing the other, equally important, values at issue.

The principles we believe ought to be central to the design of our campaign finance system, and which inform the recommendations that we present in chapter 4, are

- Political Participation
- Voter Information
- Voter Equality
- Competitive Elections
- Prevention of the Undue Influence of Campaign Financing on Governance

- Amelioration of the Burdens of Fundraising
- Effective Administration and Enforcement

A. POLITICAL PARTICIPATION

As the Supreme Court has reminded us, campaign spending involves speech and associational activity protected by the First Amendment. This is not simply an arid legal formality. Elections are our central form of collective political decision-making, and thus, they are our most important mechanism for securing democratically accountable government. The very legitimacy of our system of elections requires that candidates, political parties, and others with an interest in the election be able to participate in the process and make their cases to the voters. A free election assumes that candidates are free not simply to place their names on the ballot but to contest the election vigorously. A vigorous contest includes the freedom to communicate with the voters to persuade them to cast their ballots for a particular candidate.

Election campaigns require campaign spending. Money per se is not speech, but in our large and heterogeneous society it takes a considerable amount of money for anyone interested in an election to communicate with the voters. Campaign finances are a critical part of the election campaign. Money, in particular, is a unique campaign resource. "It buys goods, and it also buys human energy, skills, and services. . . . [I]t is the common denominator in the shaping of many of the factors comprising political power because it buys what is not or cannot be volunteered."[189] Money buys all the things crucial for a modern election campaign—broadcast and radio air time; the printing and mailing of campaign literature; transportation costs; the services of campaign professionals for crafting the campaign message, conducting polls, and producing campaign advertisements; the salaries of campaign workers; the rent for campaign offices; the costs of data-processing equipment and computer time; even the expenses incurred in raising the funds necessary to pay for the other campaign expenditures. These services are unlikely to be provided by volunteers. They require money.

---

[189] Herbert E. Alexander, *Financing Politics: Money, Elections, and Political Reform*, 3 (3d ed. 1984).

There is little controversy about the importance of respecting the value of political participation in the design of a campaign finance system. As a constitutional matter, the Supreme Court has determined that government regulation of campaign money must be subject to "the exacting scrutiny applicable to limitations on core First Amendment rights of political expression."[190] Indeed, protection of campaign spending has been central to the Supreme Court's approach to campaign finance regulation. Certainly, we should be wary of any approaches to reform that would attempt to curtail the ability of candidates, parties, and politically active groups to participate vigorously in the electoral process.

On the other hand, respect for the value of political participation does not necessarily call for a laissez-faire approach to campaign finance. Robust campaign activity can be curtailed not only by spending limits but by inadequate funding. Government regulation can promote political participation and increase the ability of candidates to speak to the voters by helping candidates obtain new campaign resources. The provision of new campaign resources may be particularly likely to open up the process to more participation by women and minority candidates.

Moreover, some restrictions on campaign money may promote popular participation. Currently, most campaign funds come from wealthy individuals and special-interest organizations, and a large and growing portion of funding comes from sources and in amounts that appear to flout existing requirements. Candidates and office-holders effectively make large donations a key to access, and personal wealth has become a factor in determining who can be a viable candidate. As a result, political participation may be depressed by the public perception that big money dominates the political process and shapes electoral outcomes. In *Buckley v. Valeo*, the Supreme Court emphasized that government could regulate campaign financing to address the politically debilitating consequences of the appearance of corruption, as well as corruption itself. The Court recently reiterated this concern in *Nixon v. Shrink Missouri Government PAC*, when it observed: "Leave the perception of impropriety unanswered, and the cynical assumption that large donors call the tune could jeopardize the willingness of voters to take part in democratic gover-

---

[190] *Buckley v. Valeo*, 424 U.S. 1, 44 (1976).

nance."[191] An important goal for campaign finance reform ought to be to win public confidence and thereby promote popular political participation.

B. Voter Information

The legitimacy of decision-making by election turns on the ability of voters to receive the information they need in order to cast informed votes. This is not simply a matter of enabling each voter to make a choice more consistent with his or her interests or beliefs. Citizens as voters are making choices that bind the polity as a whole and set the course of government policy for the next political term. There is, thus, a collective interest in increasing the amount of relevant information available to the voters in the hope of improving the quality of voter decision-making.

The goal of voter information is served by the protection of campaign speech. Although the news media provide information concerning candidates and election issues, media coverage is often wanting, particularly for lower-level elections. To a significant degree, the voters depend on candidates, parties, and other election participants to provide them with the information they need in order to cast informed votes.

But government regulation could also advance the goal of voter information. Providing candidates with funds, sponsoring debates, producing ballot pamphlets, or enabling candidates to mail campaign literature at reduced cost all facilitate voter information.

So, too, laws that require candidates, parties, and politically active committees to disclose the identities of their donors play a central role in providing voters with politically important information. As *Buckley* put it:

> [D]isclosure provides the electorate with information "as to where political campaign money comes from and how it is spent by the candidate" in order to aid the voters in evaluating those who seek . . . office. It allows voters to place each candidate in the political spectrum more precisely than is often possible solely on the basis of party labels and

---

[191] *Shrink Missouri Government PAC*, 120 S. Ct. at 906.

campaign speeches. The sources of a candidate's financial support also alert the voter to the interests to which a candidate is most likely to be responsive and thus facilitate predictions of future performance in office.[192]

Disclosure of campaign contributions has been a centerpiece of federal campaign finance law since 1910, although federal disclosure really became effective only with the enactment of FECA and the creation of the FEC to enforce its requirements. Moreover, the principle of voter information is advanced by the application of disclosure requirements to all campaign spending, not just spending by candidates. *Buckley* upheld FECA's provisions requiring disclosure of the names and addresses of people who make independent expenditures or who contribute to organizations that make such expenditures. The Court sustained these rules although it had already concluded that independent spending did not present a danger of corruption. The Court's rationale was that such disclosure "increases the fund of information concerning those who support the candidates." This informational interest in the sources of independent spending can be as strong as the interest in the sources of candidates' funds because disclosure by independent committees "helps voters to define more of the candidates' constituencies."[193] One of the troubling features about the rise of so-called issue advocacy advertising is that the organizations that sponsor issue ads are not subject to requirements that they disclose the sources of their funding, thereby depriving the voters of information that could help them evaluate such ads when they make their election choices.[194]

C. Voter Equality

Voter equality is a central premise of our democratic system. Over the course of our history, the electorate has been expanded to include all adult citizens. Recent developments like the one-person, one-vote

---

[192] *Buckley,* supra, 424 U.S. at 66–67.

[193] Id. at 80–81.

[194] See "From the Ground Up," supra, 27 *Fordham Urb. L. J.* at 112–14.

doctrine[195] and the vote-dilution doctrine[196] have sought to ensure not simply that each adult citizen has a right to vote but that each voter has an equally weighted vote and, thus, an equal opportunity to affect the outcome of the election. Our laws most emphatically deny a special place for wealth in voting. Most states long ago scrapped wealth or tax-payment requirements for voting, and the Supreme Court has made the elimination of wealth and tax-payment tests a constitutional mandate. Wealth may not be a criterion for the right to cast a vote[197] or be a candidate,[198] nor may the wealth of the voter be a factor in determining how much weight a particular vote will be given.[199]

The role of voter equality in our electoral system has implications beyond the actual casting and counting of ballots. For the election to serve as a mechanism of democratic decision-making there must be a considerable amount of election-related activity before balloting can occur. Candidates, parties, interest groups, and interested individuals need to be able to attempt to persuade voters how to cast their ballots. The election campaign is an integral part of the process of structured choice and democratic deliberation that constitutes an election.[200]

---

[195] See, for example, *Reynolds v. Sims*, 377 U.S. 533 (1964) (state legislatures required to be apportioned on one-person, one-vote basis); *Wesberry v. Sanders*, 376 U.S. 1 (1964) (congressional districts required to be apportioned on one-person, one-vote basis).

[196] See, for example, *Rogers v. Lodge*, 458 U.S. 613 (1982) (finding that at-large voting systems may be used to dilute the voting strength of minorities); *White v. Regester*, 412 U.S. 755 (1973) (finding that multimember districts can be used to dilute the voting strength of minority groups).

[197] *Harper v. Virginia Bd. of Elections*, 383 U.S. 663 (1966) (invalidating poll tax on grounds that wealth is not germane to the right to vote); *City of Phoenix v. Kolodziejski*, 399 U.S. 204 (1970) (invalidating law limiting franchise in bond issue election to taxpayers).

[198] *Bullock v. Carter*, 405 U.S. 134 (1972) (invalidating law that candidate must pay filing fee in order to have name placed on ballot); *Lubin v. Panish*, 415 U.S. 709 (1974) (same).

[199] *Hill v. Stone*, 421 U.S. 289 (1975) (invalidating law requiring that bond issue obtain approval of concurrent majorities of all voters and of tax-paying voters).

[200] As a matter of legal doctrine, the Supreme Court has often defined an election broadly to include pre-Election Day activities, or has deferred to statutes that regulate pre-Election Day activities as part of the electoral process. In *Terry v. Adams*, 345 U.S. 461 (1953), for example, the Court treated private political activity that preceded an election, and informally but effectively supplanted that election, as a part of the election. Id. at 466. The Court has indicated that Congress can treat party

The Supreme Court has acknowledged that voter equality is a factor in appraising the campaign finance system. To be sure, *Buckley v. Valeo* emphatically and famously rejected the idea that equality can justify limitations on campaign communications[201]—a conclusion sharply challenged by Justice Breyer, in an opinion joined by Justice Ginsburg, in the recent *Shrink Missouri Government PAC* case, who pointed out that "the Constitution often permits restrictions on the speech of some in order to prevent the few from drowning out the many, and that the Constitution tolerates numerous restrictions . . . to make effective the political rights of the entire electorate."[202] But the Court has relied on the voter-equality concern in validating federal and state restrictions on campaign expenditures by corporations. As *Austin v. Michigan State Chamber of Commerce* explained, corporate campaign spending can "unfairly influence elections" because a corporation's campaign funds "have little or no correlation to the public's support for [its] ideas."[203] Prohibiting corporations from using their treasury funds to finance campaign expenditures "ensures that expenditures reflect actual public support for the political ideas espoused by corporations."[204] In other words, spending that reflects the corporate spender's wealth rather than the extent of popular support for its message gives the corporate spender an undue influence on the electoral outcome. That is the voter equality point in a nutshell.[205]

To be sure, participation in and influence over an election cam-

---

nominating convention procedures as part of an election: *Morse v. Republican Party of Va.*, 517 U.S. 186, 218 n.31 (1996); and that Congress can use the notion of a preelection campaign season to define the obligations of broadcasters: *CBS, Inc. v. FCC*, 453 U.S. 367, 368–88, 397–97 (1981).

[201] *Buckley v. Valeo*, 424 U.S. 1, 48–49 (1976) ("the concept that government may restrict the speech of some elements of our society in order to enhance the relative voice of others is wholly foreign to the First Amendment").

[202] *Nixon v. Shrink Missouri Government PAC*, supra, Breyer, J., 120 S. Ct. at 912.

[203] 494 U.S. 652, 660 (1990).

[204] Id. at 660.

[205] The Court has sought to hold together its inconsistent views about the connection between voter equality and campaign finance regulation by asserting that corporations pose special problems because they enjoy a "unique state-conferred corporate structure" that is said to give them special advantages in amassing funds. Id. at 659–60. It is hard to see why this is relevant, or even that it is right. As Justice Scalia pointed out in his *Austin* dissent, corporations are not alone in receiving special advantages from the state. Id. at 680 (noting that other organizations receive government support through contracts or tax subsidies).

paign are not the same as voting. It is relatively easy to measure votes and to ensure that no person casts more votes than any other. Participation and influence take many different forms, vary widely in intensity, and are difficult to measure. It is virtually impossible to quantify the impact of a particular dollar in a particular race, nor would it be possible to quantify other modes of participation and influence—the "free media" value of a celebrity endorsement, the intensity of commitment of volunteers, the superior organization of a particular interest group—that can affect a campaign. It is not possible to truly equalize influence over elections. Indeed, given the values of robust and uninhibited political participation, and the extensive regulation it would take to ensure total equality, ensuring absolutely equal influence over elections is not even desirable. Nevertheless, when extreme inequalities of wealth bear directly on campaign financing and spending, as they do in our current privately funded campaign finance system, the norm of voter equality is undermined.

Large individual donors and large PAC contributions dominate our current campaign finance system. In 1995–96, 235,000 people, or one-tenth of 1 percent of the total population provided approximately one-third of individual donations.[206] Large donors are not a politically or demographically representative sample of the general population. A recent study of large donors—defined as those who gave at least $200 to one or more congressional candidates—found the affluent, men, whites, and people engaged in high-status occupations make up a far higher portion of the large donor group than of society as a whole.[207] Through their contributions, these large donors can have a greater impact on the outcome of the election than small donors and nondonors.

One important goal for the campaign finance system should be to reduce the tension between the goal of equal voter influence over

---

[206] See Center for Responsive Politics, "The Big Picture: Where the Money Came From in the 1996 Elections," http://www.crp.org/crpdocs/bigpicture/overview/bpoverview.htm

[207] John Green, Paul Herrnson, Lynda Powell, and Clyde Wilcox, "Individual Congressional Campaign Contributors: Wealthy, Conservative and Reform-Minded," http://www.crp.org/pubc/donors/donors.htm. The "reform-minded" in the title of the study refers to the contributors' views on campaign finance regulation.

election outcomes and the unequal influence enjoyed by wealthy individuals and interest groups capable of making large donations.

D. COMPETITIVE ELECTIONS

Elections are about giving voters choices. If one candidate is well-funded, but her or his opponents lack resources, the first candidate will have an advantage in campaigning and getting her or his message to the voters. This can affect campaign outcomes. Moreover, the legitimacy of the election may be undermined in the eyes of the voters if the better-funded candidate is perceived as enjoying an advantage.

The concern about fair competition is particularly focused on the willingness and ability of challengers to take on incumbents. The opportunity to deny reelection to incumbents, and the possibility that in any given election the people may exercise their authority to vote out current officeholders, is the ultimate security of popular control over government. The value of fair electoral competition is, therefore, especially significant when the incumbent is seeking reelection. The incumbent typically starts with many built-in advantages, ranging from the free media attention he or she gets while in office, to the opportunity to use the office to provide constituency service, to the fact that the incumbent was popular enough to win the last election. These advantages contribute to, and are typically reinforced by, the incumbent's superior ability to raise campaign money. An important goal for a campaign finance system should be to make it easier for challengers to mount effective campaigns against incumbent officeholders. This will make it more likely that incumbents will actually be challenged, and that the incumbent-challenger election will be a real contest.

Absolute funding parity is not essential for fair elections, and a challenger can do well when he or she musters a critical mass of funds even if the incumbent spends more. Nor is it necessary for challengers actually to defeat incumbents, or for there to be frequent turnovers in office. Rather, voters need to know they have a real alternative to the incumbent, and incumbents need to know there is a real possibility they may lose. This requires credible challengers, and credible challengers require adequate financing.

A central weakness of our current privately funded campaign finance system for congressional elections, as described in chapter 2 of this Report, is its failure to provide challengers with adequate funding. An incumbent can carry forward excess funds from his or her last election[208] and is well-positioned to collect funds while in office. The statistical likelihood that the incumbent will be reelected increases his or her ability to collect funds from donors who want to have "access" to the winner. Thus, incumbents usually start out well ahead in the financial arms race. In contrast, the challenger usually starts out less well-known and with less campaign money. Saddled with the presumption of incumbent reelection, the challenger is likely to experience greater difficulty raising funds as the PACs and wealthy individual donors who dominate campaign financing give their money primarily to secure and maintain access to elected officials and, thus, tend to favor incumbents over challengers.

An important goal of campaign finance reform should be to address the imbalance of candidate resources and, especially, the advantages of incumbency and to make it easier for serious candidates to undertake financially competitive campaigns.

E. Prevention of the Undue Influence of Campaign Financing on Governance

Campaign finance practices can affect not just the fairness of the election but the behavior of government after—or more accurately, between—elections. When candidates are dependent on private donations, large donors and prospective donors may obtain special access to officeholders, and their views may carry extra weight. They will, therefore, be particularly well positioned to affect government decision-making. This is rarely a matter of outright vote buying, or of donors using a large donation, or the threat to withhold a future dona-

---

[208] When the 106th Congress convened in Jan. 1999, members of the House of Representatives were already banking more than $100 million for their next re-election campaigns. More than half the members of the House—269 members to be precise—had at least $100,000 on hand for the 2000 campaign; 167 members had at least $200,000. See "Carryover Funds: 106th Congress Convenes With Over $100 Million in the Bank for 2000 Campaigns," *Political Finance and Lobby Reporter* (Jan. 13, 1999).

tion, to get a member of Congress to change her or his position on an issue. Instead, large-donor influence is typically more subtle. It is often a matter of an extra opportunity to make one's case, to be heard during negotiations while a bill is in committee, to influence a member of Congress to make one bill rather than another an agenda priority, or to affect the precise wording of a bill or amendment. Without changing votes, campaign contributions can affect what bills become law.

Concern about the undue influence of large donors and prospective donors on the operations of government has been a driving force in campaign finance regulation since the beginning of the 20th century. Congress first limited campaign contributions to curtail donor influence in 1907, and some restrictions on donations have been on the books ever since. The impact of the campaign finance system on the operations of government has been a central concern of the Supreme Court as well, which has held that the prevention of corruption and the appearance of corruption provide a constitutional basis for campaign finance regulations. To be sure, not all campaign contributions are intended to corrupt or have a corrupting influence. Many donors make contributions not to influence or gain access to officeholders but to advance the electoral prospects of candidates whose issue positions they support. Nevertheless, one of the principal concerns of campaign finance reform is controlling the disproportionate influence the sources of campaign funds can have on public decision-making.

Corruption is also implicated when officeholders who command the powers of government are able to pressure people, businesses, and organizations affected by government actions to make campaign contributions. "Every request from an elected official who influences legislation or regulatory activity is an implicit demand. The contributor fears the consequences of failing to respond. He fears that his competitors may gain an advantage if they are more generous than he." Indeed, political contributions may be not a means of engaging in political speech but simply a "cost of doing business." Under these circumstances, "[e]xtortion, or practices that differ only in being more genteel, are the Janus face of undue influence by contributors."[209]

---

[209] David W. Adamany and George E. Agree, *Political Money: A Strategy for Campaign Financing in America*, 11 (1975).

F. AMELIORATING THE BURDENS OF FUNDRAISING

The current campaign finance system places most of the burden of raising campaign funds on officeholders and candidates. A major impetus for campaign finance reform is the frustration politicians now feel concerning how much time they must devote to courting potential donors, often by methods borrowed from the marketplace that can only be described as demeaning.[210] Professor Vincent Blasi has cogently argued that our campaign finance system undermines the quality of political representation, as elected officeholders are distracted from constituent service or policy-making by the grim business of soliciting donations. Our burdensome fundraising system can skew campaign activity, too, forcing candidates to meet with potential contributors rather than formulate positions or speak with voters.

There is considerable anecdotal evidence that the rigors of fundraising have contributed to the decisions of some officials to decline to seek reelection and of potential candidates not to challenge incumbents. The burdensome fundraising process, thus, can affect the quality of governance, the extent and quality of electoral communication, political participation, and the competitiveness of elections.[211]

The burdens of fundraising do not apply to all candidates evenly. Incumbents and candidates who are personally wealthy do not have to worry as much about fundraising as do challengers and candidates who are less financially well-endowed. The fundraising system, thus, tends to reinforce the advantages of incumbency and contributes to the growing role of self-financed campaigns. The burdens of fundraising also play a part in the growing influence of campaign intermediaries who collect contributions from their associates, supporters, or members, bundle them together, and pass them on to candidates.

Consistent with the other principles of campaign finance law—particularly the values of political participation, voter equality, and minimizing the impact of the campaign finance system on governance—a well-designed campaign finance system should seek to minimize the burdens of fundraising. That could increase the willingness of some potential candidates to actually compete, free candi-

---

[210] Vincent Blasi, "Free Speech and the Widening Gyre of Fund-Raising: Why Campaign Spending Limits May Not Violate the First Amendment After All," 94 *Colum. L. Rev.* 1281 (1994).

[211] See "From the Ground Up," supra, 27 *Fordham Urb. L. J.* at 63–64.

dates for meeting with voters, and enable elected officials to devote more time to the responsibilities they were elected to undertake.

G. Effective Administration and Enforcement

Campaign finance reform will not work unless campaign finance laws are capable of effective, nonpartisan administration and enforcement.[212] This requires laws that are straightforward so that candidates, parties, organizations, and potential donors and spenders can determine whether their activities comply with legal constraints. The laws ought to be internally consistent, so that one set of restrictions or limitations are not effectively undermined and discredited by other loopholes and evasions. The laws should be congruent with legitimate campaign practices and respect the needs of candidates to raise money sufficient for their campaigns. Most importantly, there must be an administrative structure capable of detecting and punishing violations, including violations by major candidates and officeholders and by the major parties, in "real time," that is, during the election campaign that the questionable campaign finance activity seeks to affect.

Campaign finance rules will control campaign finance behavior only if they are effective and enforced and are seen as such by candidates, political committees, and contributors. Effective enforcement is also necessary to promote public faith in the integrity of the campaign finance process.

---

[212] See generally Nicole A. Gordon, "The New York City Model: Essentials for Effective Campaign Finance Regulation," 6 *J. L. & Pol.* 79 (1997).

4

Recommendations

A. The Path to Reform

WITH THE CAMPAIGN finance system produced by Congress in the Watergate Era swamped by evasion and on the verge of collapse, what direction should campaign finance regulation take? One school of thought, championed by Justices Thomas and Scalia,[213] some members of Congress,[214] and some legal scholars,[215] would say, "Go back," that is, deregulate. Deregulation would scrap FECA's prohibitions, restrictions, and contribution limitations and preserve only some reporting and disclosure requirements. Deregulation would certainly have some benefits. It would eliminate the evasions and the fine legal distinctions that make a mockery of the current campaign finance laws. By enabling candidates to obtain large contributions directly from wealthy individuals and businesses, deregulation would also ameliorate the burdens of the fundraising process, if only for those candidates favored by wealthy donors. Deregulation would certainly eliminate many of the costs of administration, too.

But deregulation, even with disclosure, would do nothing to promote competitive election contests; it would preserve, if not expand, the influence of large donors on election campaigns; and it would effectively ratify the influence of large donations over the political process. It is unlikely that disclosure alone would be sufficient to check the influence of private wealth over politics: "Full disclosure produces mountains of political finance information that must be exhaustively analyzed to reveal significant patterns of giving and spend-

---

[213] See *Nixon v. Shrink Missouri Government PAC*, dissenting opinion, 120 S. Ct. 916–27. See also *Colorado Republican*, supra, 518 U.S. at 635–44 (opinion of Justice Thomas).

[214] See H.R. 965 (the "Citizen Legislature and Political Freedom Act") introduced by Rep. John Doolittle (R-CA).

[215] See, for example, Bradley A. Smith, "Faulty Assumptions and Undemocratic Consequences of Campaign Finance Reform," 105 *Yale L. J.* 1049 (1996); Kathleen M. Sullivan, "Against Campaign Finance Reform," 1998 *Utah L. Rev.* 311 (1998).

ing; time also is needed to publicize these patterns, to allow debate and discussion about them, and finally to permit voters to ponder them and to calculate what weight political financing shall have in their ballot choices."[216]

Even voters for whom campaign finance practices are an election priority may be unable to use their votes to punish or reward particular candidates. Competing candidates and party committees may receive donations from the same PACs or wealthy individuals, or they may receive donations from different sources, but voters might find both sets of sources—or both candidates' fundraising practices—offensive. Moreover, campaign finance practices are rarely the dispositive issue in an election. A voter may be disturbed by a candidate's fundraising activities but may still believe that the candidate has a stronger record than her or his opponent on national security, healthcare, tax policy, the environment, or other issues of importance to the voter. A voter has only one vote and is likely to use it on issues the voter considers more important than campaign finance, even if she or he would vote against a candidate if campaign finance were the only issue.

Finally, regulation limited to disclosure is inadequate because it fails to provide enough money from disinterested sources, because it fails to ameliorate the burdens of fundraising, and because it fails to ensure that campaign money is distributed so as to make possible vigorous competition in all elections.

Although "deregulate and disclose" is an inadequate foundation for reform, it does suggest two steps reform might take. First, unnecessary regulations should be eliminated and unduly burdensome restrictions ameliorated. Certainly, limitations, such as the dollar limits on donations, that are more rigid than necessary to prevent undue influence should be relaxed. Second, disclosure ought to be complete. Although disclosure alone cannot carry the full burden of campaign finance reform, disclosure provides the public with critical information for evaluating candidates, campaign messages, and the post-election activities of elected officials. To be effective, however, disclosure must be comprehensive. The recent explosion of issue advocacy advertising places a growing share of campaign advertising outside the range of FECA's disclosure requirements. One goal for

---

[216] Adamany and Agree, supra, at 103.

campaign finance reform is to bring all campaign-related expenditures within the ambit of disclosure.

A second approach to reform, epitomized by the Shays-Meehan Bipartisan Campaign Reform Bill, which has passed the House of Representatives in each of the last two Congresses, would attempt to renew FECA by using the traditional techniques of contribution restrictions and disclosure to plug the holes created by soft money and so-called issue advocacy advertising. Such a reform would have the desirable benefits of checking special-interest influence, enhancing disclosure, and addressing the demoralizing effects that these blatant evasions have on public confidence in our campaign finance laws. Soft money and issue advocacy must be addressed, but capping soft money and regulating issue advocacy, without further action, would do nothing to provide underfinanced candidates with the resources they need to conduct competitive campaigns. Indeed, this approach, if unaccompanied by additional measures to inject new resources into the system, might very well exacerbate the burdens of fundraising and the difficulties experienced by challengers in trying to finance their races.

A third general approach is to go forward, build on the presidential public funding law and the growing experience with public funding in many states and localities, and create a system in which public funds are available for candidates for all federal offices. Public funding would do a better job than purely private funding in promoting competitive elections, mitigating the impact of inequalities of wealth on the electoral process, reducing the influence of large campaign contributors on the operations of government, and ameliorating the burdens of fundraising. Better than reforms that are based solely on restricting campaign spending, public funding provides new resources for election activity and, thus, actually promotes First Amendment values.

Public funding is not a panacea for our campaign finance system. As candidates may not be constitutionally compelled to take public funding, any public funding system would have to coexist with at least some private funding, so reconsideration of the rules limiting private contributions would still be appropriate. As the developments in the presidential public funding system in the 1990s demonstrated, unless some controls are placed on soft money, unregulated private money can swamp the public funding system. Moreover, adoption of a public funding system would make securing effective administration and enforcement of campaign finance laws an even more urgent issue.

Nevertheless, we believe that public funding must be the centerpiece for any serious program of campaign finance reform.[217] (See table 5.)

B. PUBLIC FUNDING

(1) History and Present Use

Public funding has been on the federal campaign finance agenda since the start of the 20th century. In the aftermath of reports about large corporate contributions in the 1904 elections, a public funding bill was introduced in Congress, and in 1907 President Theodore Roosevelt also called on Congress to enact public funding of campaigns.[218] In 1966 Congress enacted Senator Russell Long's proposal for the creation of an income-tax checkoff that would be used to provide public funding of presidential campaigns. The Long legislation was repealed in 1967, but in 1971 Congress again adopted presidential public funding, to be financed via a checkoff, although it deferred the effective date of the checkoff to 1973, and the onset of public funding until 1976. In the aftermath of the Watergate scandal, Congress revisited and strengthened the presidential public funding law. At one point during the 1973–74 debates over campaign finance reform, the Senate passed a congressional public funding measure as well, but the House refused to accept it, and congressional public funding died in conference.[219]

Public funding has provided a significant percentage of the funds available to candidates in every presidential election between 1976

---

[217] The Association of the Bar of the City of New York has previously endorsed public financing of campaigns for state and federal office. See Committee on Election Law, "Towards a Level Playing Field—A Pragmatic Approach to Public Campaign Financing," 52 *The Record* 660 (Oct. 1997); (New York state elections); Committee on State Legislation, "Campaign Finance Legislation," 41 *The Record* 746 (Oct. 1986) (same); Committee on Federal Legislation, "Federal Campaign Finance Reform," unpublished report, May 1990 (approving public financing of congressional campaigns), see 52 *The Record*, supra, at 664–65.

[218] See Mutch, supra, at 35–36.

[219] Id. at 118–31.

TABLE 5: BASIC PRINCIPLES AND RECOMMENDED REFORMS

Political Participation

- Public Funding to facilitate candidates' participation
- Public Funding, Contribution Limits, Soft Money Reform to address public's loss of confidence

Voter Information

- Issue Advocacy Reform to increase disclosure

Voter Equity

- Public Funding
- Soft Money Reform

Competitive Elections

- Public Funding
- Raising Limits on Party Support for Candidates

Prevention of Undue Influence

- Public Funding
- Soft Money Reform
- Issue Advocacy Reform

Ameliorating Burdens of Fundraising

- Public Funding
- Raising Contribution Limits

Effective Administration and Enforcement

- FEC Reforms

---

and 1996. From 1976 to 1996 public funding provided presidential candidates with $891 million, including $37 million to minor party and independent candidates. From 1976 through 1996 every major and minor party general election candidate accepted public funding in the general election.[220] From 1976 through 1992 public funding

---

[220] Ross Perot did not accept public funds in 1992, but in that election he was a

provided between 31 percent and 36 percent of candidate's primary receipts. In 1996 the public funding share of primary receipts dropped to 23 percent, due largely to the decision of Malcolm S. Forbes, Jr., to opt out of public funding and spend $42.6 million in private funds (including $37.3 million of his own money). Of some 65 serious presidential candidates between 1976 and 1996, only three (John Connally in 1980, Ross Perot in 1992, and Forbes in 1996) chose not to participate in the public funding program.[221] In the 2000 primary elections, however, two significant Republican contenders—Forbes and George W. Bush—declined to participate in presidential public funding.

Twenty-two states and a number of local governments—including New York City and Los Angeles—also have some form of public funding program. In addition, in the 1996 and 1998 elections, referendum voters in Arizona, Maine, and Massachusetts approved ballot propositions that would make most elections in those states substantially financed by publicly provided dollars. None of these laws has come into effect yet.

Of the states with older public funding systems, 10 states provide funds to political parties but not candidates; eight states provide funds to candidates but not parties; four states provide funds to both parties and candidates. The party-only programs provide only modest sums of money to the parties; several of these states rely on tax add-ons, that is, taxpayers' actions to increase their tax liabilities by one or two dollars. Generally, fewer than 1 percent of taxpayers are willing to increase their tax liabilities to pay for contributions to parties or campaigns, so these programs are quite small and have a limited impact.[222]

The 12 state programs that provide some funds to candidates are more complex. All are funded by income tax checkoffs. All of them try to encourage small contributions from individuals, either through eligibility requirements or matching-fund formulas. All of them re-

---

new party nominee and not eligible for public funds until after the election. In 1996, when Perot's Reform Party was eligible for pre-election funding as a qualified minor party, he accepted public funding with limits.

[221] See Anthony Corrado, *Paying for Presidents: Public Financing in National Elections*, 41 (1993); Joseph E. Cantor, "The Presidential Election Campaign Fund and Tax Checkoff: Background and Current Issues" (Mar. 18, 1997).

[222] See Michael J. Malbin and Thomas L. Gais, *The Day After Reform: Sobering Campaign Finance Lessons from the American States*, 53–54, 66–67 (1998).

quire candidates to abide by spending limits if they accept public funding, although some lift the spending ban if the opponent does not accept spending limits. Four of these states make public funds available for legislative races as well as elections for statewide office; in two states—Minnesota and Wisconsin—a significant number of legislative candidates participate in the public funding program. The Minnesota program has been particularly successful. More than 90 percent of the candidates for state legislative office in the past decade have participated in the program.

Most of the state public funding programs are aimed at statewide, particularly gubernatorial, elections. Between 1993 and 1996, 15 of the 22 major party general-election candidates for governor in states with public funding accepted public funds. All these state programs had spending limits, and the rate of candidate participation tended to correlate with the sufficiency of the limits.[223] In New Jersey, in 1997 the maximum public grant per candidate in the general election was $4.6 million, or two-thirds of the $6.9 million spending limit. All major party candidates for governor in New Jersey have participated in public funding since its inception in 1977.[224]

A number of local governments have public funding systems, including Los Angeles and New York City. The New York City program is particularly well-regarded. New York provides public funds to candidates for citywide office, borough president, and the city council in both primary and general elections. In 1993 all candidates for citywide office and two-thirds of the candidates for city council participated in the system.[225]

(2) Why Public Funding?

More than any other reform, public funding has the potential to ensure that our campaign finance system promotes the basic values of democratic elections: that our elections be open, fair, informed, and vigorously contested; that all adult citizens have an equal opportunity to influence the electoral process; that all serious candidates can ob-

---

[223] Id. at 62.

[224] New Jersey Election Law Enforcement Commission, "Gubernatorial Public Financing Overview."

[225] New York City Campaign Finance Board, "On the Road to Reform: Campaign Finance in the 1993 New York City Elections," 4 (1994).

tain the resources they need to bring their message to the voters; that officeholders and candidates not be unnecessarily distracted from governing and campaigning by the rigors of fundraising; and that the financing of campaigns not unduly influence government decision-making.

Public funding promotes electoral competitiveness. Challengers and political newcomers in open-seat races are simply much better able to mount campaigns when their privately raised funds are supplemented by public funds. Indeed, public funding makes it much more likely that there will be challengers in the first place and, thus, that incumbents will be forced to defend their records and engage in a public dialogue over their votes and policy preferences.[226] Presidential public funding substantially contributed to the presidential campaigns of Jimmy Carter in 1976, George Bush in 1980, Gary Hart in 1984, Jesse Jackson in 1984 and 1988, and Pat Buchanan, Jerry Brown, and Bill Clinton in 1992.[227] Public funding provided opportunities to challengers, political newcomers, and outsider candidates in the primaries and offset the built-in edge of incumbents in the general election. Indeed, in three of the five presidential elections conducted with public funding that involved challenger-incumbent contests, the challenger defeated the incumbent.

In New York City, which has run its last three mayoral elections under public funding, challengers twice defeated incumbents. In Minnesota, the only state that provides ample public funding for legislative elections (and the only state with a high level of candidate participation in the program), public funds have made legislative elections more competitive.[228] Indeed, Minnesota is the rare state in which virtually all incumbents actually had real challengers and, thus, conducted state legislative elections that were real elections. In many states that do not use public funding, half or more of all incumbents run unopposed.[229] Minnesota is also the home of perhaps the most famous beneficiary of public funding, Governor Jesse Ventura. Although he was outspent by his major party opponents, public fund-

---

[226] See, for example, "From the Ground Up," supra, 27 *Fordham Urb. L. J.* at 46–47.

[227] Corrado, *Paying for Presidents*, supra, at 39–45.

[228] See Patrick D. Donnay and Graham P. Ramsden, "Public Financing of Legislative Elections: Lessons from Minnesota," 20 *Leg. Stud. Q.* 351 (1995).

[229] See Malbin and Gais, supra, at 137.

ing provided him with the money necessary for his television ads and, thus, was critical to his success.

Public funding is necessary to bring our campaign finance system more in line with our core principle of voter equality. In privately funded systems, donors and independent spenders can have a bigger impact on the election than those who neither contribute nor spend; and big donors and spenders can have a bigger impact that smaller financial participants. Contribution and expenditure caps could ameliorate this, but they may cut into the ability of candidates to campaign effectively and may reinforce the advantages of incumbents. Public funding can break the tie between private wealth and electoral influence while simultaneously supplementing campaign resources and reducing the burdens of fundraising. Money from the public fisc comes from everyone and, thus, from no one in particular. No one gains influence over the election through public funding. The more the funds for election campaigns come from the public treasury, the more evenly is financial influence over election outcomes spread across the populace.

Moreover, public funding promotes voter equality without limiting political participation. Resistance to treating voter equality as a campaign finance norm has been sharpest when voter equality is used to justify the imposition of limits on private campaign spending. Public funding, however, increases voter equality while providing new funds for campaign communications. Even where public funding is accompanied by spending limits, public funding is unlikely to curtail electoral communications. A candidate's acceptance of public funding and a spending limit must be voluntary. Thus, each candidate has the opportunity to decide whether, on balance, public funding with limits would help or hinder her or his campaign and may opt in or out accordingly. Further, the availability of public funding for candidates has no effect on the ability of other organizations to raise and spend money in connection with the election independently of the candidates.[230] This limits the ability of public funding to promote

---

[230] See *FEC v. National Conservative Political Action Comm.*, 470 U.S. 480 (1984) (holding unconstitutional provision of presidential public funding law that would have limited the expenditures of independent committees with respect to the campaign of a presidential candidate who has accepted public funding and spending limits).

voter equality, but it ensures that even with spending limits, public funding is unlikely to reduce campaign communications.

By reducing the role of large private donors in funding elections, public funding also reduces the leverage of large donors over government. The more campaign funds come from the public fisc, the less elected officials need to be sensitive to the views of large private donors, and the more they can act on their view of what the public interest requires. So, too, by reducing the time burdens of fundraising, public funding would free officeholders to devote more time to governing and enable candidates to spend more time on campaigning.

It has been suggested that public funding would inappropriately involve government in the electoral process, but the conduct and consequences of an election campaign are matters of great public concern. It is as appropriate to use public funds to cover some of the costs of an election campaign as it is to use tax dollars to pay the costs of preparing and producing ballots and of collecting and tabulating the results. The Supreme Court acknowledged this in *Buckley* when it vindicated the use of public funding of presidential elections. Public funding, said the Court, is an effort "to use public money to facilitate and enlarge public discussion and participation in the electoral process, goals vital to a self-governing people."[231]

(3) The Design of a Public Funding System

The public funding system we propose for congressional elections would have the following major elements: (a) it would be **partial,** (b) provided to candidates who raise a **threshold amount of money in private funds,** (c) with public funds allotted on a **generous matching-funds basis**; (d) it would apply to **primary and general elections and to minor party and independent candidates as well as major party nominees**; (e) it would require participating candidates to accept a **spending limit,** (f) although **that limit would be lifted if the candidate's opponent spends above the spending limit,** and (g) it would be **funded out of regular appropriations rather than a checkoff.**

(A) PARTIAL   Under current constitutional doctrine, there probably cannot be any system that is fully publicly funded. A candidate can-

---

[231] *Buckley,* supra, 424 U.S. at 92–93.

not be prohibited from using private funds. Thus, all public funding systems are *voluntary* as well as partial, and it would be quite possible for a publicly funded candidate to have a privately funded opponent. Even if all candidates in a particular race do accept public funds, noncandidates—such as individuals, political committees, or others interested in the outcome of the election—are free to use private funds for election-related spending. Even candidates who receive public funds are unlikely to be fully publicly funded. As noted, most public funding systems require candidates to raise a threshold amount of private funds to begin with, and then use matching formulas to link the amount of public money a candidate receives to his or her ability to raise private funds.

By recommending *partial* public funding, the Special Commission is in effect stating that candidates still ought to raise some portion of their total campaign funds from private donors. This enables potential donors to participate politically by giving support to their preferred candidates directly instead of giving them an incentive to contribute to so-called independent committees. Moreover, we believe there is a value in requiring candidates to demonstrate some private support as both a condition for receiving funds and in determining the size of the public grant. The dangers inherent in private funding—of voter inequality, undue donor influence, pro-incumbent and pro-wealthy candidate bias—can be checked by limiting the matchable portion of any contribution, providing a generous public match, and requiring candidates to agree to limits on the use of their personal funds as a condition of public funding eligibility.

(B) QUALIFYING THRESHOLD   We believe that in order to receive public funds, a candidate must raise a threshold amount of money with only relatively small contributions counting toward that threshold. Specifically, **we recommend that in order to qualify for public funds, a candidate for the House of Representatives would have to collect at least $25,000 in private donations, with no more than $250 from any one donor counting toward the threshold.** We believe that the $25,000 minimum is high enough to screen out frivolous candidates without creating a barrier to serious candidates. Given the real costs in time and effort that a congressional campaign necessarily entails, we do not think the $25,000 threshold amounts to a wealth test. The provision limiting to $250 the amount of any individual contribution that counts toward the threshold ensures that backing by a small number of very wealthy individuals, or a wealthy candidate's own funds, would not be enough by itself to qualify for public funds. With these requirements, the candidate would have to obtain support from at least 100 private individuals to qualify for public funding.

In addition, **we would count only those contributions from individuals who are residents of the state in which the candidate is seeking office to count toward the threshold.** This would tie qualification for public funding to support within the candidate's voting constituency. The tie would be stronger if only contributions from within the district could count, but with decennial redistricting, district borders in many states will change, and in the election after the decennial census there could be uncertainty as to which individuals reside in the district going into the election year. Limiting qualification to contributions from within the state advances the value of linking eligibility to local support without creating unnecessary administrative complications.

For a Senate candidate to qualify for public funds, he or she would also have to attract a certain amount of private contributions, with only the first $250 of any individual's contribution—and only contributions from individuals who reside within the state— counting. The qualification level would vary to some extent with the population of the state. For a state with just one congressional district, the qualifying level would be $25,000—the same level as in the House. Thereafter, an additional $10,000 would be required for each additional congressional district in the state, but in no state would the qualifying level be more than $75,000.

(C) MATCHING FUNDS **Qualifying candidates for both the House and Senate would receive public funds on a matching-funds basis,** that is, the amount of the public grant would be based on the amount of qualifying individual contributions a candidate receives. **Only the first $250 in contributions from individuals would be matched.** A candidate could accept larger donations from individuals—up to the statutory contribution ceiling—as well as contributions from PACs and parties, but only the first $250 from any individual's total donation would be matched. We would, however, match otherwise-qualifying contributions from out-of-state donors.

Most importantly, **we would provide matching funds on a 2:1 basis, that is, for each $1 in qualifying private contributions, a candidate would receive $2 in public funds**. Thus, a $250 contribution would yield an additional $500 in public matching funds. A candidate who received all of her or his private support in small individual contributions would be two-thirds publicly funded, although given that many candidates will obtain nonmatchable donations from PACs and parties, and large individual contributions, it is likely that in many campaigns, the public share will be closer to 50 percent, or even less than that. But we believe the 2:1 match for smaller individual donations, and the possibility of two-thirds public funding, would dramatically level the playing field among candidates, significantly reduce the role of large donors, and greatly alleviate the burdens of fundraising.

Matching funds would be paid out as qualifying private funds come in, until the sum of private funds and matching public funds equaled the spending cap that a candidate agrees to accept as a condition for public funding.

(D) PRIMARY AND GENERAL ELECTIONS; MAJOR PARTY, MINOR PARTY, AND INDEPENDENT CANDIDATES   **Public funding would be available for both primary and general elections**. A candidate who qualifies for public funding before a primary would remain qualified for the general election, provided he or she is running in the general election. **Public funding would be available for any candidate, regardless of party affiliation, or the absence of party affiliation, provided he or she satisfies the threshold requirement, accepts the spending limit, and complies with the rules of the public funding program.**

(E) SPENDING LIMITS   **As a condition of eligibility for public funding, a candidate would be required to accept two spending limits. First, a candidate would have to agree not to spend more than $50,000 of his or her personal or family money on the campaign.**[232] **Second, the candidate would have to agree to limit total campaign spending.**

---

[232] We would use the same definition of "family" as is currently employed in the presidential public funding law. That would include the candidate's spouse, children, parents, grandparents, siblings, half-siblings, and the spouses of any of these persons. See 26 U.S.C. § 9035 (b).

Spending limits can serve a useful role in promoting more equal contests, curbing the influence of private donors, and controlling the arms-race mentality that currently prevails in our campaign finance system. Without some spending limit, public funding on a matching-funds basis could simply inflate the advantages enjoyed by incumbents or by those candidates receiving a disproportionate share of large, but qualifying, private contributions. Similarly, without a spending limit, candidates would still be under pressure to engage in extensive fundraising, if only to protect themselves against the war chests their opponents might be raising.

To be sure, spending limits also pose dangers. They can have the undesirable effect of limiting the amount of campaign communication. If set too low, they can discriminate against challengers.[233] Incumbents typically go into an election better known than their opponents. They benefit from greater name recognition, years of constituent service, mailings sent out under the legislative frank, "free media" coverage, and the lingering effects of their spending in prior campaigns. Challengers need to spend a critical mass of funds just to become known within the district. A spending limit set too low could prevent a challenger from ever getting his or her candidacy off the ground.

Thus, a spending limit must be set high enough to avoid the danger that it will favor incumbents or unduly burden speech. In 1996 the average House incumbent spent $750,000 on his or her campaign,[234] so any House spending limit would have to be at least that. More importantly, our data analysis determined that in 1996 and 1998 winning House challengers spent on average approximately $1 million. (See tables 6 and 7.) We, thus, recommend that the provision of public funding be tied to a **House candidate's agreement to a $1 million spending limit**. This figure, along with all other dollar figures in our public funding program, would be **indexed for inflation**.

In most districts, the spending limit would be well above recent spending levels, so that the limit would not curtail campaign speech at all. Nor would it drive up the costs of fundraising, since public funds could in theory provide as much as two-thirds of this sum, enabling candidates to raise as little as $333,000 while financing a far

---

[233] See, for example, "From the Ground Up," supra, 27 *Fordham Urb. L. J.* at 38.
[234] Herrnson in Green, supra, at 119.

TABLE 6: HOUSE OF REPRESENTATIVES:
1996 CANDIDATE SPENDING

	Number of Candidates	Total Spending	Average
Winners	435	295,705,241	679,782
Losers* (Major parties only)**	424	124,443,086	321,558
Winning Incumbents	361	232,278,629	643,431
Winning Challengers	21	22,678,435	1,079,925
Winning Open Seats	53	40,748,177	768,834
Losing Incumbents	21	23,129,152	1,101,388
Losing Challengers*	350	72,889,478	232,132
Losing Open Seats*	53	28,424,456	546,624
All Incumbents	382	255,407,781	668,607
All Challengers	371	95,567,913	285,277
All Open Seats	106	69,172,633	658,787

Source: FEC, "1996 House Campaigns Summaries.—Candidates Listed by State and District," http://www.fec.gov/finance/states.htm. Data include spending for the entire election cycle (primary + general election) for all candidates who appeared on the general election ballot. It does not include data for those candidates who lost in the primary and did not appear on the general election ballot.

*Financial information was unavailable for 36 losing challengers and one losing open-seat candidate; the general average for these groups of candidates was calculated accordingly.

**Candidates of major parties are defined as those who got 5% or more of the vote in the general election.

more extensive campaign. We believe the limit could have significant benefits in the most hotly contested districts, where it would promote spending parity, give candidates and potential candidates greater confidence that they would not be overwhelmed by a well-financed incumbent or personally wealthy candidate, and reduce the rigors of fundraising.

The same concerns go into the determination of the spending limit in Senate races. Setting Senate spending limits is a difficult task, due not simply to the differences in population across the states but to the differences in spending relative to population in very populous as opposed to less populous states. We have found that although spending in Senate races rises along with state population, spending per voting-age person (VAP) is much higher in less populous states

TABLE 7: HOUSE OF REPRESENTATIVES:
1998 CANDIDATE SPENDING

	Number of Candidates	Total Spending	Average
Winners	435	294,465,378	676,932
Losers* (Major parties only)**	308	98,136,836	320,709
Winning Incumbents	394	253,322,999	642,952
Winning Challengers	8	7,825,744	987,218
Winning Open Seats	33	33,316,635	1,009,595
Losing Incumbents	7	7,724,930	1,103,561
Losing Challengers*	271	73,703,806	273,992
Losing Open Seats*	30	16,708,100	556,937
All Incumbents	401	261,047,929	650,992
All Challengers	279	81,529,550	294,331
All Open Seats	63	50,024,735	794,043

Source: FEC, "1998 House Campaigns Summaries.—Candidates Listed by State and District," http://www.fec.gov/finance/state97.htm. Data include spending for the entire election cycle (primary + general election) for all candidates who appeared on the general election ballot. It does not include data for those candidates who lost in the primary and did not appear on the general election ballot.

*Financial information was unavailable for two losing challengers; the general average for this group of candidates was calculated accordingly.

The low number of losers relative to winners reflects both (i) elections in which the incumbent ran unopposed, and (ii) elections in which the loser raised less than $5000 and therefore was not required by law to submit a financial report before the FEC.

**Candidates of major parties are defined as those who got 5% or more of the vote in the general election.

than in more populous states. In the 1996 and 1998 Senate races, for example, the South Dakota winning challenger spent $5.61 per VAP, while in larger states like North Carolina, Illinois, and New York, the winning challengers spent between $1.23 and $1.69 per VAP, for an overall average of $1.42 per VAP. (See tables 8, 9 and 10.)

Consequently, **we recommend a two-tier system of Senate spending limits. In states with a voting-age population of less than 1 million, candidates would be able to spend $1 million plus $2 per voting-age person. In states with a voting-age population greater than 1 million, candidates would be able to spend $1 million plus $1.50 per voting-age person.** As with the House limits, these limits

TABLE 8: SENATE: 1996 CANDIDATE SPENDING

	Number	Total Spending	Average Spending	Average Spending by Population	by VAP
Winners	34	127,073,463	3,737,455	0.91	1.23
Losers	34	95,674,339	3,086,269	0.71	0.96
(Major parties only)*					
Winning Incumbents	19	79,876,169	4,204,009	0.96	1.29
Winning Challengers	1	2,990,554	2,990,554	4.06	5.61
Winning Open Seats	14	44,206,740	3,157,624	0.80	1.09
Losing Incumbents	1	4,468,434	4,468,434	6.06	8.38
Losing Challengers**	19	49,965,756	3,122,860	0.60	0.81
Losing Open Seats	14	41,240,149	2,945,725	0.75	1.01
All Incumbents	20	84,344,603	4,217,230	1.00	1.35
All Challengers**	20	52,956,310	4,115,077	0.63	0.85
All Open Seats	28	85,446,889	3,051,675	0.78	1.05

Source: (1) Spending: Federal Election Commission, "1996 Senate Campaigns—Candidates Listed by State," http://www.fec.gov/finance/state1.htm. Data include spending for the entire election cycle (primary + general election) for all candidates who appeared on the general election ballot. It does not include data for those candidates who lost in the primary and did not appear on the general election ballot.

(2) Population: U.S. Census Bureau, "State Population Estimates: Annual Time Series. July 1, 1990 to July 1, 1998. (Includes April 1, 1990 Population Counts)," http://www.census.gov/population/estimates/state/st-98-3txt.

(3) Voting-Age Population (VAP): U.S. Census Bureau, "Table 3. Estimates of the Voting Age Population, November 1, 1990 to 1996, and Percent Casting Votes for U.S. Representatives, by State: November 1994 and 1996," http://www.census.gov/prod/3/98pubs/p25-1132.pdf.

*Candidates of major parties are defined as those who got 5% or more of the vote in the general election.

**Financial information unavailable for three losing challengers.

would only rarely cut into recent or current spending levels but would set an outer bound on overall fundraising demands, with public funding available to provide up to two-thirds of the spending under the limit. In addition, to take into account the greater variability in Senate campaign costs, we would provide that in any state in which the average spending of major party candidates over the last three election cycles was more than 50 percent *above* the spending ceiling that would be produced by our formula, the average of the spending levels by the major party candidates would determine the spending ceiling.

The spending limits we propose would apply to a candidate's total spending in both primary and general elections together. In a House of Representatives contest, for example, a candidate could spend up

TABLE 9: SENATE: 1998 CANDIDATE SPENDING

	Number	Total Spending	Average Spending	Average Spending by Population	by VAP
Winners	34	154,464,643	4,543,078	0.79	1.06
Losers	34	90,461,171	2,826,912	0.46	0.62
(Major parties only)*					
Winning Incumbents	26	95,578,972	3,676,114	0.71	0.96
Winning Challengers	3	39,781,457	13,260,486	1.05	1.42
Winning Open Seats	5	19,104,214	3,820,843	0.77	1.03
Losing Incumbents	3	40,763,853	13,587,951	1.08	1.45
Losing Challengers**	26	41,731,407	1,738,809	0.31	0.42
Losing Open Seats	5	7,965,911	1,593,182	0.32	0.43
All Incumbents	29	136,342,825	4,701,477	0.79	1.07
All Challengers**	29	81,512,864	2,810,788	0.47	0.64
All Open Seats	10	27,070,125	2,707,013	0.55	1.73

Source: (1) Spending: Federal Election Commission, "1998 Senate Campaigns—Candidates Listed by State," http://www.fec.gov/finance/state198.htm. Data include spending for the entire election cycle (primary + general election) for all candidates who appeared on the general election ballot. It does not include data for those candidates who lost in the primary and did not appear on the general election ballot.

(2) Population: U.S. Census Bureau, "State Population Estimates: Annual Time Series. July 1, 1990 to July 1, 1998. (Includes April 1, 1990 Population Counts)," http://www.census.gov/population/estimates/state/st-98-3txt.

(3) Voting-Age Population (VAP): U.S. Census Bureau, "Table 3. Estimates of the Voting Age Population, November 1, 1990 to 1996, and Percent Casting Votes for U.S. Representatives, by State: November 1994 and 1996," http://www.census.gov/prod/3/98pubs/p25-1132.pdf.

*Candidates of major parties are defined as those who got 5% or more of the vote in the general election.

**Financial information unavailable for three losing challengers.

to $1 million in the primary and general elections combined. There would be no separate sub-limits for the primary and general elections.

We gave extensive consideration to providing separate limits on primary and general election spending. The question of one overall limit on election-cycle spending as opposed to separate primary and general election limits under the total spending umbrella is a close one, but we concluded that given the enormous variations in political circumstances across districts and states, primary and general election sub-limits would be unwise. In some states or districts in some years, the principal vote will be the primary, while in other states or districts or years it will be the general election. In some places and at some times, there will be contested primaries and general elec-

TABLE 10: SENATE: WINNING CHALLENGERS AND
LOSING INCUMBENTS, 1990–98

Year State	Winning Challengers					Losing Incumbents				
	Party	% vote	Spending	Spending by		Party	% vote	Spending	Spending by	
				Pop.	VAP				Pop.	VAR
1990										
Minnesota	D	51	1,380,560	0.31	0.43	R	48	6,222,333	1.42	1.93
1992										
Georgia	R	50	3,187,621	0.47	0.66	D	49	4,894,620	0.72	1.02
North Carolina	R	50	2,950,673	0.43	0.58	D	46	2,486,380	0.36	0.49
Wisconsin	D	52	1,979,488	0.40	0.54	R	46	5,427,163	1.08	1.47
1994										
Pennsylvania	R	49	6,732,849	0.56	0.73	D	46	6,300,560	0.52	0.69
Tennessee	R	56	7,017,424	1.36	1.80	D	41	4,717,147	0.91	1.21
1996										
South Dakota	D	51	2,990,554	4.06	5.61	R	49	4,468,434	6.06	8.35
1998										
Illinois	R	51	14,778,198	1.23	1.69	D	47	7,200,895	0.60	0.82
New York	D	54	16,671,877	0.92	1.23	R	44	24,195,287	1.33	1.78
North Carolina	D	51	8,331,382	1.10	1.47	R	46	9,367,671	1.24	1.65

Source: (1) Federal Election Commission, "Senate Campaigns—Candidates Listed by State," for the corresponding years. Data include spending for the entire election cycle (primary + general election) for all candidates who appeared on the general election ballot. This table in particular reflects only those elections in which a challenger defeated an incumbent in the general election. It does not include elections in which a challenger defeated an incumbent in a primary.

(2) Population: U.S.-Census Bureau, "State Population Estimates: Annual Time Series. July 1, 1990 to July 1, 1998. (Includes April 1, 1990 Population Counts)," http://www.census.gov/population/estimates/state/st-98-3txt.

(3) Voting-Age Population (VAP): US Census Bureau, "Table 3. Estimates of the Voting Age Population, November 1, 1990 to 1996, and Percent Casting Votes for U.S. Representatives, by State: November 1994 and 1996," http://www.census.gov/prod/3/98pubs/p25-1132.pdf.

tions. We would leave to the candidates the determination of how to allocate their funds and, thereby, avoid the rigidities of a uniform national rule.

The experience with the state-specific spending limits in the presidential primary public funding system is instructive. The presidential primary public funding program imposes not simply a limit on total spending in the prenomination phase of the presidential election, but also a limit on the amount that can be spent in each state, basing those limits on state population. The state-specific limits, however, completely miss the distinctive role of states like Iowa and New Hampshire, whose caucuses and primaries are of a political importance wildly out of proportion to their populations. Consequently, candidates regularly seek to evade these limits (such as by staying in hotels in Massachusetts while campaigning in New Hampshire), or violate them outright, and the FEC has regularly called for elimination of these unnecessarily restrictive limits.

Certainly, there may be difficult issues for a candidate who faces a primary and then a general election test with a major party opponent who had no primary. But that situation arises under the private funding system as well. Moreover, even if a candidate has no primary opponent, he or she still may have to go through the formalities of running in the primary and so could spend money during the primary season if the candidate so chose. Rather than trying to decide how candidates ought to split their funds between the primary and the general election, or trying to calculate how candidates faced with distinct primary and general election sub-limits would try to "game" the system through maneuvers to get more money into the election that is more vital for them, we believe that the candidates are the best judges of how to allocate their funds between a primary and a general election, and leave that question up to them.

(F) SPENDING LIMITS AND THE UNLIMITED OPPONENT   The decision to participate in the public funding program, with the concomitant spending limits, is entirely up to the candidates. Indeed, under *Buckley v. Valeo* the voluntariness of the candidate's choice is a *sine qua non* for the constitutionality of the limits. It is, thus, quite possible that one candidate could opt into the program and accept limits, while her or his major party opponent stays out and is free to spend without limit. This could pose a major challenge to the viability of the public funding program, since candidates faced with the prospect of an opponent capable of spending well above the spending limit might consider accepting public funding with a spending limit as a form of unilateral disarmament and decline to opt in.

We recommend that when a candidate who participates in the public funding program and accepts a spending limit is faced with an opponent who is not participating in the program, then the spending limit for the publicly funded candidate should be raised to 150 percent of the normal limit as soon as the privately funded opponent has received contributions equal to 80 percent of the spending limit. Moreover, if the nonpublicly funded candidate ob-

tains contributions equal to 120 percent of the spending limit, we would free the publicly funded candidate entirely of the spending limit. At that point, the value of the spending limit in curtailing the campaign money chase or in reducing the role of private contributions would already be substantially eroded, and we would not want the spending limit to interfere with the campaign. (See table 11.)

We would not provide the publicly funded candidate with additional public funds. We believe that the public funding limit does permit candidates to mount effective campaigns even if faced with opponents who spend more. But we believe that the public funding program needs to respond to the concern of candidates that they will be outspent by their unlimited opponents. We note that several courts have upheld state public funding programs that release candidates from spending limits when it appears that a privately funded opponent is about to outspend the publicly funded candidate.[235]

(G) FUNDING PUBLIC FUNDING   **We recommend that the public funding system be funded by ordinary appropriations rather than the income tax checkoff.** The checkoff has provided a shaky basis for the presidential public funding system. The percentage of tax filers

TABLE 11: PROPOSED PUBLIC FUNDING SPENDING LIMITS
FOR HOUSE CANDIDATES

Opponent Status	House Candidates Who Accept Public Funding
Publicly Funded Opponent	$1 million
Privately Funded Opponent Who Reports <$800,000 in Contributions	$1 million
Privately Funded Opponent Who Reports Between $800,000 and $1.2 million in Contributions	$1.5 million
Privately Funded Opponent Who Reports >$1.2 million in Contributions	No limit

[235] See *Gable v. Patton*, 142 F.3d 940 (6th Cir. 1998); *Rosenstiel v. Rodriguez*, 101 F.3d 1544 (8th Cir. 1996); *Wilkinson v. Jones*, 876 F. Supp. 916 (W. D.Ky 1995).

who check the federal and state checkoffs has declined since 1980, apparently reflecting the growing disenchantment of many Americans with the political process. Changes in the tax laws that raised the threshold for tax liability reduced the number of people who actually file income-tax returns, so the percentage of Americans eligible to participate in the program has dropped. Many low-income people, in particular, have no tax liability and, thus, may not participate in the public funding program. Even if the number or percentage of tax filers checking off the public funding box were to hold steady, the funds thereby made available would not keep pace with the rate of inflation. The federal checkoff had to be increased from $1 to $3 in 1993 to ensure full funding for the 1996 presidential election. It may very well have to be increased again soon.

Campaign finance is the only significant public program in which Congress has provided that the size of the appropriation would be determined not by the needs of the program to be financed "but by what amounts to an annual referendum on the program."[236] The public finance system should be financed by ordinary appropriations. New York City relies on ordinary appropriations,[237] as does public funding for the gubernatorial election in New Jersey. This is consistent with the notion that funding campaigns is a vital public function, much like the funding of the election day operations of maintaining polling places and counting ballots.

More important than the source of public funding is the amount of money in the program. Public funding will work only if it is adequately funded. Presidential public funding is in trouble with major primary contenders like George W. Bush and Steve Forbes opting out of prenomination public funding, and the major party nominees padding their funds with soft money—in part because public funding is provided at inadequate levels. The presidential public funding law pegged the grant to major party nominees at $20 million in 1974 dollars, but in the presidential election immediately before the adoption of the law, the losing major party nominee, George McGovern, had actually spent $30 million, while the winner, Richard Nixon, had spent $60 million. Indeed, only in 1996 did the public grant to the

---

[236] Mutch, supra, at 137.
[237] The New York City Charter provides special protections for the city's public funding program.

major party nominees reach the same level, in nominal dollars, that Richard Nixon spent on his reelection campaign a quarter century earlier. The combination of public funds and soft money in 1996 basically provided the major party presidential candidates with the equivalent in inflation-adjusted dollars of what their predecessors had in 1972. The benefit of soft money and the allure of private funding grow as the public grant becomes increasingly inadequate to fund an effective campaign. Public funding can induce candidates to opt in, reduce the role of private wealth in funding campaigns, promote more competitive elections, ameliorate the burdens of fundraising, and hold down incentives to evade the system's limits only if funding levels are based on the costs of competitive contemporary election campaigns.

(4) Other Public Assistance for Candidates

Public funding is the centerpiece of our program for increasing campaign communications, reducing the influence of wealthy donors on elections and government, making elections more competitive, and alleviating the burdens of fundraising. But we recommend several other, admittedly more modest, steps as well. **We recommend that all ballot-qualified candidates for federal office be given a postal frank that would cover the equivalent of one mailing to each eligible voter in the constituency. We also recommend that the federal government provide all ballot-qualified candidates for federal office with a free website for the duration of the election campaign.** These two steps would enable all candidates to have at least one opportunity to bring their messages to the attention of the community without regard to their ability to raise money.

C. Adjusting Existing Contribution Limits

The Special Commission's principal recommendation is to create a system of generous public funding for existing candidates. We believe that this could significantly increase resources for campaign activities, alleviate the burdens of fundraising, reduce the role of private wealth in elections, and reduce the influence of large donors and potential donors on government policy-makers. Nevertheless, we recognize that a private funding system is likely to coexist with public funding. Some candidates may choose not to participate in public funding, the political parties will continue to rely on privately provided funds, and individuals will continue to want to make donations to candidates, political committees, and parties. Moreover, public funding must be a voluntary choice for candidates, and unless private funding remains a viable option, the voluntariness of the choice of public funding will be subject to challenge.

Consequently, we recommend certain changes in the current limitations on contributions to candidates, contributions to and by political action committees, and contributions to and by parties. These would tend to *loosen* the existing limits, in light of changes in the cost of living as well as the experience of the last 25 years. These recommendations for loosening current statutory restraints are also tightly linked to the next two sets of recommendations concerning soft money and issue advocacy, which shut down current loopholes and place all federal election-related activity under FECA.

(1) Limit on Individual Contributions to Candidates

FECA's $1000 limit on individual contributions to candidates was adopted in 1974 and has not been changed since.[238] This $1000 has clearly been eroded by inflation. A current dollar has less than one-third the purchasing power of one 1974 dollar. Put more precisely, $1000 in 1974 dollars would be worth $3422 in January 2000.

With the cost of campaigns rising rapidly, these fixed-dollar limits greatly increase the burdens of fundraising. These fixed limits also provide the opportunity for PACs, bundlers, and other intermediaries to prove their value to candidates by ameliorating the burden of direct fundraising from individuals. The steadily declining real-dollar value of the limit also provides an incentive to candidates and potential donors alike for developing new mechanisms, such as soft money and issue advocacy, for contributing outside of FECA. These stratagems make the dollar limits increasingly meaningless to the donors,

---

[238] Former Mayor Edward I. Koch, who, as a member of Congress, sat on the House Administration Subcommittee that approved the $1000 limit, recently acknowledged, "[T]he mistake we made—and it never came up, it boggles the mind—was that we failed to provide for inflation." See "From the Ground Up," supra, 27 *Fordham Urb. L. J.* at 91.

but they have the perverse effect of giving candidates less control over their own campaigns and of magnifying the role of political committees that may be exempt from reporting and disclosure requirements and that are accountable neither to the candidates nor to the public as a whole.

Raising the contribution limits to take account of inflation would make it easier for candidates to raise funds, increase candidates' resources for campaign activity, enable potential challengers to gather the seed money necessary to launch their campaigns, and encourage large donors to participate under FECA (with its attendant reporting and disclosure requirements) rather than to provide funds outside the Act. Moreover, we believe that the corruptive potential of contributions in excess of the current $1000 limit has been diluted with the dramatic rise in campaign costs over the last quarter century and the concomitant increase in the size of candidates' campaign treasuries.

We are concerned that raising the contribution limit would exacerbate the tension between private funding and voter equality, since the size of large contributions would rise sharply, and the fraction of private funds attributable to large donors would probably rise with it. But we believe that the gains in terms of increased opportunities for political activity, voter information, electoral competitiveness, alleviation of the burdens of fundraising, and reduction in the incentive to contribute outside the system would be worth the price.

In raising the contribution limit to account for inflation, we also recommend one other change. Currently, federal election law imposes a $1000 limit on individual contributions per election, but federal law defines the primary election as a separate election—with a separate contribution limit—from the general election. Most major party candidates who appear on the general election ballot have also been through a primary election, even if they ran unopposed in the primary. Consequently, for most candidates and most donors, the real current limit is $2000 per candidate per election cycle, rather than $1000 per election.

We believe the contribution limits should be revised so as to be defined in terms of the election cycle rather than the election. This would reduce the regulatory burden of having to maintain separate accounting records for the primary and the general elections. It would also promote voter information by making the current system more transparent. If the real limit on contributions to candidates is the election cycle, not the particular balloting within that cycle, then the voters should know that, and the law should reflect that.

Consequently, **in light of changes in the cost of living, we recommend that the limit on individual contributions to candidates be raised from the current $2000 per election cycle to $6000 per election cycle,**[239] **and that the limit thereafter be indexed for changes in the cost of living, with a new limit put in place every two years.**[240]

(2) Limits on Contributions to and by PACs

FECA limits the amount of money an individual can donate to a PAC to $5000 per calendar year, and it limits the amount of money a PAC can donate to a candidate to $5000 per election. These limits are five times the limits on individual donations to candidates.

We do not see any justification for the strong preference for PACs found in current law. There is no apparent reason why PACs ought to be able to make significantly larger contributions than individuals, or why individuals should be able to contribute far more to PACs than to candidates. Moreover, given the tendency of PACs to prefer incumbents over challengers, the value of competitive elections might be better served if there were greater parity in PAC and individual contribution limits. To be sure, like the limits on individual donations to candidates, the limits on contributions to and by PACs have not been indexed for inflation and thus are worth less than one-third of their value in 1974 dollars. Nevertheless, the relative differential between PAC and individual contribution limits has not been changed.

---

[239] When a candidate must also participate in a run-off election, an individual should be allowed to make an additional contribution to that candidate above the election cycle limit. FECA currently treats a run-off as an election separate from both the primary and the general elections and with its own $1000 limit. We do not intend to deny candidates or donors the opportunity to obtain or make additional contributions in the event of a run-off.

[240] The biannual readjustment works best for House races. The election cycle for presidential and Senate races is, of course, more than two years. Congress could provide that for these offices the contribution limit would be whatever limit is in place at the start of the election cycle for a particular office. Alternatively, the limit could continue to rise at two-year intervals even for these offices, so that a person who gives an amount equivalent to the limit at the start of the election cycle would be able to give a small amount more—equal to the inflation adjustment—after the limit has been raised; a person who gives in the last two years of the cycle could be subject to the final, higher limit.

We have already proposed trebling the contribution limit for individuals. That would have the effect of significantly narrowing the PAC–individual gap. Completely closing that gap would require lowering the current limits on PACs. In light of the value of political participation, which includes contributions to and by PACs, and of avoiding any actions that would contribute to the burdens of fundraising, as well as the fact that the limits on PACs have already been eroded by inflation, we are disinclined to reduce the limits relating to PACs. Instead, **we would leave all existing limits relating to PACs in place and provide that in the future, upon the enactment of comprehensive campaign finance reform legislation, the PAC limits should be adjusted biennially for inflation as well.**

As with the limits on individual contributions to candidates, we would revise the current limits on PAC contributions to combine the formally separate limits on contributions for the primary and general elections into a single election-cycle limit. Consequently, the limit on a PAC's contribution to a candidate would be $10,000 per election cycle. The limit on individual donations to a PAC, which is based on the calendar year, would be unchanged.

(3) Aggregate Limit on Individual Contributions

Currently, FECA provides that an individual may not contribute more than $25,000 per calendar year in the aggregate to all candidates for federal office and to PACs and political party activity in support of or opposition to candidates for federal office. This number also has not been adjusted for inflation since 1974 and so is now worth about $8000 in 1974 dollars.

The aggregate limit on individual contributions also ought to be adjusted. If it were not, many of the reasons for increasing the limit on contributions to candidates would be frustrated since large donors could quickly hit the aggregate contribution ceiling after making the maximum contribution to just a few candidates. Consequently, like the adjustment in the limit on individual contributions to candidates, **we recommend that the aggregate limit on individual contributions for federal election–related purposes be trebled to $75,000 and thereafter be adjusted for inflation.** We recognize this is a very high number, that only a very tiny number of Americans have the resources to give at the level of the limit, that raising the limit so high will reinforce the tension between the inequality of wealth and the norm of voter equality, and that it may contribute to public concern about the corrupting effects of big contributions on the system.

Nevertheless, the proposed $75,000 aggregate contribution level is actually slightly less than the figure adopted by Congress in 1974, adjusted for inflation. Moreover, we make this recommendation only as part of a package that would both provide substantial public funding—thus, reducing the role of private wealth in the system overall—and eliminate soft money contributions, many of which are greatly in excess of the $75,000 figure.

(4) Limits on Individual and PAC Donations to National Party Committees

Currently, FECA provides that an individual may donate up to $20,000 to the national committee of a political party in any calendar year, with any contribution to a national party committee counting against the annual aggregate ceiling of $25,000. A PAC can donate $15,000 to a national party committee per calendar year.

As we will explain more fully in our next set of recommendations concerning political parties and soft money, we believe that the parties can and do play an important role in our system. Parties register and mobilize voters, distribute grassroots campaign materials and information, provide a shared policy platform for officeholders across the different branches of government and the federal system, and link voters and activists with candidates who share their views. Parties need to raise funds sufficient to enable them to carry out these many functions. Along with the limit on individual contributions to candidates, the limit on individual donations to the parties has also been eroded by inflation. This has contributed to the rise of soft money.

Consequently, **we recommend that the limit on donations to the national party committees be raised**. Indeed, in light of the important role of the parties, which transcends providing direct assistance to candidate, we would do more than simply adjust for inflation. **We would remove any specific limit on individual donations to parties under the aggregate cap on individual contributions per calendar year. As a result, an individual could contribute up to $75,000 per calendar year to the national party committees**—although any contribution to the parties would reduce the ability of an individual to contribute to candidates or PACs. Moreover, as the aggregate limit on individual contributions per calendar year is adjusted for inflation, the limit on individual donations to the parties would rise as well. Consistent with our approach to PACs, we would not at present raise the limit of $15,000 per calendar year on PAC donations to parties, but we would allow that limit to rise in the future to adjust for inflation, as part of the adoption of a comprehensive campaign finance reform package. (For a comparison of our proposed contribution limits for individuals and PACs, see table 12.)

D. Soft Money and the Political Parties

Soft money, that is, money that does not comply with the dollar limitations or source prohibitions of FECA, has become a major factor in the financing of the national political parties. In the last two election cycles, soft money amounted to about a third of total party receipts. In 1995–96 national party soft money donations were $263.5 million and accounted for 30 percent of total national party income. In 1997–98 the soft money share of national party income rose to 33 percent, although actual party soft money receipts declined to $224.4 million with the cyclical drop in fundraising from a presidential to a nonpresidential election.[241] National party soft money receipts in 1997–98, however, were nearly five times the $45 million in soft money receipts and treble the 10 percent soft money share of party receipts in 1993–94, the prior nonpresidential election.[242] The 1997–98 election marked the first time in which soft money played a critical role in congressional elections; in prior years, the primary use of soft money had been to enable presidential candidates participating in the public funding system to evade the spending limits that are a condition for the provision of public funds. Preliminary figures

---

[241] FEC, "FEC Reports on Political Party Activity for 1997–98," Apr. 9, 1999, http://www.fec.gov/press/ptyye98.htm (visited 10/25/99).

[242] The data on party hard money receipts in 1993–94 comes from "FEC Reports on Political Party Activity for 1997–98," supra. The data on soft money for that year is from FEC Info/Public Disclosure, Inc., "Soft Money Summary" (issued 12/28/98), http://www.tray.com/fecinfo/smrpt.htm (visited 11/17/99).

TABLE 12: CONTRIBUTION LIMITS: CURRENT LAW AND PROPOSALS

	Current Law	Proposals
Individual to Candidates	$1000 per election (primary and general are treated as separate elections) $2000 for primary and general election together	$6000 per election cycle
Individual to PAC	$5000 per calendar year	$5000 per calendar year
PAC to Candidates	$5000 per election (primary and general are treated as separate elections) $10,000 for primary and general election together	$10,000 per election cycle
PAC to National Party Committees	$15,000 per calendar year	$15,000 per calendar year
Individual to National Party Committees	$20,000 per calendar year	No limit—only limit is aggregate annual limit on individual contributions
Aggregate Limit on Individual Contributions to Candidates, PACs, and Parties.	$25,000 per calendar year	$75,000 per calendar year
		All adjusted for inflation in the future
		Adjusted for inflation in the future

for the 1999–2000 election cycle indicate the dollar volume of soft money is continuing to grow.[243]

As described in chapter 2 of this Report, there is now a substantial number of donors of very large soft money contributions. In 1997–98 there were 390 individuals or organizations—including business corporations, labor unions, American Indian tribes, and ideological groups—that gave $100,000 or more to the soft money accounts of the national political parties. Twenty-six donors gave $500,000 or more; the top four donors gave more than $1 million each. Corporate contributions prohibited by FECA dominated the soft money growth, with 218 corporations giving more than $100,000 in 1997–98 and 16 corporations giving more than $500,000 in that period. In the prior nonpresidential election cycle, only 96 corporations broke the $100,000 mark, and only four gave more than $250,000. Thirty-five trade associations also broke the $100,000 mark in 1997–98. Wealthy individuals or couples provided most of the other large soft money donations, with 114 individuals or husband-and-wife pairs giving $100,000 or more, 26 individuals or couples giving $250,000 or more, and four giving $500,000 or more.[244]

To be sure, not all soft money donations are so large. But very large donations dominate the rise of soft money. The FEC requires political committees to provide itemized data concerning only those donors who contribute $200 or more. In 1997–98 there were almost 25,000 donors who gave $200 or more to the national parties' soft money accounts.[245] Their contributions came to $176 million, or about 80 percent of total party soft money. Of these, just 700 donors (or 3 percent of those giving $200 or more) provided 40 percent of the aggregate amount provided by the $200+ donors, averaging about $97,000 each. FECA, of course, currently prohibits individuals from

---

[243] FEC, "FEC Releases Fundraising Figures of Major Political Parties—Large Gain in 'Soft Money' Contributions," Sept. 22, 1999 (Republicans raised 42 percent more in soft money during the first six months of 1999, compared with the first six months of 1997, and Democrats raised 93 percent more in the first half of 1999, compared with the first half of 1997. By contrast, party hard money receipts were up only 16 percent compared with 1997).

[244] FEC Info/Public Disclosure, Inc., "Soft Money Summary" (issued 12/28/98), http://www.tray.com/fecinfo/smrpt.htm (visited 11/17/99).

[245] See FEC Info/Public Disclosure, Inc., "Soft Money Summary" (issued 12/28/98), http://www.tray.com/fecinfo/smrpt.htm (visited 11/17/99). The parties are required to itemize by name of donor and size of donation only those donations at or above $200.

contributing more than $20,000 in a calendar year—or $40,000 in a two-year election cycle—to the national party and prohibits corporations from making any contributions at all. When all donations from a particular sector or industry are aggregated, the sums in question can be enormous.[246]

Soft money directly challenges many of the basic values of our campaign finance system. Soft money exemplifies the danger that large private contributions can have an undue influence on the operations of government. Soft money donations are part of a network of relationships in which potential large donors are linked up to federal officeholders. Both major parties regularly arrange dinners, weekend outings, and cash-for-access policy forums that enable donors of very large sums to meet with federal officials on an intimate basis.[247] Large soft money donations are tightly connected to opportunities for special access to federal officials. The DNC alone raised $27 million from the 350 people invited to attend the celebrated White House coffees with President Clinton; $3.1 million came from people who made their contributions within a week of attending the coffee.[248]

The rise of soft money mocks campaign finance law and fuels public cynicism about the political process. The current administratively created exemption for soft money is based on the theory that soft money is used for nonfederal purposes, but over the last two decades soft money has been spent largely to influence federal elections. In 1996 roughly one-quarter of all national party soft money expenditures was undertaken by the four party congressional campaign committees.[249] These are organizations composed of members of Congress whose sole raison d'être is the election of federal candidates. How is it possible for any of that money to be considered nonfederal in any meaningful sense? The remainder of the national party soft money spending was undertaken by the Democratic and Republican National Committees. The DNC in 1995–96, as is typi-

---

[246] See Jeffrey Taylor, "GOP to Get Soft Money Tobacco Aid," *Wall Street Journal* (Jan. 7, 2000):A16 (tobacco company executives say industry will donate "at least $7 million" toward the 2000 elections "mostly in unregulated 'soft money' contributions to Republican Party committee").

[247] See, for example, Phil Kuntz, "Cash-for-Access Policy Forums on Bills are Common, Controversial in Senate," *Wall Street Journal* (Jan. 25, 2000):A20.

[248] See Daniel M. Yarmish, "The Constitutional Basis for a Ban on Soft Money," 67 *Fordham L. Rev.* 1257, 1281n.217 (1998).

[249] See Biersack and Haskell, "Spitting on the Umpire," in Green, supra, at 172.

cally the case for the national committee of the party that holds the presidency, was effectively the alter ego of the President and completely subservient to him.[250] Only the national committee of the party that does not hold the presidency presents any possibility of spending money for nonfederal purposes, and once the party's presidential nominee has become apparent, even that committee also operates primarily in service to the presidential candidate. Soft money spending by state parties, in turn, is also usually controlled by the national committees that are the sources of state party soft money funds.[251]

We recommend that soft money be sharply curtailed and, to the extent possible, eliminated. To achieve this goal we recommend the following steps:

(1) Soft Money Fundraising by Federal Officials and Candidates

The national symbol of soft money is President Clinton's use of the White House coffees to raise funds for the Democratic National Committee—funds that would be used to aid his reelection campaign. **We recommend that federal officeholders and candidates for federal office, and their employees, agents, and campaign staffs, be barred from soliciting, receiving, directing, transferring, or spending any funds for their own campaigns, for any national party committee, or for any state or local party committee, with respect to any activity that is related to an election for federal office (including activities that relate to elections to both federal and state office at the same time), unless those funds comply with the limitations, prohibitions, and reporting requirements of FECA.** This would bar federal officials and candidates for federal office from having anything to do with money that comes from sources—such as corporate and union treasuries, and foreign nationals who are not residents of the United States—that are forbidden to make federal

---

[250] See Crotty, "Political Parties," in Maisel, supra, at 212. (In 1996 the DNC worked interchangeably with the White House as an extension of the President's campaign.)

[251] See, for example, Bibby, "State Party Organizations," in Maisel, supra, at 43–44.

campaign contributions, or that is in amounts larger than the maximum contributions permitted by FECA.[252]

(2) National Party Committees

Similarly, **the national party committees—this would include the congressional campaign committees as well as the national committees—and their officials and agents would be barred from soliciting, receiving, or directing to another person any contribution or from making any expenditure that does not comply with the limitations, prohibitions, and reporting and disclosure requirements of FECA.** All national party receipts and expenditures, including moneys the national parties simply pass on to state and local parties and to nonparty organizations, would have to be in "hard" dollars.

(3) State and Local Party Committees

The most knotty issue in regulating soft money is how to deal with state and local party committees. Cracking down on soft money contributions to the national parties could simply encourage soft money donors to send their contributions to the state and local party committees, which would then use the funds for activities that influence federal elections. As the Federal Election Commission has observed, "[t]he national party committees might assist their state and local affiliates by employing a type of directed donor strategy, in which the national committee solicits soft money contributions and instructs contributors to send their contributions directly to the state or local committee. Thus, instead of reducing the amount of soft money activity," restricting national parties without restricting state and local parties "may merely redirect that activity to the state and local level, where reporting may be less complete than at the federal level."[253]

Any comprehensive approach to soft money must deal with state

---

[252] We would not apply this proscription to a federal officeholder who is a candidate for state or local office and is raising or soliciting funds in connection with that campaign.

[253] FEC, Proposed Rules, "Prohibited and Excessive Contributions: 'Soft Money,' " 63 Fed. Reg. 37722, 37730, July 13, 1998.

and local parties, too. Certainly, any state and local party spending program that is aimed exclusively at federal elections must be funded entirely out of hard money. More difficult are state and local party activities—such as generic party advertising, voter registration and get-out-the-vote drives, campaign literature that mentions both federal and state candidates, and even administrative overhead expenses in federal election years—that can have an impact on both federal and state elections. Failure to impose limits on the use of soft money for such mixed federal–nonfederal activities is likely to result in an enormous loophole and the continued flow of soft money into federal elections.

On the other hand, we are wary of any rule that would impose federal election law on state campaigns. Although there are no clear Supreme Court precedents on this issue, we believe that as a matter of federalism, the states should be able to regulate their own campaigns. Where Congress and the states have adopted different campaign finance rules, requiring all state and local party mixed activities to comply with federal law could result either in displacing state law with federal law with respect to state and local elections or in forcing the state parties to sharply distinguish their campaign activities for federal candidates from their activities for nonfederal candidates. But there may be benefits, in terms of building bridges across the federal system and sharpening voter understanding of what the different parties stand for, in enabling federal and state candidates to campaign together. Moreover, forcing state parties to fund their federal and state campaigns separately—or accept federal requirements for state elections—could be financially burdensome for the parties.

For now, we would recommend that Congress amend FECA to adopt a modified version of the FEC's current practice. The FEC currently requires the national and state parties, when they engage in activities that support federal and state candidates simultaneously, to allocate the costs between hard- and soft-money accounts. The national parties are required to allocate mixed activities 65 percent to hard money and 35 percent to soft money in presidential election years, and 60 percent to hard money and 40 percent to soft money in nonpresidential election years. The allocation methods available to state parties generally permit a greater use of soft money for shared activities. The most significant allocation method for the state parties is the ballot-composition formula, in which the share of mixed activities to be funded by hard money is based on the percentage of the total number of candidates on the ballot who are running for federal office.

We believe that for state and local parties, an allocation formula is the right approach to the funding of shared federal–nonfederal activities (all national party spending even for mixed federal–nonfederal activities would have to be hard-money funded), but that the current formula is weighted much too heavily in favor of soft money. In most states, the size of the state legislature, for example, is much greater than the state's federal congressional delegation. **We believe that something like the 60/40 and 65/35 hard/soft money allocations would make more sense, and certainly there ought to be a greater hard money allocation in presidential election years.**

We would not rule out eventually requiring that all state and local party mixed activities be funded out of hard money if it turns out that our proposal permitting some continued use of soft money is abused. But for now, given our concern not to have federal law impose unduly on state elections or to force an undesirable separation of federal and state campaigns, we would recommend adoption of an allocation system, albeit one that requires that a greater percentage of state and local parties' mixed activities be funded by hard money than is currently the law. (For a summary of the Special Commission's proposals concerning soft money, see table 13.)

CONSTITUTIONALITY OF SOFT MONEY RESTRICTIONS   Restrictions on soft money contributions are constitutional. The Supreme Court has held that contributions to political committees, as well as contributions directly to candidates, can be prohibited to "protect the integrity of the contribution limits" on donations to candidates.[254] Donors can and do contribute to party committees in order to provide support to particular candidates. This can establish the same kind of quid pro quo relations that result from direct contributions to candidates. Soft money functions as a conduit for donations to candidates that would otherwise be forbidden because of their large size or because they come from proscribed sources. As a result, it under-

---

[254] *California Med. Ass'n v. FEC*, 453 U.S. 182, 197–98 (1981) (plurality opinion), 202–04 (concurring opinion of Justice Blackmun).

TABLE 13: SOFT MONEY: PROPOSALS

Federal Public Officials	ALL
Federal Candidates	FORBIDDEN FROM DEALING WITH
National Party Committees	SOFT MONEY
State Party Committees	• Forbidden from dealing with soft money for federal election activity
	• May use soft money for mixed federal-nonfederal activities subject to allocation
	—With approximately 60% of funds in hard money

mines the system created by FECA and sustained by the Supreme Court in *Buckley*. As Justice Breyer observed in *Nixon v. Shrink Missouri Government PAC*, *"Buckley's* holding seems to leave the political branches broad authority to enact laws regulating contributions that take the form of 'soft money.' "[255]

Soft money, like hard money, is used to affect federal elections. To be sure, some soft money is used to fund activities, such as voter registration and partisan voter mobilization drives, that truly benefit both federal and nonfederal candidates. Even then the nonfederal component also benefits federal candidates, since allowing any soft money to be used for such activities frees up hard money that would otherwise have been used to fund those activities and allows the parties to spend more on direct contributions to candidates or coordinated expenditures involving express advocacy that legally must be hard money financed. Moreover, soft money fundraising creates a web of relationships between large donors and federal candidates and officials that clearly raises the potential for quid pro quos and the appearance of undue influence. The size of many soft money contributions is so much larger than the current hard money limits that some restriction on soft money is required if the hard money

---

[255] *Shrink Missouri Government PAC*, supra, 120 S. Ct. at 913.

limits are to have any meaning.[256] Given the widespread use of soft money by corporations to get money to the parties, restrictions on soft money are necessary if the longstanding—and previously validated—bans on corporate hard money contributions are to continue to make any sense at all.[257]

Party spending funded by soft money can have some benefits. Some soft money–funded spending is used to support voter registration and mobilization, grassroots activities, and the strengthening of state and local parties. We believe that many of the benefits of soft money spending can be preserved through the increases in hard money spending we proposed in our second set of recommendations. But soft money also poses great dangers. It raises the specter of large donors, including corporations and unions, obtaining undue influence over government and over the parties themselves.

Cracking down on soft money is also consistent with the judgment of Congress in 1979 when it voted to permit unlimited party spending on certain grassroots activities but required that such activities be funded by contributions that comply with FECA's dollar and source restrictions. Restricting soft money would be consistent with the basic structure of campaign finance law and, especially, with the central concern about undue influence over the political process that drives campaign finance regulation.

(4) Party Support for Candidates

At present, each national party committee, party congressional campaign committee, and state party committee can contribute $5000 per election to a candidate for Congress.[258] The national party committees can together give up to $17,500 per election cycle to a Senate

---

[256] Cf. Wesley Joe and Clyde Wilcox, "Financing the 1996 Presidential Nominations: The Last Regulated Campaign?" in Green, supra, at 62 ("When individuals give $1000 to a presidential candidate they cannot expect much in return, but a contribution of $500,000 or an industrywide contribution of $4 million is perhaps a different matter.").

[257] Cf. Phil Kuntz, "Judge's Doubts on Corporate-Contribution Ban Pose Latest Test for Weakened Campaign Laws," *Wall Street Journal* (Jan. 13, 2000):A24 (federal district court judge suggests that ban on corporate contributions is unconstitutional because unregulated soft money donations by corporations to parties has " 'essentially rendered the contributions and spending limits . . . meaningless' ").

[258] 2 U.S.C. § 441a(a)(2). The limits on party donations to House candidates derive from the limits on PACs.

candidate; state party committee contributions to Senate candidates are limited to $5000 per election.[259] Parties are also allowed to undertake coordinated expenditures on behalf of candidates. The national committees (a single combined limit applies to the National Committee and the House and Senate campaign committees) can spend up to $10,000 in 1974 dollars in coordination with the general election campaign of candidates for the House of Representatives, except that in a state with just one representative, the national committees can spend $20,000 in 1974 dollars. The state party committee can also spend the same amount in coordinated expenditures. The national and state party committees can also each spend $20,000 in 1974 dollars, or two cents (in 1974 prices) times the voting-age population of the state, whichever is greater, in connection with the general election campaigns of candidates for the Senate. Moreover, a state party committee may designate a national party committee as its agent for coordinated spending. In 1998 the limits on combined national-state party coordinated expenditures came to between $130,200 (Alaska) and $3,035,874 (California) for candidates for Senate, and $65,100 for House candidates ($130,200 in single-district states).[260]

We would enhance the opportunity for parties to work with their candidates. Parties are more likely than PACs or individual donors to use their funds to support challengers. Thus, strengthening the party role would promote electoral competitiveness. Moreover, parties may present less of a "corrupting" danger than either PACs or large individual donors. Certainly, party money derives from private donors, so there is a need to cap the size and control the sources of contributions to the parties. But by aggregating large numbers of private contributions and deploying them according to the strategic concerns of the parties, party committees to some extent dilute the potentially corruptive effect of large donations.

We would also simplify the existing system by combining the contribution and coordinated expenditure restrictions and then raising the aggregate amount. In House races in states with two or more districts, national and state party committees can each currently contribute $5000 and, as of 1998, can engage in $32,550 in coordinated

---

[259] 2 U.S.C. § 441a(h).

[260] FEC, "FEC Announces 1998 Party Spending Limits: Amounts Range from $130,200 to $3 Million," http://www.fec.gov/press/441ad.htm, Mar. 6, 1998.

expenditures. **Combining and doubling those amounts, we would permit state parties to contribute to and/or coordinate $75,000 with congressional candidates; we would permit the national parties in the aggregate to contribute or coordinate the same amount. Total party committee spending for House candidates would then be $150,000 and would be adjusted for inflation. We would provide that the national and state committees could spend $150,000 apiece (or $300,000 together) in House races in single-district states and on Senate races in the smallest states, and double the current coordinated contribution limit in the larger states.** (For a comparison of the Special Commission's proposals concerning limits on party support for privately funded candidates with current law, see table 14.)

In addition, we would provide that for any candidate who participates in the public funding system and accepts a spending limit, that candidate could accept party contributions and coordinated expenditures up to the public funding spending limit applicable to that candidate's race. Party contributions and coordinated expenditures would not be eligible for matching public funds.

(5) Party Independent Spending

For the first 20 years that FECA applied to federal elections, it was universally assumed that party spending expressly supporting or opposing federal candidates would be coordinated with the campaigns of the party's own candidates and, thus, subject to FECA's coordinated expenditure limits.[261] In 1996, however, in *Colorado Republican Federal Campaign Committee v. Federal Election Commission*,[262] a Supreme Court plurality determined that party spending may be independent of the party's candidate and that such spending is entitled to the same constitutional protection from limitation that extends

---

[261] Kirk J. Nahra, "Political Parties and the Campaign Finance Laws: Dilemmas, Concerns and Opportunities," 56 *Fordham L. Rev.* 53, 97 (1987); David Adamany, "Political Parties in the 1980s," 72–73, in Michael J. Malbin, ed., *Money and Politics in the United States: Financing Elections in the 1980s* (1984); F. Christopher Arterton, "Political Money and Party Strength," 116 in Joel L. Fleishman, ed., *The Future of American Political Parties: The Challenge of Governance* (1982). Accord, *FEC v. Democratic Sen. Camp. Comm.*, 454 U.S. 27, 28 n.1 (1981) ("Party committees are considered incapable of making 'independent' expenditures in connection with the campaigns of their party's candidates").

[262] 518 U.S. 604 (1996).

TABLE 14: PARTY SUPPORT FOR PRIVATELY FUNDED CANDIDATES

House of Representatives	Current	Proposal
National Party Committee Contribution	$5000	Total National Party Support:
Congressional Campaign Committee Contribution	$5000	—$75,000 in states with two or more districts;
State Party Committee Contribution	$5000	—$150,000 in states with one district
National Committee Coordinated Expenditures	—$10,000 in 1974 dollars in states with two or more districts ($32,550 in 1998 dollars)	—Adjusted for inflation
State Party Committee Coordinated Expenditures	—$20,000 in 1974 dollars in states with one district ($65,100 in 1998 dollars)	Total State Party Support:
	Same as National Party Committee	Same as total National Party support
Senate		
National Party Contribution	$17,500	Total National Party Support:
State Party Contribution	$5000	$150,000 for smallest states and up according to VAP
National Committee Coordinated Expenditures	—Ranges from $65,500 to $1.3 million —According to VAP	Total State Party Support:
State Committee Coordinated Expenditures	Same as National Party	Same as National Committee

to PAC independent spending. *Colorado Republican* said little about the criteria for determining whether party spending is considered independent or coordinated. The spending in *Colorado Republican* took place months before either party had selected its nominee, but it is not clear from that case whether an expenditure made after a candidate has been nominated may be treated as presumptively coordinated. Indeed, a federal district court recently invalidated a state law that defined state party spending in support of a nominated candidate as coordinated.[263]

---

[263] *Republican Party of Minnesota v. Pauly*, 63 F. Supp.2d 1008 (D. Minn. 1999).

In the months following *Colorado Republican*, the national Republican Party put together a $10 million independent expenditure program for 1996, primarily supporting the party's Senate candidates.[264] The Democrats lagged with a more modest $1.5 million program. In 1998 the importance of party independent spending subsided. The Democrats again committed $1.5 million (or about 7 percent of their combined total of contributions to and spending in support of candidates) to independent expenditures, but Republican Party spending declined to under $300,000.[265] The parties' apparent lack of interest in independent spending is due to the major development in party campaign finance practices in recent years—the explosion in the use of party soft money to finance so-called "issue advocacy."[266]

Colorado Republican's holding has serious implications for both the proposed public funding program and for the limits on party support for candidates generally. There will typically be preexisting ties between the party organization and the candidate who holds the party's nomination, between the party staff and the campaign staff, or between the consultants retained by the party and by the candidate. Party committees frequently aid candidates in hiring campaign managers, consultants, media specialists and pollsters, so that parties and their committees often engage the services of the same political professionals. Party committees provide their candidates with issue and opposition research and poll and focus group data, and they assist candidates with their fundraising.[267] Party committees and candidates share pollsters, campaign strategists, and media consultants, and campaign professionals shuttle back and forth among party committees, candidate committees, and consulting firms. Even when they do not sit down to discuss the placement or content of a specific ad, parties and their candidates are structurally integrated, not indepen-

---

[264] This compares with $34.7 million in Republican Party contributions to and coordinated expenditures with candidates in 1996. "FEC Reports on Political Party Activity for 1997–98."

[265] Id.

[266] See also Paul S. Herrnson and Diana Dwyre, "Party Issue Advocacy in Congressional Election Campaigns," 90, in John C. Green and Daniel M. Shea, *The State of the Parties: The Changing Role of Contemporary American Parties* (3d ed. 1999) (Party House campaign committees declined to invest in independent spending in part because "committee officials believed that issue advocacy provided them with a better alternative").

[267] See, for example, Herrnson, "Financing 1996 Congressional Elections" in Green, supra, at 100.

dent.[268] Given the history of party involvement with candidates seeking office, party spending is likely to be quite valuable to the candidate even without formal coordination with the candidate.

The possibilities for parties to work closely with their candidates yet still engage in independent spending are nicely illustrated by the recent decision of the federal district court in *Republican Party of Minnesota v. Pauly*.[269] The Minnesota Republican Party staff provided candidates with " 'meaningful and helpful' service and 'direct support' "; kept in " 'close contact' with 'elected officials and statewide campaigns,' " " 'work[ed] directly with Republican candidates on issue research,' 'develop[ed] campaign plans,' and 'manage[d] the scheduling of candidate and party activity.' " On "numerous occasions," candidates who had been endorsed by the party attended party fundraisers, and the party encouraged its candidates to attend biweekly "coordinating meetings" at party headquarters. The party also made direct contributions to its candidates.[270] But when the party took out its own broadcast and print advertising in support of its candidates who—unlike the case in *Colorado Republican*—had already been nominated, the party officials responsible for the ads avoided direct contact with the candidates' campaigns. As a result, the party's ads were deemed independent expenditures, not subject to limitation. Although the district court found the "record in this case is replete with examples of cooperation," there was no evidence of "actual coordination" of the particular expenditures in question with candidates.[271]

PARTY INDEPENDENT SPENDING AND PUBLICLY FUNDED CANDIDATES   Independent party expenditures could upset the spending limits that are central to our public funding proposal. Given the possibilities for cooperation short of activity that would technically constitute coordination, independent spending by a party whose candidate has opted to participate in the public funding program could quickly render public funding's spending limits meaningless.

---

[268] See Jonathan Bernstein and Raymond J. LaRaja, "Independent Expenditures and Partisanship in House Elections" (paper prepared for delivery at 1999 Annual Meeting of the American Political Science Association, Sept. 2–5, 1999).

[269] 63 F. Supp.2d 1008 (D. Minn. 1999).

[270] Id. at 1012.

[271] Id. at 1017.

We recommend that if a candidate has opted into the public funding program, all spending by that candidate's party that expressly advocates the election or defeat of a clearly identified candidate (that is, either the election of the publicly funded candidate or the defeat of his or her opponent) ought to be counted against the spending limit of the party's candidate. Given the constitutional protection for independent spending, the best way to do this would be to require the candidate to agree as a precondition to the provision of public funds that the FEC could count party independent spending on behalf of that candidate, or against the candidate's opponent, against the statutory spending ceiling.

PARTY INDEPENDENT SPENDING AND PRIVATELY FUNDED CANDIDATES   Party independent spending is also a problem in elections in which the candidate benefiting from the spending is privately funded. That candidate may have a publicly funded opponent, so party spending has implications for whether the publicly funded candidate may be released from the spending limit. Even if both candidates are privately funded, party independent spending threatens to undermine the limits on party support for candidates and, thus, to undercut the constraints those limits place on the ability of large private donors to use the parties as conduits for channeling large donations to candidates.

As the Federal Election Commission has noted, "party committees are in regular contact with their candidates, help develop candidate messages and campaign strategy, and routinely share overlapping consultants, pollsters, fundraisers, and other campaign agents. . . . These consultations, discussions, and arrangements involve face-to-face meetings, telephone conversations, and exchanges of paper and electronic mail on a regular basis, sometimes daily, and take place at both the staff level and higher levels."[272]

Under these circumstances, it will be difficult to police candidate–party contacts to see whether they meet very detailed factual criteria concerning coordination. There need to be bright-line rules that would limit the ability of parties to use independent spending to avoid the limits on party donations to candidates. We recommend two such rules:

---

[272] FEC, Proposed Rules, "Independent Expenditures and Party Committee Expenditure Limitations," 62 Fed. Reg. 24367, 24369–70 (May 5, 1997).

First, FECA should be amended to provide that once a party committee has made a direct contribution to, or a coordinated expenditure with, a candidate, all subsequent expenditures by that committee—and by all committees of that party—are to be treated as coordinated with the candidate and are to be subject to the contribution/coordinated expenditure limitation.

Second, FECA should be amended to provide that once a party has nominated a candidate, all party expenditures supporting that candidate are to be treated as coordinated and, thus, subject to limits.

Together, these two proposals would mean that once a party has established a formal connection with a candidate, either by giving her money or nominating her, the party has allied itself with that candidate for purposes of the campaign finance laws. This would reconcile the Supreme Court's constitutional point that a party can act independently of a candidate affiliated with that party, with the real-world facts that parties normally work closely with their nominees and that once a party has established some formal connection with a candidate, it is exceedingly difficult to police the distinction between coordinated spending and independent spending.

E. Express Advocacy: The Definition of Electioneering Speech

The explosive rise of so-called issue advocacy advertising threatens several important values of our campaign finance system. First, electioneering ads that do not fall within the current narrow definition of express advocacy are not subject to the Act's reporting and disclosure requirements. As a result, voters may be unable to gather important information that would help them to assess the truth and persuasiveness of arguments and assertions concerning election candidates. Second, electioneering ads that do not fall within the current narrow definition of express advocacy are not subject to the Act's contribution limitations and restrictions. Consequently, such ads may be funded by corporate and union treasuries and by very large donations by individuals. This is in sharp tension with the voter equality norm and the concern about undue influence that are central concerns about campaign spending. Third, electioneering ads that do not fall within the current narrow definition of express advocacy can increase the burdens of fundraising, since candidates may feel required to respond not simply to the ads of their opponents but also to such so-called issue ads. Finally, electioneering ads that do not fall within the current narrow definition of express advocacy may be used to evade the spending limits that are part of the presidential public funding system and would be part of congressional public funding. The financing of these ads could be a means for bringing substantial amounts of private-interest money back into the system. Moreover, the possibility of electioneering ads that do not fall within the current narrow definition of express advocacy could also discourage candidates from opting into public funding for fear that the public funding spending limit would leave them unable to respond to such "issue ads."

The definition of electioneering is a more difficult problem for the campaign finance system to address than soft money, however, because protection for at least some issue advertising is rooted in the Constitution. Limiting campaign finance regulation to electioneering speech reflects the constitutional imperative of preventing campaign finance rules from impinging on non-election-related discussion of political issues and ideas. Some line between election-related speech and other political communications must be drawn, even though elections and politics are necessarily intertwined. *Buckley* was certainly right in requiring that the definition of election-related speech be precise and objective. Given the lack of experience with campaigning under FECA, *Buckley*'s suggestive reference to the "magic words" of express advocacy may have been reasonable when the case was decided in 1976. Recent campaigns, which are increasingly marked by ads sponsored by political parties and independent organizations that are virtually indistinguishable from candidate ads except for the omission of the "magic words" of express advocacy,[273] demonstrate that the "magic words" approach no longer makes sense.

We recommend that Congress take a series of steps to expand the definition of election-related speech to include much of what is now labeled issue advocacy. We believe that these steps would curtail the

---

[273] See Paul S. Herrnson and Diana Dwyre, "Party Issue Advocacy in Congressional Election Campaigns," in John C. Green and Daniel M. Shea, *The State of the Parties: The Changing Role of Contemporary American Political Parties*, 94–99 (3d ed. 1999).

worst abuses under the current system while protecting speech that is truly about issues, policy, and politics not directly related to elections. We believe that these steps are consistent with the spirit of *Buckley* in ensuring that electoral advocacy is subject to campaign finance reporting and disclosure requirements, contribution limits and restrictions, and, in the public funding context, candidate spending limits. Where we depart from *Buckley* is in our belief that, in light of recent campaign developments and current campaign techniques, the notion of express advocacy needs to be redefined away from the "magic words" approach. This can be accomplished—and vague and subjective tests still avoided—by greater attention to the relations between ad sponsors and candidates, the source of the ads, and the timing of the ads.

(1) Advocacy That Is Coordinated with a Candidate

Certainly, when the production or dissemination of an ad is coordinated with a candidate's campaign, the advertisement ought to be considered both express advocacy and a contribution to that candidate's campaign. Surprisingly, there is currently some uncertainty about whether an advertisement that is coordinated with a candidate but that refrains from the magic words of express advocacy may be treated as express advocacy.

In reports released in the fall of 1998, FEC auditors found that the Democratic National Committee and the Clinton-Gore '96 campaign had worked together on the production and placement of television ads paid for by the DNC, and that the DNC and the Clinton-Gore primary campaign committee shared a standard-form memorandum for authorization of production and purchase of air time for media advertising: "One section of this memorandum states 'The cost will be allocated _% for the DNC and _% for Clinton-Gore '96.' The next line states 'attorneys to determine.' "[274] The FEC General Counsel found that it was "difficult to distinguish between the activities of the DNC and the [Clinton] Primary Committee with respect to the creation and publication of the media advertisements at issue."[275] FEC

---

[274] See FEC, Report of the Audit Division on Clinton-Gore '96 Primary Committee, Inc., 24 (1998).

[275] Id. at 108.

auditors also found that the Republican National Committee paid more than $18 million directly and through Republican state committees on behalf of the Dole campaign for ads that were aired between April and August 1996, a period in which the Dole campaign was bumping up against the spending ceiling it had accepted as a condition for prenomination public funding.[276] Yet in December 1998 the FEC rejected the conclusions of its auditors that the party issue advocacy spending on behalf of the Clinton-Gore '96 and Dole campaigns caused those campaigns to violate the spending limits they had accepted as a condition for public funding. The FEC did not issue a formal opinion, and some members may have been unpersuaded by the evidence of coordination, but other members suggested that issue advocacy, even if coordinated with a candidate, is protected from any restriction.[277]

Such a position is clearly mistaken. It is the coordination of the expenditure with the candidate, not the content of the advertising it finances, that counts. A contribution to a candidate's campaign is subject to FECA whether or not the check to the candidate is accompanied by a cover letter containing words of express advocacy. Just as a cash or in-kind contribution to a candidate need not include the express words "Vote for Jane Doe" to be subject to regulation and limits, a coordinated expenditure—which is legally the equivalent of a contribution—need not use the magic words of advocacy in order to be subject to regulation. To remove any uncertainty, **FECA should be amended to provide that any expenditure for campaign communications that is coordinated with a campaign is express advocacy subject to regulation, regardless of its content.**

(2) Advocacy by Political Party Committees

A significant development in the last two election cycles is the growing use of issue advocacy by the major political parties. This has been fueled by the rise of soft money. By the same token, the opportunity to use soft money to pay for issue ads has stimulated party soft money fundraising. Eliminating soft money, as we have proposed, could sig-

---

[276] See FEC, Report of the Audit Division on the Dole for President Committee, Inc. (Primary), 16, 34–36, 46 (1998).

[277] See Jill Abramson, "Election Panel Refuses to Order Repayments by Clinton and Dole," *The New York Times* (Dec. 11, 1998):A1.

nificantly curtail party issue ads since parties would no longer be receiving the large corporate and union contributions that cannot be used for candidate-related activities and, thus, are targeted for issue advocacy. Nonetheless, even with the elimination of soft money, party issue advocacy poses challenges to campaign finance law. Under a public funding system, party issue ads would not be considered part of the party's support for its publicly funded candidate. Consequently, parties could use issue ads to evade spending limits. Similarly, with respect to privately funded candidates, issue ads could be used to evade the limits on party contributions and coordinated expenditures.

Moreover, major parties are unlike other political advocacy organizations. For nonparty political groups, the purpose of political activity is to advance or block certain policies or approaches to government. For them, electing candidates is a means to that end but not the end itself. When these organizations engage in speech that combines references to candidates and political issues, a relatively narrow definition of election-related speech is necessary to ensure that election law does not interfere with their ability to advocate for their policy goals. In contrast, the overarching purpose of party committee spending is the election of party candidates to office and thereby holding or winning power. To be sure, the major parties have an interest in ideology and the same right as other organizations to discuss issues. Certainly, party spending that is exclusively about issues is entitled to the same constitutional protection that applies to spending on politics by other groups or individuals. But most party spending, particularly party messages that couple issue discussions with references to candidates, is focused on winning elections. Given the overwhelming candidate-election focus of party activities, we believe that express advocacy can and should be defined more broadly for speech undertaken by the major parties than for speech by other organizations. The danger of regulating speech that is truly about issues is much diminished when party communications are involved; conversely, the danger that parties will use the issue advocacy loophole to avoid the legitimate goals of election finance regulation is much greater.

Consequently, **we recommend that FECA be amended to provide that any communication by a political party committee that mentions by name or includes the likeness of a clearly identified**

candidate for federal office be defined as express advocacy. At the point when a party communication clearly refers to a federal candidate, it can be safely assumed that the party is working to elect or defeat that candidate. Once it has mentioned a candidate, a party has crossed the line from discussion of political issues generally into participation in the election.

We recognize that, unlike our proposal concerning coordinated advocacy, this proposal departs significantly from the current judicial approach to the definition of election-related speech.[278] Nevertheless, we believe that it is consistent with the Supreme Court's concern about the prevention of corruption and the appearance of corruption and that it reflects the reality of party–candidate relations.

(3) The Temporal Context

As Justice Holmes once observed, "The character of every act depends upon the circumstances in which it is done."[279] The meaning of speech is inevitably affected by the context in which it is broadcast or published. Words can be understood to convey a message that goes beyond their literal terms, with the meaning of those words determined by the context in which they are uttered. This is particularly true of modern advertising, which rarely uses literal words of advocacy but can be quite effective in persuading people to buy things. As Justice Ann Walsh Bradley of the Wisconsin Supreme Court recently observed,

> Few advertisements will directly say "Buy Nike rather than Reebok" or "Drink Maxwell House coffee." Be they in the print or electronic media, advertisements normally do not include a call for action or use "magic words" to relay their message. Yet every reader, listener, or viewer knows that "Less filling, tastes great" is an unambiguous exhortation to purchase a particular type of Miller beer. And "They're Gr-r-reat" is Tony the Tiger's unambiguous appeal to buy a box of sugar-coated corn flakes.[280]

This is as true of campaign ads as of ads intended to sell beer or cornflakes. Few campaign ads, whether aired by candidates or inde-

---

[278] Current judicial treatment of the definition of electioneering speech is considered at pp. 51–57 of this Report.

[279] *Schenck v. United States*, 249 U.S. 47, 52 (1919).

[280] *Elections Board of Wisconsin v. Wisconsin Manufacturers & Commerce*, 597 N.W.2d 721, 742–43 (Wis. S. Ct. 1999).

pendent groups, use literal words of advocacy. But when heard and understood in context, they can be powerful forms of advocacy.

The most important part of a political ad's context is its timing. The timing of a political message is quite likely to affect its meaning. An election-eve message that combines references to candidates and to issues is far more likely to affect voter thinking about the election than about political issues in general precisely because the message is mailed, published, or broadcast on the eve of the election. A denunciation of President Clinton's healthcare policies will mean one thing and can have one effect when those policies are being debated by Congress more than a year before the election and will have another meaning and a different effect a few weeks before an election, when Congress is in recess and the President and members of Congress are campaigning for reelection.

The Annenberg Center study showed that issue ads aired in the immediate pre-election period differ from issue ads broadcast at other times. The study, which examined 423 ads, found that issue ads released in the immediate pre-election period were far more likely to refer to candidates or officeholders by name, far less likely to discuss legislation, and far more likely to be attack ads than those aired in the preceding 20 months. In 1997–98 only 35 percent of the ads released before September 1, 1998, mentioned a candidate; but 80 percent of ads aired after that date named a candidate.[281] Conversely, 81 percent of issue ads aired before September 1 mentioned pending legislation, while only 21.6 percent of ads disseminated after September 1 mentioned pending legislation.[282]

The pre-election period is the high point of the election campaign, when the voters are most likely to be considering their Election Day decisions. It is unlikely that communications referring to candidates that are disseminated in this period will have an impact on political activity other than the election itself even if the communications refer to issues or ideas as well as to candidates. Typically, in the days and weeks before Election Day, politics focuses on the election. Legislative bodies whose members are up for election generally go out of session. Executive branch officials who are up for election devote themselves to their campaigns. In this period, political activity in-

---

[281] "Issue Advocacy Advertising," supra, at 4.
[282] Id.

volving clearly identified candidates is likely to be election-related activity. As a result, presuming that election-eve, candidate-identifying speech is election-related speech will place little burden on other political speech.

We recommend that Congress provide by law that any communication broadcast, printed, mailed, or distributed within 30 days before a primary or general election that includes the name or likeness of any clearly identified candidate for federal office shall be presumed to be express advocacy, but that such presumption may be rebutted on a showing that, based on the content and context of the speech, viewers, listeners, or readers are unlikely to treat it as an election-related communication. A one-month pre-election period is the period in which voters are most focused on the upcoming elections and political actors are least likely to be engaged in political activity unrelated to the election.

Like our proposal concerning party issue advocacy, a 30-day or similar temporal rule would depart from existing judicial approaches to the definition of express advocacy and is certainly likely to be subject to constitutional attack.[283] It is arguably both underinclusive—in the 1995–96 campaign, the Democratic Party engaged in issue advocacy more than a year before the 1996 general election—and overinclusive.

The underinclusive aspect of the definition will be supplemented by the more inclusive rules concerning coordinated and party advocacy. Moreover, like the *Buckley* Court, we would rather err on the side of protecting the speech of independent organizations and individuals who have genuine political goals other than the election or defeat of candidates.

A temporal test would be overinclusive when it applies to advertisements that mention an elected official but are aimed at influenc-

---

[283] Thus far, courts have rejected the use of the temporal pre-election period to define express advocacy. See *West Virginians for Life, Inc. v. Smith*, 960 F. Supp. 1036, 1039 (S.D. W. Va. 1996) (invalidating a West Virginia law providing that voter guides distributed within 60 days of an election are presumed to be election-related for purposes of a state law requiring reporting and disclosure of election expenditures); *Right to Life of Michigan, Inc. v. Miller*, 23 F.Supp.2d 766 (W.D. Mich. 1998) (holding unconstitutional a Michigan administrative rule that prohibited corporations and other entities from using treasury funds to pay for communications, made within 45 days prior to an election, that contained the name or likeness of a candidate).

ing the elected official's exercise of his or her official powers, as when an ad calls upon a candidate who is also a member of Congress to vote a particular way on a matter up for a legislative vote during the pre-election period. To deal with the danger of overinclusiveness, Congress should provide that the presumption that a communication that mentions the name or includes the picture of a clearly identified candidate within the pre-election period is election-related may be rebutted on a showing by the speaker that based on the content and context of the speech, viewers, listeners, or readers are unlikely to treat it as an election-related communication. The opportunity to rebut the definition of express electoral advocacy would raise some question of vagueness or uncertainty, but whatever uncertainty results would be due to the law's desire to give some extra opportunity to exempt true issue advocacy from regulation.

The exact determination of the pre-election period is bound to be somewhat arbitrary. But like the number of petition signatures needed to place a candidate on the ballot,[284] the number of feet from the polling place in which a state may bar electioneering,[285] or, more pertinently, the dollar thresholds for FECA's reporting and disclosure requirements and contribution limits, this seems like an issue in which the courts ought to give Congress some leeway. Just as there are no magic words, there are no magic days. But election-eve communications that mention clearly identified candidates are more likely to affect readers', viewers', or listeners' views about their election choices than their views about political issues unanchored to candidates. Regulating such communications is not likely to interfere with a robust issues debate because most political debate on the eve of the election is about the election itself. A bright-line test, with an opportunity to rebut the definition of express advocacy on a showing that the speech concerned actual government action—or potential government action under active consideration—during the pre-election period is constitutionally desirable even if no particular bright line is empirically decisive. We believe that in light of *Nixon v. Shrink*

---

[284] See, for example, *Jenness v. Fortson*, 403 U.S. 453 (1971) (affirming a Georgia law requiring 5 percent of eligible voters to sign a candidate petition to gain ballot access if that candidate's party received less than 20 percent of the state vote at the most recent presidential or gubernatorial election).

[285] See *Burson v. Freeman*, 504 U.S. 191 (1992) (upholding a Tennessee law prohibiting campaigning within 100 feet of a polling station on Election Day).

Missouri Government PAC's reiteration of deference to the political branches concerning the precise level of the contribution limit necessary to prevent the danger of corruption, any reasonable period selected by Congress would be entitled to receive judicial deference.

(For a summary of the Commission's proposals concerning the redefinition of express advocacy, see table 15.)

F. THE FEDERAL ELECTION COMMISSION

Effective enforcement of campaign finance law is essential if the principles of campaign finance regulation are to be attained and public confidence in the system restored. Effective enforcement, in turn, requires a vigorous and nonpartisan FEC with the legal authority and resources to determine in a timely fashion that candidates, contributors, and other participants in the process are abiding by the rules and to seek appropriate penalties when they are not. The FEC's current organization and powers fall short of these goals. The Commission is too often bipartisan, rather than nonpartisan, winking at violations by the major parties and major party candidates and focusing instead on lesser actors. Its cumbersome enforcement process guarantees delays, and its limited investigative powers fail to deter.

TABLE 15: EXPRESS ADVOCACY: PROPOSALS

√ Any communication coordinated with a candidate should be treated as express advocacy.

√ Any communication by a political party committee that mentions by name or includes the likeness of a clearly identified candidate for federal office should be treated as express advocacy.

√ Any communication within 30 days before an election that mentions by name or includes the likeness of a clearly identified candidate for federal office should be presumed to be express advocacy. That presumption may be rebutted on a showing that, based on the context and content of the communication, viewers, listeners, or readers are unlikely to treat it as an election-related communication.

Its resources have failed to keep pace over time with the growth in campaign activity.

Many of the FEC's problems may be beyond statutory solution. The Commission is charged with the thankless task of regulating the very elected officials who have the authority to appoint and confirm its members, control its budget, and determine its legal powers. Vigorous exercise of its responsibilities can result in a loss of authority and cuts in its budget. Moreover, the elected officials—the President and members of the Senate—responsible for selecting and approving commissioners have too often prized partisanship and close ties to the politicians to be regulated over nonpartisanship and a commitment to appropriate enforcement. The partisan culture that has often resulted produces deadlock and failure to enforce the law.

We believe that the recommendations that follow have the potential to strengthen the FEC and improve enforcement, but we also recognize that the ultimate success of enforcement and of the election laws themselves will require that the President nominate and the Senate confirm qualified, independent men and women who have experience with politics but are not tied to any political figures or parties, and who are committed to working together to enforce the law.

(1) Commission Membership

The FEC consists of six members—three Democrats and three Republicans—who serve for six-year terms. The FEC needs the affirmative votes of four of the six members. There is no presidentially appointed chair; rather, the position of chair rotates annually among the members.

Of all federal administrative agencies, only the FEC and the International Trade Commission consist of an even number of commissioners—and the ITC is empowered to act on the affirmative vote of three out of six commissioners, whereas four votes are required for FEC action. The even number of members compounded by the partisanship of the commissioners can lead to deadlock when decisions have partisan implications. Although the vast majority of FEC decisions are taken without closely divided votes and "three-three splits occur in a very, very small number of cases,"[286] the three-three splits, particularly the partisan three-three splits, "tend to be on very important questions of law."[287]

We recommend that the FEC be expanded to seven members to reduce the likelihood of deadlock. To avoid the danger of narrow partisan majorities, **we also recommend that the Commission be required to have one member not affiliated, either at the time of appointment or in the three preceding years, with any political party.**[288] We also believe that the FEC would benefit from a strong chair who can give direction, set enforcement and policy priorities, and raise the public profile of campaign finance enforcement. **We recommend that the President be authorized to designate a member to serve as chair for a two-year term.** To reduce the dangers of partisanship, **we recommend that if a chair is affiliated with a particular political party, his or her successor may not be affiliated with that party.**

We also urge the President and the leaders of Congress to consider the creation of a nonpartisan advisory panel that would be authorized to recommend qualified, vigorous, independent candidates for nomination to the FEC. The constitutional doctrine of separation of powers precludes any requirement that the President be limited to nominating only persons recommended by such an advisory panel. Yet we note the paradox that although the President in theory must enjoy unfettered power to make nominations to the FEC—subject to the advice and consent of the Senate—in practice the congressional

---

[286] FEC General Counsel Lawrence Noble in "Federal Election Commission Panel Discussion: Problems and Possibilities," 8 *Ad. L. J.* 223, 252 (1994). According to a 1998 FEC Press Release, only 22 out of 1587 votes in open session resulted in 3–3 deadlocks.

[287] Elizabeth Hedlund of the Center for Responsive Politics in id. at 252–53. Until 1997 the dangers of partisan deadlock were reinforced by the fact that commissioners were eligible for reappointment. A FEC member might fear to vote in such a way as to anger his or her party and, as a result, be denied reappointment. In 1997, however, Congress provided that henceforward newly appointed commissioners would be limited to one term (and currently serving commissioners would be eligible for reappointment for just one more term).

[288] Cf. "From the Ground Up," supra, 27 *Fordham Urb. L. J.* at 152–53 (comments of FEC General Counsel Lawrence M. Noble supporting the current six-member FEC with a requirement of four votes for action because it provides the courts some assurance that an enforcement action is supported by more than one partisan faction on the Commission).

leadership, operating on a partisan basis, has a decisive role in determining who will be nominated to the Commission. We acknowledge that the appointment process is ultimately political, but we hope that the President and Congress will look for ways to make it less partisan.

(2) The Civil Enforcement Process

Civil enforcement is hampered by a cumbersome multistep enforcement process, with a four-member majority of the FEC required to approve advancing a case from one step to the next. The General Counsel may not initiate enforcement action without an affirmative vote of four members of the Commission—based on a preliminary investigation and papers submitted by the General Counsel—that there is "reason to believe" (RTB) a violation has occurred. Only at that point is an investigation officially opened. If after the investigation the General Counsel is persuaded that the respondent violated the Act, he or she must return to the FEC to secure four affirmative votes that there is "probable cause to believe" (PCTB) a violation has occurred. Before getting to the PCTB step, the General Counsel and the respondent must attempt a pre-probable cause conciliation. Even after the Commission votes PCTB, nothing actually happens to the respondent. The General Counsel and the respondent must again try conciliation; under the statute the conciliation effort must last at least 30 and as many as 90 days.[289] In practice, the conciliation period may run much longer than 90 days because many respondents are skilled at protracting the process. If conciliation fails, then, if four commissioners approve, the FEC may institute a judicial proceeding against the respondent. That proceeding is a de novo action. The burden is on the FEC to prove its case. Its finding of PCTB is not entitled to judicial deference.

Note that the failure to get four votes for any action—the finding of RTB, which is necessary to begin a full investigation; the finding of PCTB; the decision to file a civil action—effectively terminates a matter.[290] Moreover, the General Counsel may have to return to the full FEC at several points during the investigation because the af-

---

[289] 2 U.S.C. § 437g(a)(4).

[290] See Lawrence M. Noble, "Federal Election Commission Enforcement," 1019 PLI/Corp 599, 607 (1997).

firmative votes of four commissioners are necessary for the General Counsel to obtain subpoenas to compel production of documents, attendance at depositions, and responses to interrogatories.

This process is cumbersome and protracted, provides respondents with opportunities for delay, and produces few decisive results. **We recommend that Congress eliminate the requirement that the FEC must vote that there is reason to believe a violation exists before formally opening an investigation.** There is no reason for this step. The RTB has no direct impact on a respondent; any penalty must await later action by the Commission. Yet the requirement of a formal submission to and vote by the FEC slows down the investigative process. In a few cases, the failure through partisan or other deadlock to obtain four affirmative votes has cut off an investigation before it is fully under way. By the same token, the person under investigation has no opportunity to participate in the pre-RTB phase of the case, so requiring an RTB vote burdens the respondent's procedural interests, too. Eliminating this step would expedite the process.[291] It would also make sense to couple the elimination of the RTB step with some requirement that the General Counsel resolve a matter under investigation by either closing it or formally finding a reason to investigate after a certain period.

We also recommend elimination of the multiple conciliation requirements. There is evidence that the conciliation process is subject to abuse by respondents, who, relying in part on the FEC's limited staff, are able to extend the process in order to delay the finding of violation and reduce the negotiated penalty. We believe that under appropriate circumstances conciliation may be preferable to a formal administrative determination, but we believe the decision whether to seek conciliation should be left to administrative flexibility and not formal mandate. This is especially true since, even if the conciliation fails, the FEC lacks the power to impose penalties and must go to court to enforce its determinations.

A significant number of FEC cases involve relatively minor violations, such as late or incomplete filings. The FEC must gear up its full enforcement process—RTB, investigation, conciliation, PCTB,

---

[291] If this proposal is adopted, it would make sense to rename the "reason to believe" step something like "reason to investigate" to dispel any implication that RTB implies guilt.

with full commission votes at each stage—to go after these violations. Otherwise, as is increasingly the case under the current enforcement priority system, these matters remain inactive for a time and are then dismissed. By legislation enacted in September 1999 and effective for a two-year period starting January 1, 2000, Congress authorized the FEC to create a so-called "traffic ticket" system under which the Commission could adopt a schedule of fines for violations of FECA's reporting requirements and could impose those fines directly, without having to go through a full hearing, conciliation, or a de novo civil action in federal court. The schedule of fines would be required to take into account the amount of the violation involved, the existence of previous violations by the person, and such other factors as the FEC considers appropriate. Respondents would be entitled to written notice and an opportunity to be heard before the Commission and would be permitted to seek judicial review of the fines.[292]

We applaud this experiment. In our deliberations, we gave serious consideration to changing the basic structure of the FEC's enforcement process by authorizing the FEC to impose penalties directly on a finding of a violation. We recognize that increasing the FEC's power would also require greater formal procedural protection for respondents within the FEC's internal processes. We believe that the newly authorized system of FEC-imposed penalties for reporting violations can provide an excellent test of this alternative approach to campaign finance law enforcement. Consequently, we defer any recommendation now on whether the FEC's enforcement process should be changed further, in addition to the elimination of the RTB and mandatory conciliation steps, until there is more information on how well the new system of FEC-imposed penalties works.

(3) Detecting Violations: The Need for Random Audits

The FEC's enforcement process may be triggered either by an external complaint or by an internal referral—the latter typically from the FEC's audit staff. As a result of legislation adopted in 1979, the FEC is banned from undertaking random audits. The Commission initially had random-audit authority, and following the 1976 election it under-

---

[292] Treasury and General Government Appropriations Act, 2000; Sec. 640, Pub. L. No. 106–58.

took random audits of 10 percent of House and Senate candidates. Those audits turned up minor but embarrassing inaccuracies in the reports of many incumbents.[293] Congress then stripped the FEC of the authority to conduct random audits. As a result, it is unlikely that contribution, expenditure, or disclosure violations of campaign committees that know enough to submit a formally correct report will ever be detected.

We recommend that Congress restore the FEC's power to undertake random audits of political committees within its jurisdiction. The authority to undertake random audits needs to be restored if there is to be any possibility of catching, punishing, or deterring FECA violations. Indeed, the FEC ought to be required to undertake random audits as part of its enforcement responsibilities.

(4) Expedited Relief

All FEC determinations concerning FECA violations and penalties occur long after the violation in question occurred and long after the election that was the subject of the contribution or expenditure in question. The FEC has no authority to seek expedited relief, such as a temporary restraining order, against campaign finance law violations occurring during the election period. **We recommend that the FEC be given the authority to seek expedited injunctive relief during the election period when there is evidence that a serious violation has occurred or is unfolding.**

We recognize that this creates the potential for direct government agency intervention into an election. But without the authority to seek expedited relief in appropriate cases, key provisions of federal election law may never be enforced. Too often, parties and candidates who are focused on winning elections are willing to risk a finding that their actions violate the law, knowing that the penalty, if any, will be a relatively small fine imposed long after the election is over.[294]

We would limit expedited relief to cases involving serious violations, such as spending above the public funding limit or contributions that violate the Act's source prohibitions or dollar limitations.

---

[293] Brooks Jackson, *Broken Promise*, supra, at 12.

[294] See, for example, "Federal Election Commission Panel Discussion: Problems and Possibilities," supra, 8 *Ad. L. J.* at 232.

We also note that we would give the FEC the authority only to *seek* expedited injunctive relief. The decision whether to grant such relief would have to be made by a court, which would hear from, and assess the arguments of, the parties opposed to such relief.

(5) Resources

In the years FECA has been in place, the FEC's budget has failed to keep pace with the increased magnitude and complexity of federal campaign finance activity. As the recent audit by the Commission authorized by Congress and undertaken by PricewaterhouseCoopers LLP put it, "the current election process has evolved into a high-velocity system of complex transactions and litigious recourse, punctuated by the actions of a few participants engaging in behavior designed to push the limits of the traditional campaign finance system."[295] Yet the FEC lacks the resources for field investigators—one study found it has only two field investigators—audit analysts, and lawyers.

The resource problem will be compounded if public funding is adopted. Although the FEC's handling of the presidential public funding program has been praised, presidential public funding involves at most two dozen candidates every four years. With congressional public funding, there could very well be more than 1000 publicly funded candidates in every election cycle.[296] Public funding will involve review of a huge number of private contributions to see if they satisfy the criteria for qualifying a candidate for public funding and/or for matching the private contributions with public funds, and policing the expenditures of the candidates to see if they comply with the spending ceiling.

It is difficult to determine what resources the FEC needs to carry out its current duties and to administer a congressional public funding law. Resources for the FEC, relative to its statutory responsibili-

---

[295] PricewaterhouseCoopers LLP, "Technology and Performance Audit and Management Review of the Federal Election Commission," vol. 1 Final Report, Jan. 29, 1999, at ES-2.

[296] This assumes 435 House races, 33 Senate races, two major party nominees in each race—for a total of 936 candidates—plus some primary candidates and independent candidates who qualify for public funding in the general election. If there is at least one losing primary candidate in each race, the total number of candidates would be approximately fourteen hundred.

ties, declined from the mid-1970s to the mid-1990s. In 1976 the appropriation for the agency was $6 million; it had a staff of 197; and federal election campaigns cost about $300 million. By 1995–96 the budget was $26.5 million (up about 350 percent); the FEC's staff had increased by about 50 percent (to around 300); but federal election spending subject to FECA regulation had increased by well over 600 percent. The ratio of campaign finance activity subject to regulation to the FEC's budget went from about $48:$1 in 1976 to $86:$1 in 1996.[297] In recent years, the agency's budget has grown. The FY 1998 budget was $31.7 million, and the budget for FY 2000 was $38.2 million.[298]

Certainly, the effectiveness of the FEC is as much related to how efficiently it uses its resources as to the level of resources. While more money would be needed to implement public funding—as well as to secure more timely compliance with disclosure requirements and enforcement of contribution restrictions—it is likely that the amount needed would be modest relative to overall campaign costs. We could speculate that the FEC's budget might have to rise to $100 million by the time public funding is fully effective. Although that would be nearly a 200 percent increase over the current budget level, the increase is small relative to the overall cost of elections. In 1996 the total cost of federal election campaigns came to about $2.2 billion.

We have considered whether there are ways to ensure that the FEC's budget is adequate to its tasks and to protect the budget from congressional retaliation, but short of a constitutional amendment comparable to the provisions of the California constitution or the New York City charter offering special protections for campaign finance agency budgets, there is no statutory mechanism for taking the FEC's budget out of the political process. Some commentators have proposed that Congress adopt a two-year rather than a one-year budget authorization for the agency,[299] or that the budget be indexed for inflation. Such steps would certainly add desirable predictability

---

[297] The 1996 figures were actually a small improvement over the previous presidential elections in which the activity/agency appropriation ratios were $99:$1 (1984); $96:$1 (1988); and $95:$1 (1992).

[298] FEC, "FEC Submits FY2001 Budget Request," http://www.fec.gov/press/budg01.htm (Dec. 9, 1999). In FY 2000, the Commission had a staff of 356 authorized personnel.

[299] ABA Standing Committee on Election Law.

concerning the agency's level of funding but could not ensure the budget's adequacy. In the end, the sufficiency of resources for enforcement must turn on the commitment of the President and Congress, and on the role of public opinion in reminding our elected officials of the importance of campaign finance law enforcement to our democratic system and to public confidence in government.

(6) Improving Disclosure

Observers have generally praised the FEC's handling of the disclosure of campaign finance reports, but there is consensus among those who have studied the Commission's work that the process could be expedited, administrative costs reduced, and public benefits increased if the FEC could require committees that handle more than a threshold level of contributions to file electronically according to a standard form prescribed by the Commission. A comprehensive mandatory electronic data filing system is one of the principal recommendations of the 1999 PricewaterhouseCoopers audit. According to the audit, "Electronic filing offers the most cost-efficient and effective method to capture campaign finance transactions."[300] Disclosure information submitted electronically is on the public record well within 24 hours of receipt. Filing electronically would reduce errors and substantially reduce the resources necessary to process reports.[301] PricewaterhouseCoopers states that the move from paper-based to electronic filing would "eventually allow the FEC to shift some resources from its disclosure activities to its compliance programs."[302]

In September 1999 Congress finally gave the FEC the necessary authority to mandate electronic filing—starting after the 1999–2000 election cycle.[303] We regret that Congress chose to defer computerized disclosure for one more election cycle, although we applaud the decision to couple the electronic filing requirement with the requirement that the FEC make any report filed in electronic form accessible to the public via the Internet within 24 hours of receipt.

(For a summary of the Commission on Campaign Finance Reform's proposals concerning the FEC, see table 16.)

---

[300] PricewaterhouseCoopers Audit at 5–2.

[301] Id. at 4–30 to 4–36.

[302] Id. at 5–1.

[303] Treasury and Government Appropriations Act, 2000, Sec. 639, Pub. L. No. 106–58.

TABLE 16: FEDERAL ELECTION COMMISSION: PROPOSALS

√ Seventh commissioner to be appointed. Must not be affiliated with a political party.

√ Strong chair to be appointed for a two-year term.

- If she/he is affiliated with a particular party, her/his successor may not be affiliated with that party.

√ Simplification of the Civil Enforcement Process: elimination of the "reason to believe" step, and the multiple conciliation requirements.

√ Random-Audit Authority to be restored.

√ Power to seek expedited injunctive relief during the election period.

√ Additional resources to keep pace with the increased magnitude and complexity of federal campaign finance activity.

5

Conclusion

FREE AND FAIR ELECTIONS are at the heart of American democracy. Campaign money, in turn, is essential for free and fair elections. But the methods by which campaign money is collected and spent have a critical impact on elections and on the democratic process.

We believe that the recommendations presented in this Report can improve the way our elections are financed and, ultimately, how well our democracy works. Public funding, together with an increase in the limits on individual and party donations, the curtailment of soft money, an expanded and more realistic definition of election-related speech, and reforms in the organization and operation of the FEC can make our political process more open and competitive, promote the norm of voter equality, assure that the voters are better informed, reduce the burdens of fundraising, improve administration of the campaign finance laws, and ameliorate the dangers of undue influence that are endemic to any system that relies heavily on large private contributions to cover the costs of election campaigns.

We would like to stress three points. First, that this is an integrated package of reforms. The proposals are intertwined and are intended to reinforce one another. Adoption of just one category of recommendations, such as those for adjusting contribution limits, would do little to achieve many of the goals of campaign finance reform and might very well make the system worse overall.

Second, although our proposals are intended to be comprehensive, this Report is not all-inclusive. We have focused on what we consider to be the most critical issues in federal, particularly congressional, campaign finance. There are many other important issues, which, due to time and resource constraints, we have been unable to address. These include such questions as the funding, eligibility criteria, and spending limits of the presidential public funding system; an improvement in the disclosure of the fundraising activities of intermediaries who collect contributions from donors for transmission to candidates' campaigns;[304] and incumbents' use of public resources for campaign purposes. We believe that these matters deserve careful scrutiny by Congress, by bar associations, and by the public.[305]

Third, we do not think our Report or these proposals or any one set of proposals can be the final word on campaign finance reform. Campaign finance regulation must be a dynamic process. It is impossible to know in advance how a particular legal change will work in practice. Candidates, parties, and donors may develop new campaign finance techniques unanticipated by existing laws. Campaign technologies may change in ways that challenge legal structures. Legal changes that affect other aspects of the campaign process—the rules governing the timing and openness of primaries, or voter registration requirements—can also have an impact on campaign finance. A central problem with the current federal campaign finance laws is that they have scarcely changed despite significant changes in the political process over the last two decades. Campaign finance reform is not a one-time event. It is an ongoing process that requires careful monitoring of campaign practices and revision of the law in light of future developments.

Our proposals will not produce the perfect campaign finance system. Given the different, and often competing, values that ought to go into the design of a campaign system, there is no perfect campaign finance system. But we believe our proposals, if adopted together, would constitute a significant improvement over the status quo and over the likely future of campaign finance law in the absence of meaningful reform. Indeed, they would constitute a significant step toward a campaign finance system that embodies the principles of our democratic system.

---

[304] These intermediaries are known colloquially as "bundlers."

[305] We note that the Bar, and particularly this Association, has been actively engaged in considering the special questions of professional ethics posed by the contributions by lawyers to officeholders and candidates who are in position to determine the selection of counsel in government legal matters. In February, 2000, the American Bar Association House of Delegates passed an ethical rule addressing this issue.

SOURCES

CASES

Austin v. Michigan Chamber of Commerce, 494 U.S. 652 (1990)

Brown v. Socialist Workers '74 Campaign Committee, 459 U.S. 87 (1982)

Buckley v. Valeo, 424 U.S. 1 (1976)

Bullock v. Carter, 405 U.S. 134 (1972)

Burson v. Freeman, 504 U.S. 191 (1992)

California Medical Association v. FEC, 453 U.S. 182 (1981)

CBS, Inc. v. FCC, 453 U.S. 367 (1981)

City of Phoenix v. Kolodziejski, 399 U.S. 204 (1970)

Clifton v. FEC, 114 F.3d 1309 (1st Cir. 1997)

Colorado Republican Federal Campaign Committee v. FEC, 518 U.S. 604 (1996)

Faucher v. FEC, 928 F.2d 468 (1st Cir. 1991)

FEC v. Christian Action Network, 894 F. Supp. 946 (W.D. Va. 1995), affd mem., 92 F.3d 1178 (4th Cir. 1996); 110 F.3d 1049 (4th Cir. 1997)

FEC v. Democratic Senatorial Campaign Committee, 454 U.S. 27 (1981)

FEC v. Furgatch, 807 F.2d 857 (9th Cir. 1987)

FEC v. Massachusetts Citizens for Life, Inc., 479 U.S. 238 (1986)

FEC v. National Conservative Political Action Committee, 470 U.S. 480 (1985)

FEC v. National Right to Work Committee, 459 U.S. 197 (1982)

Gable v. Patton, 142 F.3d 940 (6th Cir. 1998)

Harper v. Virginia Bd of Elections, 383 U.S. 663 (1966)

Hill v. Stone, 421 U.S. 289 (1975)

Jenness v. Fortson, 403 U.S. 453 (1971)

Lubin v. Panish, 415 U.S. 709 (1974)

Maine Right to Life Committee, Inc. v. FEC, 98 F.3d 1 (1st Cir. 1996)

Morse v. Republican Party of Virginia, 517 U.S. 186 (1996)

Nixon v. Shrink Missouri Government PAC, 120 S.Ct. 897 (2000)

Republican National Committee v. FEC, 487 F. Supp. 280 (S.D.N.Y.), affd mem. 445 U.S. 995 (1980)

Republican National Committee v FEC, 1998 U.S. App. LEXIS 28505 (D.C. Cir. 1998)

Republican Party of Minnesota v Pauly, 63 F.Supp.2d 1008 (D. Minn. 1999)

Reynolds v Sims, 377 U.S. 533 (1964)

Right to Life of Michigan, Inc. v Miller, 23 F.Supp.2d 766 (W.D. Mich 1998)

Rogers v. Lodge, 458 U.S. 613 (1982)

Rosenstiel v. Rodriguez, 101 F.3d 1544 (8th Cir. 1996)

Schenck v. United States, 249 U.S. 47 (1919)

Elections Bd. of Wisconsin v. Wisconsin Mfrs. & Commerce, 597 N.W.2d 721 (Wisc. Sup. Ct. 1999)

Terry v. Adams, 345 U.S. 461 (1953)

Wesberry v. Sanders, 376 U.S. 1 (1964)

West Virginians for Life, Inc. v. Smith, 960 F. Supp. 1036 (S.D. W.VA. 1996)

White v. Regester, 412 U.S. 755 (1973)

Wilkinson v. Jones, 876 F. Supp. 916 (W.D. Ky 1995)

Wisconsin Manufacturers & Commerce v. Wisconsin Election Board, 978 F. Supp. 1200 (W.D. Wisc. 1997)

Books, Articles, and Other Sources

Abramson, Jill. "Election Panel Refuses to Order Repayments by Clinton and Dole." *The New York Times* (December 11, 1998).

Abramson, Jill, and Leslie Wayne. "Democrats Used the State Parties to Bypass Limits." *The New York Times* (October 2, 1997).

Adamany, David W. "Political Parties in the 1980s." In *Money and Politics in the United States: Financing Elections in the 1980s,* edited by Michael J. Malbin. Chatham House Publishers, 1984.

Adamany, David W., and George E. Agree. *Political Money: A Strategy for Campaign Financing in America.* John Hopkins Univ. Press, 1975.

Alexander, Herbert E. *Financing Politics: Money, Elections, and Political Reform,* 3d ed. CQ Press, 1984.

Alexander, Herbert E., and Monica Bauer. *Financing the 1988 Election.* Westview Press, 1991.

American Bar Association, Report of the Standing Committee on

Election Law (Report No. 100, 1994, approved at the ABA Mid-year Meeting, 1995).

Arterton, F. Christopher. "Political Money and Party Strength." In *The Future of American Political Parties: The Challenge of Governance,* edited by Joel L. Fleishman. Prentice Hall, 1982.

Association of the Bar of the City of New York. "Campaign Finance Legislation." 41 *The Record* 746 (1986).

―――. "Towards A Level Playing Field—A Pragmatic Approach to Public Campaign Financing." 52 *The Record* 660 (1997).

Barnes, James A. "Wobbly Watchdog" *The National Journal* (April 2, 1994).

Beck, Deborah, et al. *Issue Advocacy During the 1996 Campaign.* Annenberg Public Policy Center, 1997.

Bernstein, Jonathan, and Raymond J. LaRaja. "Independent Expenditures and Partisanship in House Elections." Paper prepared for delivery at 1999 Annual Meeting of the American Political Science Association.

Bibby, John F. "State Party Organizations: Coping, and Adapting to Candidate-Centered Politics and Nationalization." In *The Parties Respond: Changes in American Parties and Campaigns,* 3d ed., by L. Sandy Maisel. Westview Press, 1998.

Biersack, Robert, and Melanie Haskell. "Spitting on the Umpire: Political Parties, the Federal Election Campaign Act, and the 1996 Campaigns." In *Financing the 1996 Election,* edited by John C. Green. M. E. Sharpe, 1999.

Blasi, Vincent. "Free Speech and the Widening Gyre of Fundraising: Why Campaign Spending Limits May Not Violate the First Amendment After All." 94 *Colum. L. Rev.* 1281 (1994).

Briffault, Richard. "Issue Advocacy: Redrawing the Elections/Politics Line." 77 *Tex. L. Rev.* 1751 (1999).

Cantor, Joseph E. "The Presidential Election Campaign Fund and Tax Checkoff: Background and Current Issues." (March 18, 1997).

Carroll, Michael W. "When Congress Just Says No: Deterrence Theory and the Inadequate Enforcement of the Federal Election Campaign Act." 84 *Geo. L. J.* 551 (1996).

"Carryover Funds: 106th Congress Convenes With Over $100 Million in the Bank for 2000 Campaigns." *Political Finance and Lobby Reporter* (January 13, 1999).

Center for Responsive Politics. "The Big Picture: Where the Money

Came From in the 1996 Elections." http://www.crp.org/crpdocs/
bigpicture/overview/bpoverview.htm

———. "The Big Picture: Who Paid for This Election?" http://www.opensecrets.org/pubs/bigpicture2000/overview/whopaid.ihtml

———. "Election Statistics at a Glance." http://www.opensecrets.org/pubc/bigpicture2000/overview/stats.ihtml

———. "Enforcing the Campaign Finance Laws: An Agency Model." http://www.opensecrets.org/pubs/lawenforce/enforceindex.html

———. "Money and Incumbency Win Big on Election Day, November 4, 1998." http://www.crp.org/pressreleases/nov0498.htm

Committee for Economic Development. "Investing in the People's Business: A Business Proposal for Campaign Finance Reform." (1999).

Corrado, Anthony. *Paying for Presidents: Public Financing in National Elections.* Twentieth Century Fund Press, 1993.

———. "Party Soft Money." In *Campaign Finance Reform: A Sourcebook,* edited by Anthony Corrado, Thomas E. Mann, Daniel R. Ortiz, Trevor Potter, and Frank J. Sorauf. 1997.

———. "Financing the 1996 Presidential General Election." In *Financing the 1996 Election,* edited by John C. Green. M. E. Sharpe, 1999.

Donnay, Patrick D., and Graham P. Ramsden. "Public Financing of Legislative Elections: Lessons from Minnesota." 20 *Leg. Stud. Q.* 351 (1995).

Eisele, Albert. "Your Money, Their Views: Playing Partisan Politics With Nonprofits." *The New York Times* (December 9, 1997).

Epstein, Leon. *Political Parties in the American Mold.* Wisconsin Univ. Press, 1986.

"Federal Election Commission Panel Discussion: Problems and Possibilities." 8 *Ad. L. J.* 223 (1994).

Federal Election Commission. Advisory Opinion 1976–72.

———. Advisory Opinion 1978–10.

———. Advisory Opinion 1979–17.

———. Advisory Opinion 1995–25.

———. *Annual Report 1997.*

———. Proposed Rules. "Independent Expenditures and Party Committee Expenditure Limitations." 62 Fed. Reg. 24367, May 5, 1997.

————. Report of the Audit Division on Clinton-Gore '96 Primary Committee, Inc. (1998).

————. Report of the Audit Division on the Dole for President Committee, Inc. (Primary) (1998).

————. "FEC Announces 1998 Party Spending Limits: Amounts Range from $130,200 to $3 Million." March 6, 1998: http://www.fec.gov/press/441ad.htm

————. Proposed Rules. "Prohibited and Excessive Contributions; 'Soft Money.' " 63 Fed. Reg. 37722, July 13, 1998.

————. "Political Party Fundraising Continues to Climb." January 26, 1999: http://www.fec.gov/press/pty3098.htm

————. "FEC Reports on Political Party Activity for 1997–98." April 9, 1999: http://www.fec.gov/press/ptye98.htm

————. "FEC Reports on Congressional Fundraising for 1997–98." April 28, 1999: http://www.fec/gov/press/canye98.htm

————. "Both Major Parties to Receive Public Funding for 2000 Conventions." June 28, 1999: http://www.fec.gov/press/conv00.htm

————. "If the Presidential Election Were Held in 1999." July 7, 1999: http://www.fec.gov/press/spend99.htm

————. "FEC Releases Fundraising Figures of Major Political Parties—Large Gain in 'Soft Money' Contributions." September 22, 1999: http://www.fec.gov/press/ptymy99.htm

————. "Reform Party to Receive Public Funding for 2000 Convention." November 22, 1999: http://www.fec.gov/press/refconv.htm

————. "FEC Submits FY2001 Budget Request." December 9, 1999: http://www.fec.gov/press/budg01.htm

————. "FEC Issues Semi-Annual PAC Count." January 14, 2000: http://www.fec.gov/press/paccnt12000.htm

FEC Info/Public Disclosure, Inc. "Soft Money Summary." (issued 12/28/98): http://www.tray.com/fecinfo/smrpt.htm

Feigenbaum, Edward D., and Palmer, James A. *Campaign Finance Law 98: A Summary of State Campaign Finance Laws With Quick Reference Charts.* 1998.

"From the Ground Up: Local Lessons for National Reform." 27 *Fordham Urb. L. J.* 5 (1999).

Gierzynski, Anthony. *Legislative Party Campaign Committees in the American States.* Univ. of Kentucky Press, 1992.

Gordon, Nicole A. "The New York City Model: Essentials for Effective Campaign Finance Regulation." 6 *J. L. and Pol.* 79 (1997).

Green, John, Paul Herrnson, Lynda Powell, and Clyde Wilcox. "Individual Congressional Campaign Contributors: Wealthy, Conservative and Reform-Minded." http://www.crp.org/pubc/donors/donors.htm

Gross, Kenneth A. "The Enforcement of Campaign Finance Rules: A System in Search of Reform." 9 *Yale L. and Pol. Rev.* 279 (1991).

Herrnson, Paul S. "National Party Organizations at the Century's End." In *The Parties Respond: Changes in American Parties and Campaigns,* 3d ed., by L. Sandy Maisel. Westview Press, 1998.

———. "Financing the 1996 Congressional Elections." In *Financing the 1996 Election,* edited by John C. Green. M. E. Sharpe, 1999.

Herrnson, Paul S., and Diana Dwyre. "Party Issue Advocacy in Congressional Election Campaigns." In *The State of the Parties: The Changing Role of the Contemporary American Parties,* 3d ed., by John C. Green and Daniel M. Shea. Rowman and Littlefield Pub., 1999.

Jackson, Brooks. *Broken Promise: Why the Federal Election Commission Failed.* Twentieth Century Fund, 1990.

Jacobson, Gary C. *Money in Congressional Elections.* Yale Univ. Press, 1980.

Joe, Wesley, and Clyde Wilcox. "Financing the 1996 Presidential Nominations: The Last Regulated Campaign." In *Financing the 1996 Election,* edited by John C. Green. M. E. Sharpe, 1999.

Kuntz, Phil. "Judge's Doubts on Corporate-Contribution Ban Pose Latest Test for Weakened Campaign Laws," *Wall Street Journal* (Jan. 13, 2000):A24.

———. "Cash-for-Access Policy Forum On Bills Are Common, Controversial in Senate." *Wall Street Journal* (January 25, 2000).

Malbin, Michael J., and Thomas L. Gais. *The Day After Reform: Sobering Campaign Finance Lessons from the American States.* The Rockefeller Institute Press, 1998.

Mann, Thomas E. "The Campaign Finance System Under Strain." http://www.brookings.edu/views/Articles/Mann/SNP.htm

Mitchell, Alison. "The Making of a Money Machine: How Clinton Built His War Chest." *The New York Times* (December 27, 1996).

Mutch, Robert E. *Campaigns, Congress, and Courts: The Making of Federal Campaign Finance Law.* Praeger, 1988.

Nahra, Kirk J. "Political Parties and the Campaign Finance Laws: Dilemmas, Concerns and Opportunities." 56 *Fordham L. Rev.* 53 (1987).

New Jersey Election Law Enforcement Commission. "Gubernatorial Public Financing Overview." http://www.elec.state.nj.us/gub-pub.htm

New York City Campaign Finance Board. "On the Road to Reform: Campaign Finance in the 1993 New York City Elections." (1994).

Noble, Lawrence M. "Federal Election Commission Enforcement." 1019 PLI/Corp 599 (1997).

Note. "The Toothless Tiger—Structural, Political and Legal Barriers to Effective FEC Enforcement: An Overview and Recommendations." 10 *Admin L. J.* 351 (1996).

PricewaterhouseCoopers LLP. "Technology and Performance Audit and Management Review of the Federal Election Commission." January 29, 1999.

Seelye, Katherine Q. "GOP's Reward for Top Donors: 3 Days With Party Leaders." *The New York Times* (February 20, 1997).

Smith, Bradley A. "Faulty Assumptions and Undemocratic Consequences of Campaign Finance Reform." 105 *Yale L. J.* 1049 (1996).

Sorauf, Frank J. *Inside Campaign Finance: Myths and Realities.* Yale Univ. Press, 1992.

———. "What *Buckley* Wrought." In *If* Buckley *Fell: A First Amendment Blueprint for Regulating Money in Politics*, edited by E. Joshua Rosenkranz. 1999.

Sullivan, Kathleen M. "Against Campaign Finance Reform." 1998 *Utah L. Rev.* 311.

Taylor, Jeffrey. "GOP to Get 'Soft Money' Tobacco Aid." *Wall Street Journal* (January 7, 2000).

Yarmish, Daniel M. "The Constitutional Basis for a Ban on Soft Money." 67 *Fordham L. Rev.* 1257 (1998).

ADDENDUM

Separate Statements by Commission Members

A SEPARATE STATEMENT

Mark Alcott, Andrea Berger, Richard Briffault, Marilyn Friedman, Nicole A. Gordon, Lance Liebman

IT IS IN THE NATURE of committees that their work is based on compromise. Few members are likely to endorse every conclusion adopted by the entire group. Nevertheless, commitment to the common enterprise and support for the overall thrust of a set of recommendations ordinarily counsel acquiescence in the views of the majority even over particular points with which one disagrees. These general observations apply to this Report. There are several specific items on which we disagree with the group as a whole, but they are not important enough to prompt a separate opinion. With respect to two recommendations, our disagreements are more profound. Given that critical support for those two points was provided by members of the Commission on Campaign Finance Reform who disagree with both the overall thrust and many of the specific decisions of our compromise package, we feel compelled to record our disagreement.

We believe that the Commission's decisions (i) to raise the aggregate individual contribution limit to $75,000 per calendar year, and (ii) to permit political party committees to make contributions to or coordinated expenditures with a publicly funded candidate up to the publicly funded candidate's total spending limit are seriously mistaken. The unfortunate consequences of these two decisions are interrelated and compound each other.

(1) AGGREGATE CONTRIBUTION LIMIT

The factors that counsel raising the limits on individual donations to candidates per election cycle simply do not apply to the same degree with respect to the annual aggregate contribution limit. The individual donation limit cuts directly into a candidate's ability to raise funds and thereby compete effectively. The aggregate limit has a more attenuated effect on candidate fundraising since it does not limit how much any individual donor may give to any individual candidate. Instead, the limit operates to restrict the influence of very wealthy individual donors on the political process as a whole.

Some adjustment in the aggregate limit is certainly necessary to make the increase in donations to individual candidates workable, but trebling the limit is unwarranted: $75,000 per calendar year—effectively $150,000 per election cycle—is an extraordinarily high limit. Only a few hundred Americans currently make soft money contributions at that very high level. Indeed, with such a high annual limit—and with our elimination of any other cap on individual donations to parties—the Report comes perilously close to legalizing individual soft money donations, not eliminating them.

(2) Party Support for Publicly Funded Candidates

The dangers of undue influence posed by the very high aggregate limit on individual contributions are compounded by the decision to eliminate all limits on party support for candidates who opt into the public-funding program other than the limit on the publicly funded candidate's total spending. Eliminating all limits on party support for publicly funded candidates could be easily manipulated to permit the channeling of very large private donations to ostensibly publicly funded candidates. A candidate could nominally participate in the public-funding program by obtaining the threshold amount of small matchable private funds, but then once certified for public funding, the candidate could rely entirely on private funds collected by the parties. In House of Representatives elections, the Commission has recommended that publicly funded candidates be permitted to spend up to $1 million per election cycle. If, as the Commission also proposes, the aggregate ceiling on individual donations is raised to $75,000 per calendar year/$150,000 per two-year election cycle, then a mere handful of very large donors could finance virtually the entire costs of a nominally publicly funded House candidate's campaign.

Elsewhere in the Report, the Commission recommends that the

limit on party hard money support for privately funded candidates be roughly doubled from current levels. That would enable the national and state parties together to give up to $300,000 for a candidate in a House election. The same limit should apply to party support for publicly funded candidates. This would give the parties ample opportunity to aid their publicly funded candidates. But it would also mean that publicly funded candidates would have to look to small, matchable private donations, and, especially, to public matching funds, to cover their campaign costs. This would be far more consistent with the goals of the public funding program than a rule that would enable an ostensibly publicly funded candidate to rely entirely on private funds—and on private funds potentially composed of very large donations at that.

By applying the private funding limit to the public funding setting, a House candidate who raises as little as $235,000 in matchable private contributions would receive $470,000 in public funding and could finance the rest of her or his expenses up to the public funding $1 million limit for House elections with party funds. Such a balance of small private donations, public funds, and party money would be a far better means of advancing our goals of voter equality, promoting competitive elections, and reducing the potential for wealthy private donors to obtain undue influence by channeling money through the parties than the proposal for unlimited party support (up to the $1 million spending limit in House elections and the various state limits in Senate elections) in the Report.

STATEMENT OF DISSENTING VIEWS

Joel Gora, Constantine Sidamon-Eristoff, Peter J. Wallison, Michael S. Weinstock, Paul Windels III

THE COMMISSION ON CAMPAIGN FINANCE REFORM'S Report is an impressive document. It is the result of a careful, thoughtful, two-year study of the seemingly intractable campaign finance dilemma. Accordingly, we are pleased to associate ourselves with many of its principal elements. The Commission's chairs, Robert Kaufman, John Feerick, and Cyrus Vance, deserve great praise for their leadership and the spirit of fairness and objectivity with which they approached this task. Professor Richard Briffault and his assistant Miriam Jimenez did a truly extraordinary job of outlining in writing and in briefings the principal arguments for and against each issue to be decided by the Commission, and the report they drafted for the Commission will surely become a classic of its kind. Not only does it clearly and succinctly outline the current law, but its explication of the decisions of the Commission is exemplary for its clarity and the logic of its presentation. We are all proud to have been part of this process.

I. INTRODUCTION

The Commission began its work by deciding, with the invaluable assistance of Professor Briffault, on a set of goals for campaign finance reform summarized in chapter 1 of the Report. It is probably true that no campaign finance proposal could meet all these goals with equal success, and indeed some are in conflict with others. For example, the goal of informing the public—which is undoubtedly a function of the amount of spending by candidates—conflicts with the goal of reducing the appearance of corruption or excessive influence by limiting large contributions. Limiting the size of contributions in turn conflicts with the goal of easing the fundraising burden on candidates. In part, the Commission's task was to choose the most important goals, and structure its proposal to meet these objectives, without slighting the less important goals or other objectives and values that are important in our free and democratic constitutional system.

To a large extent, our dissent from many of the Commission's principal recommendations rests on our disagreement with the priorities and weights it placed on particular goals. For example, a majority of the Commission seemed uncritically to accept the proposition that large individual contributions to candidates or to parties create undue influence or even have a corrupting effect on lawmakers. Indeed, if there is one organizing principle around which the Report seems to be organized, it is the Commission's effort to mitigate the supposed corrupting effect of hard money contributions to candidates and soft money contributions to political parties. As a result, in too many areas, the Commission's recommendations place limits on contributions to candidates and parties that we regard as unnecessary and unwarranted.

While we do not doubt that contributions can, to some extent, influence the decisions of lawmakers, or contribute to an appearance of such influence, we doubt that this effect is so significant and pervasive that it should be used to justify a system of public finance for political campaigns, or the restrictive rules adopted by the Commission on the total amount that an individual can contribute to all candidates or to the party of his or her choice. Nor do we think that the danger of undue influence or corruption is sufficient to justify the severe restrictions that the Commission's majority proposes to place on soft money contributions to parties or the independent activities of groups.

Supporters of campaign finance reform often *assume* that contributions to political campaigns are intended to purchase influence. It is the power of this assumption that often drives reform proposals. Indeed, the majority's report echoes this widely held belief: "Campaign finance practices can affect not just the fairness of the election but the behavior of government after, or, more accurately, between elections.

When candidates are dependent on private donations, large donors and prospective donors may obtain special access to officeholders and their views may carry extra weight. They will, therefore, be particularly well positioned to affect government decision-making."[1]

Regrettably, it is this fear of quid pro quo corruption that frequently dominates the campaign finance reform debate. If we allow this easy assumption to determine the course of campaign finance reform, we will pay a steep price in the deprivation of our liberties and the loss of vigor in our contests for political office. The real focus of campaign finance reform should be maintaining a system in which challengers can mount an effective campaign against officeholders while all interested individuals and groups can express their First Amendment rights. The false assumption of undue influence should not be allowed to determine the direction of reform.

Although the notion that campaign contributions result in undue influence has the patina of common sense,[2] a substantial majority of those who have studied voting patterns on a systematic basis agree that campaign contributions affect very few votes in the legislature.[3] The factors that truly play a role in determining a legislator's votes, these studies conclude, are party affiliation, ideology, and constituent views and needs.[4] When contributions and voting patterns meet, it is a result of contributors donating money to candidates they support, not the other way around.[5] There are, of course, dissenters from these views,[6] but the fact that the underlying reasons for a legislator's vote

---

[1] Commission Report at 92.

[2] Bradley A. Smith, "Faulty Assumptions and Undemocratic Consequences of Campaign Finance Reform," 105 *Yale L. J.* 1049, 1068 (1996): "Experience and human nature tell us that legislators, like most people, are influenced by money, even when it goes into their campaign funds, rather than directly into their pockets."

[3] Id. at 1068 (citing data from Stephanie D. Mousalli, "Campaign Finance Reform: The Case for Deregulation," 6 [1990]; Frank Sorauf, "Money in American Elections," 316 [1988]; Janet Grenzke, "PACs and the Congressional Supermarket: The Currency Is Complex," 33 *Am. J. Pol. Sci.* 1 [1989]; Larry Sabato, "Real and Imagined Corruption in Campaign Financing," in *Elections American Style*, 159–62 [a. James Reichley ed., 1987]; cf. W. P. Welch, "Campaign Contributions and Legislative Voting: Milk Money and Dairy Price Supports," 35 *W. Pol. Q.* 478, 479 [1982]). ("The influence of contributions is 'small,' at least relative to the influences of constituency, party, and ideology.")

[4] Smith, supra note 2, at 1068.

[5] Id. at 1068–89.

[6] Daniel H. Lowenstein, "On Campaign Finance Reform: The Root of All Evil Is Deeply Rooted," 18 *Hofstra L. Rev.* 301, 313–22 (1989) (arguing that such studies are deeply flawed).

are difficult to disentangle should warn us against distorting our vigorous democratic system in pursuit of a debatable goal.

A congressman from North Carolina, for example, would probably be a strong proponent of the tobacco industry and, accordingly, would likely favor a bill that is being pushed heavily by the tobacco lobby. To suggest that he voted in such a way because he may have received a contribution from Philip Morris would be erroneous. It would be equally inaccurate to suggest that a congressman from New York City was voting against the bill simply because he never received such a contribution. Both members of Congress would likely take into consideration their party's reaction, their personal feelings about the bill, as well as the reaction of their constituents, long before they thought about any PAC money that might be changing hands. Legislators clearly will not accept a campaign contribution in exchange for a vote that would anger their voters.

When considering the possible effect that contributions have upon votes, it is also important to remember that people who are drawn to public office usually have clear and established views on most major issues. Contributions are not going to convince an elected official to sacrifice those core beliefs.

If campaign contributions are truly to have a sinister effect upon votes, such activity would be directed toward specialized issues that do not normally arouse much public interest.[7] On these narrow issues, prior contributions may indeed provide the donor with access to legislators or their staffs. But such instances are not commonplace, and before we distort our democratic system we should consider whether they can be addressed through meaningful disclosure requirements as well as legitimate enforcement mechanisms.

Rather than elevating the elimination of undue influence by contributors to the highest level of concern, we believe the Commission should have given greater weight to some of its other goals—particularly political participation, voter information, competitive elections, ameliorating the burdens of fundraising, and effective enforcement and administration. In addition, the Commission should have given greater weight to values outside its explicit goals, including the values of free expression and the preservation of a vigorous political-party system.

---

[7] Smith, supra, note 2 at 1070.

Political participation. Despite all the discussion in the media about soft money and individual maxing out, the parties and candidates still raise most of their funds in small contributions from individuals, and these contributions represent an important form of political participation and commitment. We are concerned, as we discuss below, that this aspect of political participation will be stifled by the availability of public financing dollars.

Voter information. The amount of information available to voters is a direct function of the amount of money available to candidates and parties, and for this reason we are reluctant to set limits on campaign expenditures. Such a limit is an inherent element of a public campaign finance system and is included in the system adopted by the majority of the Commission. As discussed more fully below, we believe that a limit on campaign expenditures under a public finance system will reduce the amount of information available to voters and ultimately benefit incumbents.

Competitive elections. Thus, despite the Commission majority's belief that a public finance system will promote competitive elections, we are concerned that it will diminish competitiveness by enabling incumbents to manipulate the system, by enabling the majority parties to freeze out minority parties, by limiting the funds available to challengers, and by imposing an overall limit on expenditure to inform and engage the public.

Reducing the burdens of fundraising. Although a public financing system clearly reduces the burdens of fundraising, as we suggest above its cost is very high in terms of the Commission's other goals of political participation, voter information, and competitive elections. As we discuss below, there are other ways to reduce the burdens of fundraising for candidates and officeholders without creating a system of direct government support for campaigns.

Enforcement and administration. The Commission paid relatively little attention to the problems of enforcement of the campaign finance laws that were thrown into sharp relief by the depredations of the 1996 campaign. We do not believe that limitations on soft money and the establishment of a publicly funded campaign finance system—coupled with the Commission majority's proposed changes in the Federal Election Commission (FEC)—are sufficient to address this problem. In the most general sense, the country's leaders—those charged with enforcement of the laws—manipulated the system and justified their actions as necessary to secure their re-election. This is a very dangerous precedent, especially when—under the Commission's proposal—the entire campaign finance system could one day be in the hands of similarly unscrupulous officeholders. We have proposed what we believe is a better way to ensure enforcement of the campaign finance laws.

Having said all this, there are elements of this Report that we fully support, particularly its recommendations for (i) an increase in the permissible amount of individual contributions to candidates; (ii) an increase in the amount individuals may contribute to the political parties; (iii) the adjustment of these limits for inflation; (iv) the increase in permissible party contributions to candidates; and (v) in the context of the increase in permissible contributions to parties, the regulation of soft money contributions to political parties.

The Report also provides certain public benefits, such as one free mailing to all eligible voters by all ballot-qualified candidates, a simple and equitable reform that will help expand political participation and opportunity. Indeed, recommending more than one free mailing would have been even better.

These recommendations will, we believe, advance the goals of making adequate funds available for political campaigns—thereby contributing to a more informed electorate—and reducing the fundraising burden on lawmakers. It also enhances the likelihood that challengers—either directly or through contributions from their political parties—will be able to raise the necessary funds to overcome the inherent advantages of incumbents, thus contributing to more competitive races.

However, we have a rather long list of objections to the recommendations in the Report. Some of these refer to matters or recommendations to which we believe the Commission did not give sufficient attention or consideration; others refer to limitations the Commission placed on recommendations with which we, on the whole, agree. Our concerns about public financing of campaigns, the Commission's efforts to control independent expenditures by groups or issue advertising by parties, and the enforcement mechanism the Commission ultimately devised are treated separately and more extensively below.

II. General Concerns

Immediate and Full Disclosure

The Commission did not seriously consider the advantages of a system of immediate disclosure as a way of addressing the supposed problem of corruption arising from hard money contributions by individuals or political action committees (PACs). As noted above, we believe the Commission's concern about corruption or the appearance of corruption was somewhat exaggerated, and that in large part accounts for its apparent view that immediate disclosure would be an insufficient reform. However, we believe that—especially in the age of the Internet—immediate and full disclosure of contributions and contributor affiliations will allow the question of excessive influence or corruption to be settled in the most appropriate forum—the voting booth.

Tax Deductions and Credits

The Commission's most controversial recommendation is a public financing system for congressional and Senate campaigns. It should be controversial, for the reasons outlined in our extended discussion below. However, there was an alternative to public financing that the Commission did not fully consider—a system of tax deductions and credits that would encourage large and small individual contributions to political campaigns. In both cases, the public would be paying for election campaigns, but a system of tax deductions and credits would mean that these contributions would be in an important sense voluntary.

To be sure, the Commission considered and ultimately rejected the idea of a system of tax deductions and credits, but for very small contributions. This, we believe, was a mistake. In the Internet era, as Senator McCain has demonstrated, it could be relatively easy for candidates to raise large amounts of campaign funding over the Internet, through large numbers of small contributions. The Report shows no awareness of this possibility. Encouraging small contributions through tax deductions and credits would have been a major step forward in campaign finance reform; it would encourage political participation in a significant way and substantially ameliorate the fundraising burden for candidates.

But the Commission also made a mistake in not considering a system of tax deductions and credits for contributions—of at least the size the Commission has now authorized for individuals—in lieu of its public financing proposal.

Many taxpayers will be seriously distressed by the sight of the government contributing to—indeed supporting—the political campaigns of candidates they abhor. Ultimately, as we discuss more fully below, that distress will be translated into restrictions that will impair the financing of minority views. This result will not be so likely if campaigns were to be supported by individual contributions for which the contributors get a full or partial tax deduction or credit.

Such a system would also be superior to the Commission's public-finance proposal in the following ways: (i) it will continue the voluntary and individual-based contribution system we have today, promoting commitment and political involvement by individuals; (ii) it will provide some degree of public support for campaign finance without the unfortunate need to impose a ceiling on expenditures or put the government in a position to control the flow of campaign funds; and (iii) it will significantly reduce the effort that candidates would have to make in order to obtain financing for their campaigns.

The Role of Parties

The Commission has proposed a significant expansion of the amount that an individual can contribute to a political party, and the amount that a party can in turn contribute to its candidates. In exchange, the Commission has proposed the elimination of soft money contributions to the political parties. As outlined below, we do not agree with the Commission's effort to restrict soft money contributions to parties insofar as these contributions are to be used solely for issue advertising or party building. Nor do we agree with the Commission's restriction on the amount of their hard money contributions that political parties could contribute to their candidates.

The Commission had an opportunity in this Report to structure its recommendations so that more campaign finance would be funneled through parties. The benefits of this would be considerable in our political system. For most of the last century, political scientists have remarked the decline of the two political parties in the United States. The consequences of this decline are visible all around us today—

particularly the voting public's difficulty in determining what a candidate stands for, or in holding anyone or any group accountable when promises are not kept or policies fail.

The phenomenon of legislative gridlock—so frequently noted in the media—should not be surprising when the ability of the parties to mediate differences among contending groups in order to gain or retain power has been largely eviscerated. A likely reason for the decline of the parties is the structure of the current campaign finance laws, which emphasize contributions to individual candidates and limit the intermediation of parties. As a result, candidates—although they bear party labels—are independent of the parties, in elections as well as in their official actions. Without having to consider the broader interests of their respective parties, lawmakers have a strong incentive to hold to a position that will advance their own re-election prospects rather than vote for a compromise that will produce necessary legislation. This is the very definition of gridlock.

Although the Commission expanded the amount that individuals may contribute to political parties—a step that we approve—it maintained limitations (although higher ones) on contributions by the parties to the campaigns of their candidates. There is no obvious policy basis for this restriction. Even within the terms of the Commission's own objectives—to limit the likelihood of corruption or excessive influence—allowing parties to contribute as much as they can to the campaigns of their candidates would have made sense. At the very least, contributions to parties tend to attenuate the supposed undue influence of large individual or PAC contributions.

But permitting unlimited contributions by parties to their candidates would have significant additional benefits, some of which were among the stated objectives of the Commission: (i) it would ameliorate the burdens of fundraising by candidates and officeholders; the parties would do this for them, much more efficiently, with permanent staffs, and from a far broader base of contributors; (ii) parties would use their funds efficiently, funneling money to campaigns where the party's candidates have the best chance of winning, thus enhancing the competitiveness of campaigns (another goal of the Commission) and solving the problem of incumbents having a surfeit of campaign money while challengers are starving for funds; and (iii) it would permit political parties to intermediate among interest groups and regional interests, reducing the gridlock that has made it so difficult over the last quarter century to achieve necessary reforms through legislation.

III. The Commission's Public Financing Proposal

We cannot support the Commission's public financing proposal, or indeed any public financing proposal in which the Treasury is the sole source of funds and the government itself is the only paymaster.

Our opposition is based on concern about what a public financing system might become, combined with a view that it is not necessary to achieve the purposes for which it was proposed. We have already noted our skepticism about the need for public financing as a mechanism for addressing the undue influence or corruption that is alleged to arise from the current system of individual contributions. Indeed, the Commission majority itself must believe that a private financing system can be structured in such a way as to avoid undue influence, since the Commission has proposed just such a private financing system for candidates who do not accept public financing of their campaigns.

Moreover, even if undue influence were the result of a private system of campaign finance, there is no reason to believe that it would be eliminated by a system of public finance. Under the Commission's public finance system, and indeed under any conceivable public finance system, there must be a limit on the amount that can be spent on a publicly financed campaign. This means that influence by individual donors and PACs could be replaced by the influence of groups that have large amounts of money to spend for and against candidates—including labor unions, business groups, and single issue advocacy organizations. In addition, the voice of the media will be significantly enhanced, since candidates will not have the funds to contradict false reports in the news and editorial pages. This is also undue influence, since it will affect the election prospects of candidates, and hence their voting behavior.

Finally, we do not believe that a public financing system will achieve the Commission's stated goal of reducing the influence of money on the political process. Funds used in political campaigns are only part of the moneys raised and spent under the auspices of political figures. Many officeholders, for example, have created their own political action committees or even Section 501(c)(3) nonprofit corporations that study and debate public policy, for which they actively raise funds and which play an active role in the political process.

If the Commission believes that lawmakers can be influenced by campaign contributions to give access or political favors to campaign contributors, then donations to lawmakers' controlled PACs or favored charities or community groups should also be restricted. The point here is that a public finance system—for all the problems it creates for our political system—can accomplish very little of what the Commission majority hopes to achieve.

In other words, the mere fact that wealthy individuals and PACs are no longer contributing to campaigns obviously does not mean that only the voters will be exerting influence on candidates and lawmakers. In fact, a system of public finance may effectively disarm candidates in their efforts to overcome or correct inaccurate information about them. So public financing might not achieve, indeed we believe is unlikely to achieve, the very purpose for which it has been advanced by the Commission—the curbing of undue influence on candidates and lawmakers.

Moreover, by structuring a private system of campaign finance that will not, in its view, give rise to undue influence or alleged corruption, the Commission majority has further reduced the policy reasons for using public funds to finance campaigns. If a system of private finance is possible, the burden on the Commission majority to demonstrate why a public financing system is necessary is correspondingly greater. We do not think this burden can be met by any system of public finance, and was not met by the Commission in this Report, for the following reasons:

1. *Manipulation by and for incumbents.* One serious flaw of any system of public campaign finance administered by the government is its susceptibility to manipulation by and for incumbents. There is probably no way to prevent this, and the Commission makes no substantial effort to do so. Manipulation by and for incumbents can occur in two ways: (i) by enhancing the natural advantages of incumbents without a corresponding increase in the funding available to challengers, and (ii) by making it difficult for challengers to obtain the funding to which they should be entitled.

That incumbents have natural advantages is clear. Incumbent

members of Congress have staffs paid for by the federal government, many of whom "moonlight" on their employer's campaigns[8] or can transfer to the campaign payroll at the moment most convenient for the incumbent. A challenger must find campaign staff where he or she can, frequently employing them before they are necessary so as to assure their availability when the campaign begins.

Members of Congress receive full salaries for the time they spend campaigning, while nonincumbents are required to take unpaid leaves of absence from their jobs or campaign part-time, a huge disadvantage to anyone who is not independently wealthy or already an elected official.

Incumbents mail newsletters to their constituents that strongly resemble campaign literature and can schedule official engagements (for which they travel at the expense of the federal government) to parallel campaign events.[9]

More fundamentally, however, incumbents have an advantage in creating news simply by virtue of holding office. We believe that if any ceiling is to be placed on expenditures it should be accompanied by measures that deflate the advantages of incumbency.

A system of public finance does nothing to overcome these advantages. To be sure, it increases the likelihood that challengers will have sufficient funds—if they can gain access to them—to put on a credible campaign, but there is no way to prevent incumbents from increasing their own inherent advantages without correspondingly increasing the funds available to challengers. Larger appropriations for staff, in Washington and in district or state offices, and larger

---

[8] Prior to 1993, such conduct was illegal under the Hatch Act: *The New York Times* (July 21, 1993):A8, (Aug. 26, 1993):A20. The potential for abuse is enormous. In a 1996 New York State legislative primary, "more than 100 [public employee volunteers] were bussed from Albany" to assist one of the campaigns: *New York Post* (Sept. 16, 1996):7.

[9] One example, that of the current campaign for the U.S. Senate in New York, demonstrates the extent of this advantage as well as the limitations on the current and proposed laws relating to campaign finance. Throughout the fall of 1999, the mayor of New York City and the First Lady of the United States—neither of whom was a declared candidate—traveled throughout the state and elsewhere ostensibly on official business while engaging in what was universally recognized in the press as campaign activities. For example, *The New York Times* (Sept. 1, 1999):B5. Although the conduct of both individuals may have been entirely legal, the situation demonstrates the ability of officeholders to take advantage of the present system and the need for any credible public finance system to offset these advantages.

budgets for constituent service and communication are two likely vehicles for this purpose.

2. *Misuse by the government.* Another and more troubling aspect of a public funding system's susceptibility to manipulation is the possibility that it will be misused by an administration in power to perpetuate itself and its supporters in office. In the 1996 campaign, by common agreement, the administration in power stretched the existing campaign finance laws to their very limits—if not beyond—and justified its actions by citing the superior fundraising success of the opposition. It is not far from this position to manipulating a government financing system in order to keep the opposition from gaining power.

The fact that the Justice Department has done little to prosecute offenses in this scandal, despite scores of participants fleeing the country or taking the Fifth Amendment, reminds us that there are worse and more dangerous forms of corruption than the undue influence that may accompany campaign contributions from wealthy individuals. The 1996 experience leaves us with deep skepticism that the government can be trusted to administer a system of public funding of campaigns without manipulating it for its own purposes.

3. *Freezing out minority parties.* The only real check on an effort by the administration in power to manipulate the campaign financing system for its own benefit is the existence of a large party that is currently out of power. However, both political parties have incentives to prevent the success of new minority parties, and in that case it is unlikely that any significant force will be brought to bear to prevent the stifling of minority-party growth through manipulation of the public financing system.

This process will, regrettably, be aided by the fact that many minority parties will be unpopular with the majority population, and acting to deprive them of campaign funds—it will be taxpayers' money, after all—will be politically popular. The standards established in such a case will be available in later cases to deprive the candidates of less offensive minority parties of the campaign funds that could give them a voice in the political process.

4. *Withering of the private campaign finance system.* Proponents of the Commission's approach will no doubt argue that the continued existence of a private campaign finance system—as proposed and enhanced in the Commission's Report—will always permit minority

parties and challengers to incumbents to obtain the necessary financing for campaigns, even if the public system is manipulated to the benefit of the two parties, the administration in power, or incumbents generally.

However, this is not necessarily the case. A private campaign finance system cannot be established at will, whenever necessary. Like any other system, it is a network of participants, many—perhaps most—of whom participate because they know that (i) it is their duty as citizens, or (ii) there is no other source of campaign funds for the candidates they prefer or with which to defeat the candidates they oppose.

The tone of most fundraising letters reflects this. They are frequently based not on the qualities of the candidate for whom support is solicited but on the dangers of allowing the opposition candidate to gain power. Once it becomes clear that public financing is available from the government—both for the primary and the general election—the incentives to contribute funds to candidates will decline. Where an incumbent is accepting public funds for his or her campaign, a challenger will have a difficult time explaining why he or she needs private support. The incumbent will be limited in the amount he or she can spend, so the challenger can't argue that a large war chest is essential. The parties will not be able to raise funds for support of their candidates, since the public will be aware that there is government money available for the parties' candidates.

Once the private financing system falls into general disuse, it will be difficult to reconstruct. The names of regular contributors will not be current, the skills and contacts of fund solicitors will be lost. We will be forced back to wealthy individuals using their own money in support of their campaigns as the only way to keep a public finance system honest.

5. *Limits on expenditure.* The public financing system proposed by the Commission entails expenditure limits for both House and Senate races. The Commission believes these limits are at levels that will permit strong races by both incumbents and challengers. However, any spending limits are by their nature limits on the amount of information the public receives. In some cases, the ceilings will be adequate to inform the public, in others they will not be. Every district and state is different, as is every contest for office, and we are reluctant to establish any level as adequate for all contests.

Moreover, there is a sense in which the Commission majority believes that campaigns are too expensive, and that a public financing system will have the salutary result of placing a reasonable lid on the constant growth of campaign costs. We do not favor this constant growth, and we can agree that in some cases campaign spending has grown beyond the bounds of what most people would consider reasonable. However, we believe that there is greater danger in limiting campaign spending than in allowing it to continue to grow to its natural limits, whatever they are.

For one thing, limits on spending favor incumbents, for the reasons outlined above; for another, they almost inevitably mean that in some cases—perhaps many cases—the public will not be adequately informed or drawn into the process by the spending of the candidates. Finally, and perhaps equally important, limitations on spending by the candidates themselves will foster independent spending by interest groups. While this may have the salutary effect of educating the public in the issues, the fact that this spending is not under the control of the candidates will make it very difficult for the public to separate truth from fiction or to place blame for false statements. Outside, independent spending will also benefit incumbents, who are in the best position to obtain this kind of voluntary, independent support from organized groups.

While the $1 million figure for House races seems adequate, and is slightly below the level of spending by winning challengers in recent House elections, it can and probably will be dwarfed by independent spending that is clearly constitutionally protected. The AFL-CIO, for example, has recently pledged to spend $40 million to defeat (presumably mostly Republican) candidates in 70 key House races—an average of almost $600,000 per race.[10] Candidates who are subject to a limit on their spending because they have elected to receive public funds will be swamped by independent expenditures of this kind, yet there is no question that these expenditures are constitutionally protected.

In such a situation, an approach involving floors without ceilings, one that would provide widely available public benefits without overall ceilings, would help the challenger much more than a limit that ties the challenger to the incumbent and provides no way to counter a vigorous interest group or media attacks.

---

[10] *Washington Post* (Feb. 16, 2000):A14.

The Report recognizes this problem, providing that the limits are lifted if a publicly funded candidate is running against a privately funded candidate who will be spending more than the limit. But how to determine whether this is happening will be fruitful grounds for dispute and even litigation (the Report suggests that the ceiling be raised or eliminated when a privately financed opponent has raised substantial percentages of the ceiling), and it is doubtful that a challenger—or perhaps even an incumbent—would be able to raise significant private funding on short notice in the middle of a campaign.

6. *The effect on parties.* The limits-driven public funding scheme proposed by the Commission also compels it to propose unprecedented and unfortunate limits on party activity and issue advocacy in order to try to shore up its candidate campaign limits. The publicly funded candidate would have to agree that any supportive independent party spending, which again is constitutionally protected, could nonetheless be counted against the candidate's limit. Not only does this presume, contrary to law and fact, that parties and their candidates always have an identity of interests, but it requires candidates to cede their speech rights to others in exchange for public funding.

Efforts to deem one person's advocacy to be on another person's behalf have been consistently invalidated.[11] Even parties should not be allowed to put words in the mouths of their candidates. Likewise, the Supreme Court has rejected the idea that protecting public funding ceilings can justify restraining independent advocacy beneficial to a publicly funded candidate.[12]

Public Funding Issues Not Addressed by the Commission

A system of public financing can itself be manipulated, and the Commission's report leaves a number of loopholes. Because the entire theory of public financing for political campaigns is to provide campaigns with the funds necessary for the contest at hand, any publicly financed campaign that has a surplus at the end of the election cycle

---

[11] See *Colorado Republican Federal Campaign Committee v. FEC*, 518 U.S. 604 (1996); *Republican Party of Minnesota v. Pauly*, 63 F.Supp. 2d 1008 (D. Minn. 1999); see also *United States v. National Committee for Impeachment*, 469 F. 2d 1135 (2d Cir. 1972); *American Civil Liberties Union v. Jennings*, 366 F. Supp. 1041 (D.D.C. 1973), vacated as moot, sub.nom.; *Staats v. American Civil Liberties Union* (1975).

[12] See *FEC v. National Conservative PAC*, 470 U.S. 480 (1985).

should return that surplus to the government. There is no reason to permit the use of public financing to accumulate war chests for future campaigns (including campaigns for higher office or campaigns that do not participate in the public-financing process), and that result would again provide additional advantages to incumbent office-holders.

By the same reasoning, publicly financed campaigns should not be permitted to make contributions to other political committees or campaigns. Absent such a restriction, one campaign that did not face a competitive challenge could accept public financing and channel it to other campaigns, in disregard of the basic premise that the purpose of public funding is to support the campaigns that receive it.

In "Towards a Level Playing Field—A Pragmatic Approach to Public Campaign Financing," 52 *Record* 660 (Oct. 1997), the Association recommended a public campaign financing system in New York State using block grants in amounts designed to offer campaigns an opportunity to become competitive, which would then be refundable after a participating campaign had raised enough funds to wage a competitive campaign.

This approach is preferable to the matching-funds approach followed by the Commission for two reasons. First, it does not place a premium on the services of "bundlers" of campaign contributions, whose services would, under the Commission's public funding proposal, be matched two for one up to the first $250 of each contribution "bundled." If there is undue influence under the current system, the "bundler" may have it more effectively than the contributor, and the Commission's proposal would only enhance that influence.[13] Second, a system of block grants as proposed in "Towards a Level Playing Field" would not continue to subsidize campaigns that do not need help.

IV. Free Speech and Political Campaigns

One of the remarkable things about many of the proposals for campaign finance reform is their limited regard for the First Amendment

---

[13] The identity and amount raised by "bundlers" is rarely required to be disclosed under current law, and it would be difficult if not impossible to draft a rigorous disclosure requirement that would not place an impossible burden on campaign treasurers trying to comply with the law.

value of free speech. One would suppose that in a democracy—especially a successful constitutional democracy such as our own, where free expression is guaranteed by the Constitution and valued by the public—the proponents of reform would pay somewhat more attention to the free speech values their proposals would impair.

This should be especially true in the context of elections. If individuals and corporations have the right to publish salacious material on the Internet for their own profit and the titillation of children of all ages, one would suppose that anyone should have the unrestricted right to communicate with the American people about how to exercise their votes. It should be obvious that the core value of free speech is its contribution to a public's understanding of what is at stake in an election. Regrettably, we believe that the Commission majority has also succumbed—apparently in the interest of achieving a reduction in the purported influence of money on political candidates—to a slighting of this basic element of our democracy.

Thus, in order properly to assess the Commission's recommendations, it is appropriate to outline the first principles that are pertinent to any proposal for government regulation of campaign finance. In the leading case of *Buckley v. Valeo*,[14] the Supreme Court reminded us of why any campaign funding restrictions must be subject to the closest examination: "[c]ontribution and expenditure limitations operate in an area of the most fundamental First Amendment activities. Discussion of public issues and debate on the qualifications of candidates are integral to the system of government established by our Constitution."[15]

Restrictions on the funding of such discussion and debate constitute direct and gross restraints on that liberty. As the Court put it: "[a] restriction on the amount of money a person or group can spend on political communication during a campaign necessarily reduces the quantity of expression by restricting the number of issues discussed, the depth of their exploration and the size of the audience reached."[16] Or, more pointedly, "[b]eing free to engage in unlimited political expression subject to a ceiling on expenditures is like being free to drive an automobile as far and as often as one desires on a

---

[14] 424 U.S. 1 (1976).
[15] 424 U.S. at 14.
[16] Id. at 17.

single tank of gas."[17] For these reasons, the principles and the public policies embodied in the First Amendment require that all proposals to restrict the funding of core political speech and association be given the most rigorous scrutiny.

In this respect, we find the Report's recommendations deficient. They would, in our view, impose unprecedented restraints on the political funding and advocacy of candidates, parties, and issue groups. The proposals, we fear, would weaken political parties and undermine issue advocacy organizations. Implementation of those proposals would require the kind of command-and-control bureaucratic mechanism that would be fundamentally antithetical to the system of freedom of speech and association in the political realm.

1. Contribution Limits

The Report offers hard money fundraising benefits to candidates and parties that are certainly more generous than many reformers would advocate. We support these increases but feel compelled to point out that they do no more than keep pace with the inflation that has occurred since the original limits were enacted a quarter century ago. And the price of this rectification for parties is a total abolition of soft money to fund a wide variety of laudable party-building activities far removed from corruption of federal elections. The Report also reduces the relative role of PACs, which can be important sources of group advocacy and political support across the political and economic spectrum. While we support the raising of the hard money limits to facilitate campaign and party fundraising, we oppose the relative downgrading of the advocacy and political participation of PACs, and we dissent from the proposal to outlaw all soft money political party activities.

2. Independent Party Spending

We are concerned by the Commission's proposal that would automatically deem all party spending in support of a party's candidate as coordinated with the candidate. For the government-funded candidate, it would have the limiting consequence described in our discus-

---

[17] Id. at 19n.18.

sion of the Commission's public finance proposal above. For the privately funded candidate, the rule seems both unnecessary and unconstitutional. It is unnecessary because, with soft money gone, and parties allowed to spend only hard money, there seems no reason not to let a party spend as much as it wants independently in support of a privately funded candidate.

The automatic presumption of coordination between a party and its candidate in order to limit the party's honestly independent expenditure is inconsistent with *Colorado Republican,* where the plurality opinion stated: "[s]imply calling an independent expenditure a coordinated expenditure cannot (for constitutional purposes) make it one."[18] Even independent party expenditures made after a candidate has become the party's nominee and made in consultation with the party cannot be conclusively presumed to be coordinated without violating the First Amendment.[19] Nor can express advocacy expenditures made by independent groups be presumed to be coordinated with the candidate supported if they are not disavowed within 72 hours.[20]

3. Soft Money

To try to protect limits-driven public funding, and to safeguard against claimed corruption, the Report recommends a total ban on all fundraising by national political parties that does not conform to the rigid contribution and source limitations and requirements of FECA. To be sure, the Report sweetens the deal by raising the limits on individual hard money contributions to parties up to $75,000. But that barely keeps up with the inflation since the enactment of FECA in 1974, and the soft money ban will still appear to be a poison pill to those political leaders who view party soft money funding as essential to the strength and vitality of political parties.

The health of our parties should be a major concern of any campaign finance reform. Yet the Report, in its concern with 1996 campaign excesses in the soft money area, would prescribe a cure that is far worse than the malady and, indeed, is overkill.

---

[18] 518 U.S. at 621.

[19] See *Republican Party of Minnesota v. Pauly,* 63 F.Supp. 2d 1008 (D. Minn. 1999).

[20] *Iowa Right to Life Committee v. Williams,* 187 F. 3d 963 (8th Cir. 1999).

It must be remembered that soft money activities by political parties are those that do not involve direct and express electoral support for federal political candidates, even though the activities may exert an influence on the outcome of an election in the broadest sense of that term. Parties are surely advocates for their candidate's electoral success, but they are also issue organizations that influence the public debate. Get-out-the-vote drives, voter-registration drives, issue advocacy, policy discussion, grassroots development, and the like are all activities fundamentally protected by the First Amendment and engaged in by a wide variety of individuals and organizations. An issue ad by the ACLU is as much an example of soft money activity as an editorial in *The New York Times*. We need more of such activity during an election season, not less, from parties and from all others as well.

The right of individuals and organizations, corporate and otherwise, to engage in such issue advocacy traces back to the holding of *Buckley v. Valeo* that the only kind of independent political expenditures that could validly be subject to federal control were those that expressly advocated the election or defeat of identified federal political candidates. All other expenditures were totally beyond governmental control: "[s]o long as persons and groups eschew expenditures that in express terms advocate the election or defeat of a clearly identified candidate, they are free to spend as much as they want to promote the candidate and his views."[21] That is why such activity like issue advocacy and voter mobilization can be funded from sources that would be restricted in making federal political contributions and expenditures.

Twenty years later, in the *Colorado Republican* case, the Supreme Court recognized the legitimacy of soft money funding of political parties:

> [w]e also recognize that FECA permits unregulated "soft money" contributions to a party for certain activities, such as electing candidates for state office . . . or for voter registration and get out the vote drives. . . . But the opportunity for corruption posed by these greater opportunities for contributions is, at best, attenuated. Unregulated "soft money" contributions may not be used to influence a federal campaign,

---

[21] *Buckley,* 424 U.S. at 46.

except when used in the limited, party-building activities specifically designated by statute.[22]

And even in its recent regrettable decision upholding a $1075 limit on contributions made directly to candidates, the Court's opinion was silent on the whether soft money could be similarly regulated, although individual justices discussed whether Congress had the power to do so.[23]

To be sure, to the extent soft money funds issue advocacy and political activities by political parties, it becomes something of a hybrid: it supports protected and unregulatable issue speech and activities, but by party organizations closely tied to candidates and officeholders. Despite the fact that there is an attenuated relationship linking party contributors through the party committees to the party candidates, the structural relationship between political parties and political officials might permit greater regulatory flexibility than would be true with respect to issue advocacy and activity of other organizations.

Thus, for example, disclosure of soft money contributions to political parties, as is currently required, might be acceptable, even though it would be impermissible if imposed on nonparty issue organizations. A limitation on the amount of soft money parties could receive might be prudent. A restriction on coordination of soft money–funded issue advertisements between the party and its candidates or officeholders might be permissible as well. But the Report's approach of a total ban on all soft money activity by political parties is a substantially overbroad response to whatever legitimate concerns of corruption may be posed by large soft money contributions to major parties.

Lastly, there is also an Equal Protection issue in the Report's recommended ban on the raising or spending of soft money by parties. As proposed by the Commission, anyone else—corporations, foundations, media organizations, labor unions, bar associations, wealthy individuals—could use their resources without limit to attack a party and its programs and even its candidates, but the party would unable to respond except by using limited hard money dollars. A regulatory regime that lets one side of a debate speak while silencing the other poses both First Amendment and Equal Protection problems.

---

[22] *Colorado Republican,* 518 U.S. at 616.
[23] See *Nixon v. Shrink Missouri Government PAC,* 120 S.Ct. 897 (2000).

In our view, reasonable regulation, rather than flat prohibition, of soft money funding by political parties is the more appropriate and measured response to the current situation.

4. Issue Advocacy

The Report's partial and flawed answer to the equality issue is to broaden the Act's coverage to regulate and restrict issue groups as well. It is here that the Commission's recommendations stray furthest from constitutional acceptability or sound policy.

The Report proposes to outlaw the use of soft money by political parties and to mandate that the funding of issue advocacy by other organizations be done wholly under the rigors and restrictions of FECA—in effect, federalizing political speech. Those stringent FECA restrictions on the funding of political speech would apply to all persons, groups, and organizations—except for the organized news media (whatever that is)—that engage in the new and dramatically expanded definition of express advocacy. The FECA regime would impose the following restrictions on the funding of issue advocacy:

(1) It can only be subsidized by hard money.
(2) It cannot be pursued by any corporation (except, perhaps, a purely ideological and ad hoc one), labor union, foundation, or charitable or educational institution.
(3) It cannot be supported by funds from any corporation, labor union, foundation, charitable institution, or educational institution.
(4) It must be fully disclosed to the Federal Election Commission.
(5) The organizational PAC-creating strictures of FECA must be complied with.
(6) No one person can contribute more than the relevant hard money contribution limits to supporting that activity.

The Report would apply all of those restraints to three situations that are not subject to such controls under the current law.

First, the Report would declare that any issue advocacy coordinated with a campaign, ipso facto, is express advocacy subject to regulation, regardless of its content. This Alice-in-Wonderland fiat ignores the fact that coordination can span a spectrum from President Clinton's apparent editing of the text of DNC anti-Republican television ads to the ACLU's determining a candidate's stand on abortion in order to prepare a voter's guide. Courts have indicated that just because an issue organization discusses matters with a candidate does not by alchemy transmute the subsequent speech of the issue group into either express advocacy or a coordinated expenditure.[24]

Like the Report's proposed total ban on all party soft money, the presumption here is not carefully tailored as restrictions in the First Amendment area must be. And it could wreak havoc on issue organizations that communicate with candidates and campaigns in order better to engage in public discussion of issues of concern to them.

Second, the Report would treat as express advocacy any party communication that "mentions by name or includes the likeness of a clearly identified" federal candidate. Since we believe that even "express advocacy" by parties, in the form of independent party expenditures, should be permitted if they are in fact independent, the case of party issue discussions is even easier and the case for blanket automatic regulation even harder to sustain.

Finally, the Report mandates treating as express advocacy, and therefore subject to all of the FECA controls outlined above, "any communication that is broadcast, printed, mailed, or distributed within thirty days before a primary or general election that includes the name or likeness of any clearly identified candidate for federal office." This is an unprecedented redefinition of the established constitutional concept of express advocacy. By expanding and shifting the boundary line, it would subject to regulation precisely the kind of issue advocacy that the courts have consistently held immune from government regulation.

In addition, although the redefinition has a "temporal" limitation of 30 days before a general or primary election, it has no monetary floor or threshold, which means that, literally, it applies to the first dollar spent on any covered communication that "includes the name or likeness" of any federal candidate. Read literally, the language would subject to FECA control every high school civics class project for which the students prepare reports on the positions of the opposing presidential candidates and the teacher uses personal or school funds to distribute them to the rest of the class.

At a more serious level, the proposal would subject to FECA con-

---

[24] See *FEC v. Christian Coalition*, 52 F. Supp. 2d. 45 (D. D.C. 1999); *Iowa Right to Life Committee v. Williams*, supra.

trols all organized group discussion or communication of any political or policy issue that mentions the name of a candidate. If the NYCLU wants to run an ad criticizing New York Mayor Rudolph Giuliani on the issue of police conduct in October, when he's running for the U.S. Senate, it would either have to form a PAC, subject to all the relevant controls and restrictions—which its charter prohibits—or be silent. If an issue organization in corporate form, such as Planned Parenthood, were to send a mailing to its members urging them to write to a named senator, the organization would be committing a crime if that senator happened to be up for re-election; under the Commission's proposal, corporations would be banned from engaging in such redefined "express advocacy."

Since almost every organized issue-advocacy group in America is a corporation, all would effectively be silenced in the month before any primary *or* general election from making any covered communication. During the presidential primary season, that cone of silence barring even mentioning a presidential candidate could cover a six-month period.

Thus, for example, if the NAACP wants to mail out a press release condemning Governor George W. Bush's visit to Bob Jones University, it could do so only if it first formed a PAC, which its nonpartisan and nonprofit status might preclude, and be prepared to publicly disclose the names of its contributors. Likewise, if the Christian Coalition wanted to run an advertisement in *The New York Times* urging the Senate to reject the McCain-Feingold campaign finance bill, that could be considered an illegal corporate expenditure for express advocacy under the Report's proposal if Senator McCain were the Republican nominee for President.

The concern with the asserted increase in the use of so-called or "phony" or "sham" issue ads, which are claimed to be campaign ads in disguise, does not justify the kind of severe impact this proposal would have on suppressing issue advocacy during an election season.

For more than 25 years, the courts have made it clear that issue advocacy that mentions, criticizes, praises, or condemns public officials who happen to be up for election or re-election, even during an election season, cannot for that reason be subject to campaign finance controls. From the Second Circuit's earliest ruling in 1972 in the National Committee for Impeachment[25] case, to the recent Virginia

---

[25] 469 F.2d 1135.

District Court's decision granting a nationwide injunction against the FEC's expanded and flawed redefinition of "express advocacy,"[26] the courts have spoken with almost one voice in holding that campaign finance controls cannot regulate issue advocacy and can only regulate express advocacy, defined in terms of the explicit content of the communication.

The Supreme Court fashioned the constitutional standard in *Buckley* by defining "express advocacy" as "communications that in express terms advocate the election or defeat of a clearly identified candidate for federal office. . . ."[27] We believe the Court defined express advocacy so carefully precisely to avoid the kind of proposal that the Report puts forward, one that would effectively silence issue discussion during an election season: "Discussion of issues and debate on the qualifications of candidates are integral to the operation of the system of government established by our Constitution."[28] "The distinction between discussion of issues and candidates and advocacy of election or defeat of candidates may often dissolve in practical application. Candidates, especially incumbents, are intimately tied to public issues involving legislative proposals and governmental actions. Not only do candidates campaign on the basis of their positions on various public issues, but campaigns themselves generate issues of public interest."[29] Accordingly, the Court reasoned, any rule that controlled all discussion "relative to" a federal candidate would impermissibly and sweepingly control a wide range of vital issue discussion.

The Court was well aware that the express advocacy standard could be manipulated by speakers to skirt controls: "It would naively underestimate the ingenuity and resourcefulness of persons and groups desiring to buy influence to believe that they would have much difficulty devising expenditures that skirted the restriction on express advocacy of election or defeat but nevertheless benefitted the candidate's campaign."[30] Nonetheless, the Court concluded that maintaining the secure express advocacy standard to protect public

---

[26] See *Virginia Society for Human Life, Inc. v. Federal Election Commission*, 2000 U.S. Dist. LEXIS 643 (D. Va. 2000).

[27] 424 U.S. at 45.

[28] Id. at 14.

[29] Id. at 42.

[30] Id. at 46.

discussion of issues was more important than guarding against the risk of such manipulation. Courts have followed suit ever since.[31]

We cannot support a proposal that would restrain citizens and organizations and individuals from discussing candidates and issues they stand for during the 30 days preceding any election, the very time when the need for such public discussion is at its zenith. That would effectively leave the organized press (an ill-defined concept in any event) as the only unrestrained voice on issues and candidates during that critical period. All other speakers would be forced into the regulatory straitjacket of FECA. Such a regime raises severe First Amendment problems since it would regulate the very issue advocacy that, for more than a quarter of a century, has been held categorically immune from government control.

5. Disclosure

We are also concerned that the Report does not address the problem of the extremely broad disclosure of the names of people who donate even relatively modest amounts to a federal candidate, campaign, or organization. Under current law, all contributors of more than $200 must be publicly disclosed to the FEC and the public. We believe that these extremely low disclosure thresholds cut too deeply into the established rights of political anonymity and freedom of association.[32]

Whatever valid information such disclosure might afford in terms of bundling of multiple contributions from the same company or firm, there has been no showing that this is a serious problem at the $200 level. Moreover, since we are recommending a threefold increase in the contribution ceilings, to compensate for inflation, we should recommend a comparable increase in the contribution disclosure floor as well. We would include in the Report a recommendation that the threshold for public disclosure of campaign contributions be raised to those in excess of $500.

---

[31] Finally, we would note that the proposed language, regulating any public communication that "includes the name or likeness" of a federal candidate is directly contrary to the unanimous en banc D.C. Circuit decision in the *Buckley* case declaring unconstitutional a part of FECA that required reporting and disclosure only by any organization that communicates any material "referring to a candidate. . . ." See *Buckley v. Valeo,* 519 F.2d 821, 843–44 (D.C. Cir. 1975).

[32] See *McIntyre v. Ohio Elections Commission,* 514 U.S. 334 (1995).

V. Enforcement

The Commission's proposal does not directly address the conduct that has led to the call for campaign finance reform, which includes allegations of laundered campaign contributions (including contributions from donors who are otherwise barred from making such contributions) and alleged receipt of political favors or "access" to public officials in return for contributions. Most of that conduct violates existing laws, which have simply not been enforced adequately, or in which attempts at enforcement have failed. We believe that any reform of the campaign finance system must address these failures under the existing system head-on and propose the following.

1. *Money Laundering.* The entire system of campaign finance law (both present and under the modifications proposed by the Commission) is predicated on full and accurate disclosure of campaign contributions. The lack of such disclosure—or alternatively the toleration of false or misleading disclosure—nullifies that system. As but one example, a contribution limit is meaningless if a contributor can simply reimburse others for making contributions to a candidate to whom that contributor has already made the maximum contribution.[33] Moreover, the reports filed by the candidate who receives laundered funds would fail to disclose the true amount of the contribution actually made—and thus its true significance.

The difficulties that have been encountered in prosecuting such violations of the current law (such as the successful defense at trial that a contributor did not realize that his concealed donation would mislead the Federal Election Commission),[34] suggest that the existing law should be modified to place contributors and campaigns on notice that contributions as reported must disclose the true donor and amount of the contribution.

Accordingly, we would have the Commission recommend that candidates and campaign treasurers state—under penalty of criminal liability and significant personal civil fines—on every financial report filed with the Federal Election Commission, a statement that (i) they are not aware of any contribution (direct or indirect) required to be disclosed other than as listed on the report; (ii) they are not aware of

---

[33] This practice is alarmingly common. See, for example, *Wall Street Journal* (Mar. 3, 2000):A1, A18; *The New York Times* (Mar. 6, 2000):B1, B5.

[34] *The New York Times* (July 2, 1999):A14.

any contribution listed on the report for which the contributor has or will receive reimbursement from another source; and (iii) they have taken reasonable steps to discover whether any illegal contribution has been made.

The purpose of these certifications is to create a strong incentive for candidates and campaign treasurers to inquire into the sources of the funds they receive. It is not unlike the severe penalties placed on directors and officers of banks and S&Ls if they knowingly file a false report with a bank or S&L regulator.

2. *Law Enforcement.* We doubt that the problems of enforcing the present law or any reform package will be solved simply by reformulating the FEC, as proposed by the Commission. In the first place, even as reformulated, the FEC could be subject to political pressure. In 1994, for example, Trevor Potter, then chairman of the FEC, charged that Congress had cut the federal election fines levied against the campaigns of congressmembers.[35] Whether this was true or not, the possibility of such retaliation can seriously diminish the ardor with which a regulatory commission such as the FEC pursues its responsibilities.

In order to create a majority on the FEC that could take action against a major party or one of its candidates, the Commission has recommended that a seventh member be added to the FEC as its chair, and that this member be unaffiliated with either major party. This is a sensible recommendation as far as it goes but does not address those instances in which neither party wants its circumventions of the law to be interfered with. A better enforcement mechanism is necessary, perhaps arming local U.S. Attorneys with post-election civil as well as criminal prosecution authority to enforce the law— and the FEC's regulations—before the courts.

3. *The Federal Election Commission.* The Report makes a series of recommendations for improving the enforcement capability of the

---

[35] *Wall Street Journal* (Aug. 2, 1994):A14. The New York City Campaign Finance Board has also faced heavy political pressure. During 1993, after a mayoral campaign in which the Board had levied a substantial fine against his reelection campaign, the Mayor in effect ousted the chairman, who had recently received praise for an impartial and strong performance overseeing New York City's public finance program. Public outrage ultimately resulted in the resignation of the Mayor's appointee and the reappointment of the original chairman by the incoming Mayor. *The New York Times* (Oct. 21, 1993):11, 3; (Jan. 6, 1994):A20.

FEC. We have no position on most of those suggestions. However, there are three issues with respect to the FEC that should be noted.

First, the Commission's Report, if enacted into law, would dramatically increase the workload of the FEC. The FEC would have an enormously wider range of new—and, we think, ill-advised—regulatory controls to enforce against candidates, campaigns, political parties, and, now, issue organizations as well. And it would have to administer perhaps a billion dollars worth of public funding involving thousands of federal candidates in primary and general elections. Since almost every action of the FEC has a First Amendment consequence, this enormous expansion of authority must be accompanied by a comparable degree of public scrutiny.

Second, because of the dramatic increase in FEC workload, we are particularly concerned about the Commission's recommendation that the FEC be given the power to go to court during the height of an election season and seek injunctive and enforcement relief against candidates, campaigns, parties, and now issue organizations for alleged violations of FECA. The power to seek such injunctive relief, tantamount to a prior restraint, poses severe First Amendment concerns. Since the FEC is subject to political appointment and congressional oversight by a Congress full of incumbents, and with an enormously expanded workload, we worry about the dangers of selective enforcement in the FEC's determining against which candidates, parties, or organizations to seek pre-election enforcement in court. Will the FEC prosecute suits against incumbent politicians or the major political parties, or will it instead bring politically popular proceedings against troublesome issue organizations, as it has often done in the past? These concerns reaffirm our belief that the granting of pre-election enforcement power to the FEC is fraught with the potential for abuse, and we would oppose it.

Finally, the Report fails to note that there are serious grounds for concern about the pattern of excessive enforcement by the FEC against protected issue advocacy. Over a span of two decades the FEC has been faulted by courts for excessive zeal in enforcing the Act against issue organizations. From the Second Circuit's 1980 ruling in *Federal Election Commission v. Central Long Island Tax Reform Immediately Committee*,[36] through the Fourth Circuit's decision

---

[36] 616 F.2d 45 (2nd Cir. 1980) (en banc).

in *Federal Election Commission v. Christian Action Network, Inc.,*[37] to the recent ruling granting a nationwide injunction against the FEC's expanded unconstitutional definition of express advocacy,[38] the courts have had to step in and protect issue organizations from FEC harassment. The chilling effect of such a pattern on protected issue speech is clear. Our Report should note that pattern and recommend steps to see that it is not repeated for another twenty years.

VI. CONCLUSION

There is much to be applauded in the Commission's Report. But there is much cause for concern. In our view, there are three essential measures that should be the essence of any campaign reforms. First, we should raise the limits on contributions to candidates and parties to enable them to fund their campaigns and get their messages out. Second, we should improve disclosure of the kinds of large contributions to candidates and campaigns that the public should know about when it decides how to cast its votes. Finally, to the extent that any form of public assistance is extended to campaigns, this assistance should not involve government determinations on who should receive it, should not be manipulable to the advantage of incumbents, and should not entail government limitations or controls on expenditure.

To the extent the Commission's Report goes in other directions, we must respectfully dissent.

---

[37] 110 F.3d 1049 (4th Cir. 1997).
[38] See *Virginia Society for Human Life, Inc. v. Federal Election Commission,* supra.

COMMENT OF JEROME S. FORTINSKY

I SUPPORT THE REPORT issued by the Commission on Campaign Finance Reform (the Report). I write separately to highlight three areas where I disagree with the views expressed by the majority.

POLITICAL ACTION COMMITTEES

The Report makes a persuasive case that the contribution limits established by the Federal Election Campaign Act (FECA) nearly 30 years ago are now hopelessly outdated. But the Commission has declined to endorse an increase in the limit on contributions to candidates by political action committees (PACs), even as it has recommended tripling the current limit on contributions to candidates by individuals. I think the Commission, because of its legitimate concern about the uses of fundraising as a means of purchasing political access, has lost sight of the essential role organized groups have historically played, and continue to play, in the American political system. If, as is widely acknowledged, it is time to raise contribution limits generally, then it is also appropriate to raise the limits on contributions by PACs. Although the original ratio between the limits on individuals contributions and the limits on PAC contributions need not be regarded as immutable, the limits should be raised at least approximately in tandem.

Under the system that the Commission would establish, individuals would be able to donate $6000 to each candidate per "election cycle" (that is, in each two-year period, including both the primary and the general election), up from the current limit of $1000 in each of the primary and the general elections. By contrast, PACs would remain subject to the current contribution limit of $5000 to each candidate per election (which permits contributions totaling $10,000 when donations are made for both the primary and general elections). As a result, the Commission is recommending a system in which PACs, which are intended to represent large groups of people acting together on matters of shared concern, would be able to donate less to each candidate than a husband and wife.

Underlying the Commission's recommendation to freeze the ceiling on contributions to PACs at its current level (pending future adjustments for inflation) is its concern about the "primacy of access over ideology in patterns of business PAC giving." I share this concern. But this concern applies to contributions by individuals as well. As the Report acknowledges, what it calls "large individual contributions" account for a larger proportion of the funding for congressional elections than donations by PACs.

Moreover, the well-founded suspicion that business PACs (like many large individual donors) are motivated by a desire for access does not justify reducing the role that organized groups play in the system of campaign finance to less than that of a married couple. As the *Federalist Papers* recognized, and as Alexis de Tocqueville famously observed, organized groups are central to the functioning of American democracy. Organized groups, which in the campaign finance system take the form of PACs (or, as FECA refers to them, "political committees"), are not all nefarious business interests. They are abortion-rights activists and gun owners, supporters of foreign aid and defenders of gay rights, sugar farmers and advocates of public education. To the extent that our system continues to permit nonpublic sources to play a role in financing our elections, citizens should be able to participate not only in their own name but also by banding together as groups dedicated to their favorite cause.

The Report is filled with language about putting individual and PAC donors on a "more level playing field." But the "playing field" analogy is inapposite. Individuals and PACs are not opposing forces competing against each other, like rival football squads or even like Republicans and Democrats. There is no reason to suppose that individuals, who themselves may donate to PACs, are disadvantaged if PACs are subject to a different contribution limit.

In short, I would have preferred to see the Commission recommend an increase in the contribution limits on PACs that parallels the increase recommended for individuals.

FREE MAILINGS

I enthusiastically endorse the Commission's proposal to give each ballot-qualified candidate for federal office one mailing, at federal expense, to the voters in that candidate's constituency. I regret that the Commission did not recommend more than one such mailing.

Providing free mailings to candidates for public office is an extraordinarily efficient way to promote many of the objectives set forth in the Report (and broadly shared by the American public, including both supporters and opponents of campaign finance reform): disseminating information about the candidates, promoting competitive elections, and reducing the burdens of fundraising. In general, the cost of most forms of public assistance for political candidates is approximately the same as the benefit the candidate receives. For each dollar that the candidate receives from the public campaign finance program, the cost to the public treasury is a dollar. But providing free mailings to candidates for public office—in effect, extending to them a limited version of the franking privilege enjoyed by members of Congress for official business—would enable them to save mailing costs far out of proportion to the incremental cost to the U.S. Postal Service of delivering a few additional pieces of mail per person per election year.

One free mailing for each candidate is a good idea. One or two more such mailings, which would enable candidates to use these mailings to engage one another in political debate, would be even better.

PRE-ELECTION ADVOCACY AND ADVERTISING BY NON-CANDIDATES

For the reasons set forth in the statement by the dissenting members of the Commission, I cannot support the Commission's recommendation to treat as "express advocacy," and thus to subject to the reporting requirements and other restrictions of FECA, any "communication broadcast, printed, mailed, or distributed within 30 days before a primary or general election that includes the name or likeness of any clearly identified candidate for federal office." I write separately to object to one aspect of this recommendation that is particularly disturbing.

Acknowledging that this recommendation is likely to be subject to constitutional attack on the grounds (among others) that it would regulate political speech that was not directly related to the upcoming election, the Commission calls on Congress to provide that communications within the 30-day period preceding an election "shall be presumed to be 'express advocacy' but that such presumption may be rebutted on a showing that, based on the content and context of the speech, viewers, listeners, or readers are unlikely to treat it as an election-related communication." As the Report acknowledges, this "rebuttable presumption" would result in considerable uncertainty as to what kinds of communications are permissible during this period. In my view, such uncertainty as to the permissibility of political speech is intolerable, and perhaps unconstitutional. The purpose of law is, in part, to give the public proper notice as to what conduct will be tolerated and what conduct will be punished. The proposed 30-day rule, by itself, is a "bright line" test that does just that; the "rebuttable presumption," however, robs the rule of its clarity and forces the public to guess what types of communication a future decision-maker (whether a regulator or court) might determine, after the fact, to be of the sort that voters would be "unlikely to treat . . . as . . . election-related."

I see the 30-day rule proposed by the Commission as a close call, with good arguments on both sides, although in the final analysis I oppose it. The added wrinkle of a "rebuttable presumption" of election-relatedness, however, weakens the proposal rather than strengthens it.

ADDITIONAL STATEMENT OF JOEL M. GORA

I FULLY SUBSCRIBE to the principal Statement of Dissenting Views, as well as the separate statement of Constantine Sidamon-Eristoff. But I wanted to add a few additional words of my own.

There is much in the Report of the Commission on Campaign Finance Reform that is positive and praiseworthy. I appreciate the recommendation for raising the restrictively low hard money contribution limits for federal campaigns, which have made it difficult for many candidacies to gain a foothold. I think that the proposal for one free mailing for all ballot-qualified federal candidates is a welcome suggestion for expanding the range of political opportunity.

The Commission's proposal for public financing of congressional elections is particularly noteworthy. This is a serious and relatively generous public financing proposal, far advanced over the few comprehensive proposals that have gathered any significant support in Congress. It has an admirably low threshold of eligibility. It provides a very expansive two-for-one match for small contributions. Coupled with the provision for a free mailing, it might very well nourish candidacies that might otherwise falter. If one were to support a limits-based, government-supplied public financing scheme, the one the Commission proposes is a good model. It might have been even better had the Commission determined to include the provision for modest tax credits or deductions as an incentive for direct and across-the-board citizen financing of political activity.

At the end of the day, however, to my mind the benefits of the Commission's proposals are overcome by the burdens I fear they would impose on the political freedom that is at the core of the First Amendment and of democracy.

It is not at all clear that the kind of sweeping, limits-based public financing plan the Commission proposes, in an effort to avoid the well-known failures of the presidential public financing scheme, will work. Candidates and parties will be compelled to try to get their messages out in other ways. The alternatives, then, become either to let them, which breeds public cynicism but protects speech, or to restrict them as the Report would seek to do, which, to the extent it does work, will come at the expense of speech. In my view, "floors without ceilings" is the only public financing/subsidy approach that is consonant with the First Amendment. That approach was tried in a handful of states in past years with no obvious untoward consequences. Providing a mix of benefits—free mailings, tax deductions or credits, government-provided matching funds for small contributions—without the comprehensive system of controls the Report proposes, would be a far better First Amendment–friendly approach.

The Report's recommendations would impose unprecedented restraints on the political funding and advocacy of candidates, parties, and issue organizations. Implementation of these proposals would require the kind of command-and-control bureaucratic mechanisms that are fundamentally antithetical to freedom of political speech and association.

For these reasons, I must respectfully dissent from the Commission's Report.

SEPARATE STATEMENT OF NICOLE A. GORDON

I AM LOATH TO DEPART from an excellent report, notwithstanding disagreements any member of a committee must have with a consensus document. There are three items, however, that I must comment on, even before the Commission on Campaign Finance Reform's ideas have had a chance to be tested.

First, the Commission recommends a single spending limit covering both the primary and general elections. I strongly disagree with this. It works a basic unfairness on candidates who are not similarly situated. This unfairness cannot be overcome by the notion that a single limit gives more flexibility to candidates, because the candidates are not getting the same flexibility vis-à-vis the same limits when one has a contested primary and the other does not.

Consider: Candidate A, who has a hotly contested and bruising primary, and is left with half of his overall spending limit as prescribed by the Commission, finds himself at the starting gate in a general election contest against candidate B. Candidate B had no primary and has the full amount to spend for the general election. The general election covers a different period and has a different set of candidates and even a different set of issues, as well as a different population eligible to vote (all registered voters) from the population eligible to vote in the primary (enrolled party members). The result is that candidate A—already perhaps damaged by spending by his opponents during the primary period—will have one-half the spending limit to spend against candidate B, who will have the entire spending limit available. I cannot see how this can be considered fair.

I am not aware of any jurisdiction that has a spending limit covering two separate elections, which suggests that it is generally understood that primaries and general elections are realistically viewed as distinct. I realize that often the contest is "only" in the primary or "only" in the general election, but as long as the expenditure limits are on the high side, and candidates can all spend up to their primary limit during the primary period even if they do not have a contested primary, I think having separate limits is fairer in the end. In addition, given the purpose of spending limits to "even the playing field" and promote competition, we ought to be encouraging and providing for a norm in which both primary and general elections involve meaningful contests.

Second, as indicated by my concurrence in the separate statement of Richard Briffault et al., I think that an aggregate cap on contributions from individuals of $75,000 is extraordinarily high.

Finally, I believe more emphasis is needed on creating a structure to assure the appointment of non-partisan FEC commissioners, and on creating a mechanism for ensuring periodic review and refinement of the operation of the proposed law.

DISSENT OF CONSTANTINE SIDAMON-ERISTOFF

I WISH TO REGISTER my dissent to the overall thrust of our Report.

In doing so, I do not in any way mean to derogate the extraordinarily hard work and many hours of effort put into the Report by Professor Richard Briffault, his staff, and the members of the Commission on Campaign Finance Reform. Given the thrust of the report, it is an excellent job.

I must, however, state that at the beginning of the process, in early 1997, I felt that it was important that the Commission reexamine the fundamental bases upon which the present federal and, to some extent, state and local campaign finance laws have been erected. I do not think that these have been sufficiently explored.

THE PRESENT SYSTEM IS "BROKE"

Any "reform" system that is finally adopted must meet certain general, but obvious criteria, including:

1. Access to the political system, by candidates and others, should be broadened, and not limited, by whatever system is adopted.
2. First Amendment freedoms, particularly freedom of speech, must not be infringed in any way.
3. The system must be even handed and not skewed toward incumbent challenges or parties.
4. At least in my opinion, the political parties must be strengthened.

The present thrust toward reform, as stated in the report, stems from a feeling, well stoked, that "soft money," illegal or improper campaign fundraising, and the arms race are sufficiently prevalent and evil to warrant changes or improvements to the current system.

Unfortunately, by building on the present system, the Commission is trying to do the impossible. This system is broken, and adding

more restrictions, changing contribution or spending limits, and tin-
kering with the details of the system will not in any real way improve
it.

I believe the current system is not only broken but enormously
complicated, impossible for the average person to understand, and it
could be perceived to exist primarily for the benefit of lawyers and
accountants.

I personally would scrap the whole system, including limits on
spending, limits on contributions, and the rest of the present requirements, and in all cases go back to a system based on the essential,
vital core of any true campaign finance reform, which is full and
immediate disclosure. Internet disclosure will allow voters to know
immediately who is supporting whom and for how much. That is all
you really need to know.

THE ARMS RACE

Are we spending too much money on politics in this country? Com-
pare the entire amount of money spent on the 1996 federal elections
with the advertising budget of one company such as Proctor and
Gamble, and see which is greater? It will be the Proctor and Gamble
budget. A good case can be made for the fact that we are not spending enough, and that enough different people are not giving enough
money to candidates. What the Commission should be doing is encouraging more people to give money, perhaps by allowing a federal
deduction from income tax, or a credit, or one of the other suggestions from Commission member Peter Wallison.

In the Report (see page 118) it is noted that the combination of
public funds and soft money in 1996 provided the major party presidential candidates with the equivalent in inflation-adjusted dollars of
what their predecessors had in 1972. In other words, Richard Nixon,
who spent $60 million, would have spent in 1994-inflated dollars ap-
proximately what Clinton did. This means that the amount of spending for campaigns, whether it is soft or hard money, has not really
increased. As also is pointed out on the same page, when the public
grant became insufficient to fund an effective campaign, candidates
began to cultivate soft money and to decline public funding. The
Report goes on correctly to state that public funding can work by

inducing candidates to opt in, and by reducing the role of private wealth in funding campaigns, *only* if funding levels are based on the costs of competitive contemporary election campaigns.

I would do away with all campaign spending limits and all campaign contribution limits. By raising the effective $2000 limit on contributions for House of Representative campaigns to $6000, some of the imbalance would be redressed, but note again that if the original $1000 plus $1000 was raised from 1974 dollars to 1998 dollars, the amount would be $6636, that is, still greater than the new ceiling.

It is also true, as has been pointed out recently, that with the advent of the Internet, attempts to control spending by wealthy donors will become very, very difficult, particularly since anybody can get to the Internet and do anything they want. The wealthy can simply, as Walter Dellinger of the Duke University School of Law suggests, start new opinion magazines on the Internet or buy radio and T.V. stations instead. Further limiting campaign contributions and campaign spending essentially only increases the overall power of the media. The owner of Time Warner or the *New York Post* will have increased power, other wealthy persons will lose power. Is this really what we want to accomplish?

As pointed out in the Report, the primary recommendation of the Commission is to recommend public funding for U.S. Senate and House of Representatives campaigns. I might support such public funding, if it is only meant to be a supplement and not used as a way to force spending limits on candidates. But, unfortunately, what has been recommended is that those who qualify for public funding adopt limitations on what they themselves can use of their own personal or family funds, and also adopt spending limits.

It should also be noted that making public money available for campaigns does not lower the cost of campaigns or limit the amount spent on campaigning per voter. Public money can also be perverted, as can be seen by this curious beast called the Reform Party, started with the use of enormous personal funds by Ross Perot and now existing because it is going to get federal money. Does this make any sense?

If the Commission is concerned about the cost of a campaign, it should go to the root of the cause, which is the cost of television and other media. One way or the other, a free television system might work wonders. But just simply increasing the contribution limits and the spending limits does not do the job.

Regrettably, the Supreme Court has not thrown out the contribution limits, which were left in place by the *Buckley v. Valeo* decision, but essentially made it plain that reasonable limitations on contributions could be left in place to avoid the appearance of corruption. That was a bad decision.

What the Supreme Court did not accomplish, Congress should. All of these limits make for a totally unreasonable, incomprehensible, and unmanageable problem, and they are all based on the assumption that there is too much money in politics, which if it is true, is more easily accomplished by providing free access to means of communication by candidates. The system is totally broken and frankly cannot be fixed.

ADDITIONAL STATEMENT OF PAUL WINDELS III

I SALUTE THE COMMISSION on Campaign Finance Reform for its efforts and for a clearly written Report that comprehensively states the case for its proposals. I agree with the Commission that the system as it operates today is unacceptable. I believe, however, that the Commission's Report and proposal focus too much on the regulation and limitation of *all* campaign contributions and expenditures as opposed to those contributions that *actually* corrupt the process. At the same time, the Commission has not paid adequate attention to what I believe to be the most promising and fundamental hope for reform—reducing the *need* for money in politics. With that in mind, I have participated in drafting the joint separate statement of Peter Wallison, Joel Gora, Constantine Sidamon-Eristoff, Michael Weinstock, and myself and join the separate statement of Constantine Sidamon-Eristoff subject to the following.

1. As a matter of black-letter constitutional law, contributions to political campaigns and spending by campaigns have been held as core political speech, subject to the highest protection under the First Amendment. The constitutional standard for any regulation on campaign finance is therefore one of strict scrutiny. To date, the only justification for such regulation that has passed constitutional muster is the prevention of graft and corruption or the avoidance of the appearance of graft and corruption.

I believe that this standard—first set forth in *Buckley v. Valeo* and adhered to ever since—represents sound constitutional policy that is rooted in the founding of our nation. In our diverse and pluralistic society, speech has little impact unless it is heard. Without the ability to publish, therefore, the freedom of speech carries little meaning. Political campaigns, which after all involve the exercise of our constitutional functions as voters, must be able to get their messages out to the voting public.

2. The elimination of corruption or its appearance is a constitutionally sound goal and indeed one that fulfills the constitutional mandate of a republican government. Less drastic and more focused means are available to serve this goal than the wholesale limitation of political speech of those who are not trying to corrupt the governmental system. This Association has endorsed an across-the-board two-year ban on "pay-to-play" political contributions by persons or entities doing business with New York State in the context of the New York State Election Law as well as restrictions in the context of lawyers engaged in municipal securities practice.[39] A similar ban belongs as the centerpiece of federal campaign finance reform. To the extent that the Commission predicates its recommendations here on corruption or the appearance of corruption caused by campaign contributions, that problem can and should be directly addressed by restrictions of "pay-to-play" political contributions not limited solely to the municipal securities business but to government contractors, lobbyists, and other persons or entities who do business with the government (including regulated or licensed industries). These restrictions should include a ban on contributions by persons or entities "doing business" with the government within a certain period of the contribution or business (or further restrictions on the amount of the contribution to a token level) and additional disclosure by the contributor and/or campaign or political party receiving the donation.

Although restrictions must be drawn so as not to infringe on legitimate free-speech rights, there is a fundamental difference between a contribution made by a citizen who supports the political ideology of a candidate and a contribution made for the purpose of self-enrichment. As the Association has noted, "a line [has] to be drawn between contributions and solicitations in furtherance of constitutionally protected expression and such contributions and such solicitations that could be regulated because designed to advance a business

---

[39] In 1996 the Association offered a resolution before the American Bar Association recommending ethical restrictions on contributions made or solicited by lawyers to municipal officers responsible for awarding municipal bond business received by the firms of those lawyers. That resolution is discussed in "Towards a Level Playing Field—A Pragmatic Approach to Public Campaign Financing," 52 *Record* 660, 686 (Oct. 1997), in which the Association proposed that political contributors to public officeholders having the direct or indirect ability to award state business be barred from receiving such state business within two years of making any contributions to those officeholders.

purpose—a purpose of corrupting the political process ('pay to play'). . . ."[40] Restrictions on "pay-to-play" would also go a long way toward eliminating the use of campaign contributions as a means of gaining access to political figures and at least improve voter morale with respect to campaign financing.

A restriction on "pay-to-play" politics thus strikes at the very contributions that raise the concerns underlying the calls for reform and is consistent with the positions the Association has taken in the context of New York State law and the municipal bond practice. By contrast, under the Commission's proposal, "pay-to-play" contributions would actually be increased from $2000 per election cycle to $6000, subject only to the largely unenforced (or unenforceable) laws against bribery.

3. The Commission's proposal implicitly treats the notion that political campaigns have an infinite and inelastic desire for money as axiomatic. I believe that any reform proposal should be built upon a systematic analysis of why money is needed in political campaigns, how much money campaigns truly need, and whether that need can be addressed through alternate means.[41] As the Association has observed in "Towards a Level Playing Field—A Pragmatic Approach to Public Campaign Financing," 52 *Record* 660 (Oct. 1997), political

---

[40] Report of the Association to the American Bar Association in support of the its "pay-to-play" resolution (quoted in "Towards a Level Playing Field—A Pragmatic Approach to Public Campaign Financing," 52 *Record* 660 (Oct. 1997). The Association's Report to the ABA noted the example of bond lawyers who made substantial contributions to *both* major party candidates for New York State Comptroller in the 1994 campaign. Under *Buckley v. Valeo*, the prevention of graft or the appearance of graft is a constitutionally valid basis for restricting the amount of a campaign contribution.

[41] For example, in most of the congressional races in which incumbent members have been defeated in recent years, the incumbent has actually outspent the successful challenger by a substantial margin. See Malbin, *Campaign Finance Reform—Some Lessons from the Data,* 1993 Rockefeller Institute Bulletin at 47–49; Ornstein, Mann, and Malbin, *Vital Statistics on Congress 1995–1996* (CQ Press 1996), table 3–6 at 88–89. Statistics such as these—and the number of high-spending campaigns that have not proved successful—indicate that the effect of spending money on a political campaign is subject to the law of diminishing returns. As Professor Michael Malbin has summed up: "This confirms that money, or having the ability to communicate, is essential to campaigning in contemporary congressional politics; but that money is not enough by itself to win. Having money means having the ability to be heard; it does not mean that the voters will like what they hear. Incumbents who had worn out their welcome were heard and rejected." Ornstein, Mann, and Malbin, supra, ch. 3 at 76.

campaigns need money primarily in order to reach voters in today's society. The best means of diluting the effect of money on political activity is, therefore, to augment other means of access between politicians and citizens. Many such improvements have been achieved outside the law, such as the creation of C-SPAN and the use of the Internet, both in the creation of political websites and through the use of e-mail to communicate with large groups of voters.[42] More can be done in this sphere, including more coverage of campaigns in the media, free television time for candidates, the public sponsorship of candidate fora, debates, and a public website for all congressional candidates who have filed reports with the Federal Election Commission. The more that is done along these lines and the easier it becomes for candidates to compete with less money, the less impact campaign contributions will have on politicians.

4. Nor do I subscribe to the notion that large contributions or the spending of significant amounts of a candidate's own money is per se a bad influence on politics. It is worth noting that one of the most significant insurgent campaigns in modern American history, that of Senator Eugene McCarthy for President in 1968, was largely funded by a few individuals.[43] In addition, the 1996 presidential campaign of Steve Forbes opened the door for reforming New York's ballot-access process (which the Association has strongly supported) by bringing a successful constitutional challenge to that process in federal court, which ultimately resulted in the first statewide Republican presidential primary in the history of New York that includes all of the candidates still in the race.[44] Moreover, the frequency of unsuccessful campaigns in which the candidate spent significant amounts of personal wealth—a fact often used against those candidates—refutes the notion that an election can be bought simply by outspending the opposition out of personal assets.[45]

5. Any reformation of the campaign finance system should attempt

---

[42] See "Towards a Level Playing Field—A Pragmatic Approach to Public Campaign Financing," 52 *Record* 660 (Oct. 1997) for further discussion of this issue.

[43] See *The New York Times* (May 20, 1968):1, 31; (Jan. 7, 1972):14; (Jan. 18, 2000):A21; *Wall Street Journal* (Oct. 13, 1998):A22. It is unlikely that the McCarthy campaign could have achieved what it did had it been subject to the current law.

[44] *Rockefeller v. Powers,* 917 F. Supp. 155 (E.D.N.Y. 1996), affd, 78 F.3d 44 (2d Cir. 1996); *Molinari v. Powers,* No. 99 Civ. 8447 (ERK) slip op. (E.D.N.Y. Feb. 10, 2000); "The Petition Process," 41 *Record* 710 (Oct. 1986).

[45] See Ornstein, Mann, and Malbin, supra, ch. 3 at 76.

to offset the advantages of incumbency through a number of means, including the provision of additional free mailings to challengers against incumbents and the sponsorship of candidate fora and debates in order to afford the opportunity to gain exposure. I also recommend returning to the original Hatch Act ban on congressional staff and civil service employees working on federal campaigns. Finally, some remedial steps should be taken with respect to compensating challengers for their time spent campaigning. Recognizing the potential for abuse, candidates should at a minimum be permitted to continue to receive preexisting health and insurance benefits from their employers while on leave, and those candidates who cannot continue to receive their salaries should also be permitted a salary allowance from their campaigns for the months of September and October equal to the pay of the office they are seeking, which allowance would not be counted against any expenditure ceilings.

6. Enforcement of the election law is not solely the province of the Federal Election Commission but also that of the Justice Department. No structural changes in the administration of the law through the FEC, however well-intentioned, can substitute for a will and ability to enforce the law impartially and thoroughly, which in turn requires accountability to the electorate. Public groups such as the Association and the press can lead by praising officials who enforce the law rigorously and fairly and by not hesitating to criticize in the strongest terms possible those who fail to do so or who seek to intimidate attempts to enforce the law.[46]

7. A good test of any proposed reform of the law is to measure the burden of compliance by citizens who wish in good faith to follow the law. The Special Commission's proposed system would saddle campaigns and treasurers with a serious potential dilemma by counting independent expenditures made by political parties against the campaign's expenditure limit. Given the multiplicity of party com-

---

[46] In one recent example, the *Wall Street Journal* and *The New York Times* praised the efforts of the U.S. Attorney for the Southern District of New York for the successful prosecution for embezzlement of a union official who caused union funds to be contributed to the Democratic National Committee, which were then contributed in turn to the reelection campaign of the president of the union, and the *Times* simultaneously criticized the Attorney General of the United States for her lax performance in enforcing campaign finance laws. *The New York Times* (Nov. 23, 1999):A26; *Wall Street Journal* (Nov. 22, 1999):A22.

mittees, especially at the state and local level,[47] and their ability to spend independently of the campaign, a campaign that itself spends the maximum (or close to it) would run the risk of violating the law based on expenditures made by persons or entities beyond its control.[48] Moreover, the proposal flouts basic fairness. It is a fact of political life that candidates from time to time have differences of opinion with party leaders. A party committee of some sort, for example, could view one issue as important and run advertisements stressing that issue, while the candidate might want to stress different issues. Can it be fair to impute expenditures to a candidate that the candidate did not make and would prefer not to have been made? Even more troubling, in some instances, party leaders have allegedly opposed candidates of their own party.[49] In such a case, the absurdity of permitting party leaders to spend the money of a campaign they were trying to defeat is self-evident. Having served as a campaign treasurer, I would advise any candidate to be extremely chary of opting into a system under which his or her campaign may be held accountable for activities beyond its control.

8. With respect to deterring laundered campaign contributions, I would not only require the candidate and treasurer to certify that they are not aware of any improper contributions, I would also require either (i) that all donors of contributions required to be reported sign a statement on their donor cards[50] to the effect that they have not received and will not accept any reimbursement for their contribution from any source and that they understand that such reimbursement would violate federal election law, or (ii) that an officer of the campaign certify that those donors have been advised of that fact in writing contemporaneously with the contribution. This addi-

---

[47] In New York, for example, there is a New York State Republican Committee made up of two members elected from each of the assembly districts in the state. In addition, each county has a separate Republican County Committee, and there is at least one separate committee for each assembly district (also elected), not to mention unofficial Republican clubs such as the Women's National Republican Club and the Log Cabin Republican Club.

[48] If a party committee expenditure is actually coordinated with the campaign, this does not pose a problem, since the campaign can anticipate the expenditures that will be chargeable against its ceiling.

[49] See *The New York Times* (Nov. 27, 1994):57.

[50] Donors of contributions required to be reported (that is, over $100) are typically required to complete a donor card listing their name, address, and employer in order that the campaign may include that information on its reports to the FEC.

tional certification will send an unambiguous message that no one in the process—candidates, treasurers, or contributors—can safely look the other way with respect to laundered contributions. Placing an affirmative duty on candidates and treasurers to prevent laundered contributions and placing donors on notice of their duty to provide complete and accurate information regarding their contributions will likely deter many illegal contributions (and lighten the burden of prosecuting such offenses), but should have no chilling effect on legitimate donations (since the donor would be certifying to a fact that he or she knew to be true).

9. Finally, while I agree with the proposal to increase the maximum amount an individual may contribute to $6000 per election cycle, I see no reason to increase the maximum that political action committees may contribute above $6000. A citizen has at least the same free-speech rights as a corporation or a political action committee and should, therefore, be permitted to contribute the same amounts to political campaigns.